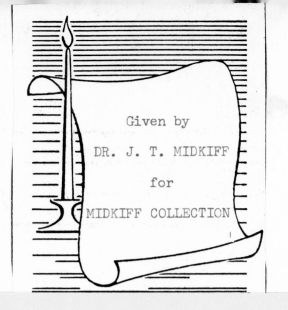

The Kent Affair

Documents and Interpretations

Edited by

Ottavio M. Casale

Louis Paskoff

Kent State University

Houghton Mifflin Company · Boston

New York · Atlanta · Geneva, Illinois · Dallas · Palo Alto

" 'V' Sign for Peace at Kent Services," by Lynn Langway, from the *Chicago Daily News,* May 11, 1970. Reprinted with permission from the Chicago Daily News.

"Life Story," by Erich Segal, from the *Ladies' Home Journal,* October, 1970. Reprinted by permission of William Morris Agency, Inc. Copyright © by Downe Publishing Company, Inc. "Life Story" originally appeared under the title "Death Story" in the *Ladies' Home Journal.*

"Kent State Gag" (excerpts) and "The Indicted Professor," both by David Sanford, from the *New Republic,* November 7, 1970. Reprinted by Permission of The New Republic, © 1970, Harrison-Blaine of New Jersey, Inc.

"A Drama of Blood (& Corn)," from the *New York Post,* May 6, 1970. Reprinted by Permission of New York Post. Copyright © 1970, New York Post Corporation.

"Death on the Campus," from the *New York Times,* May 6, 1970; "In the Nation: The Dead at Kent State," by Tom Wicker, from the *New York Times,* May 7, 1970; "Violence on the Right," from the *New York Times,* May 9, 1970; and "Excerpts from Summary of F.B.I. Report on Kent State U. Disorders Last May," from the *New York Times,* October 31, 1970, all © 1970 by The New York Times Company. Reprinted by permission.

" 'My God.' They're Killing Us," Copyright Newsweek, Inc., May 18, 1970.

"Kent State: Martyrdom That Shook the Country," from *Time,* May 18, 1970. Reprinted by permission from Time, the Weekly Newsmagazine. Copyright Time, Inc., 1970.

Cover montage from photograph by John Paul Filo. Copyright Valley Daily News, Tarentum, Pennsylvania.

Printed in the U.S.A.

Library of Congress Catalog Card Number: 70–148112

ISBN: 0–395–12361–5

Contents

Preface

The events at Kent, Ohio, in the spring of 1970 have been among the most widely reported and analyzed in recent history. The complex and tragic nature of these events has prompted thousands to speak, reflecting every degree of exploitation and restraint. This collection seeks to present the first balanced, representative, and objective sampling of this huge mass of material. It includes local and national news coverage ranging from the underground press to the *Wall Street Journal*, and transcriptions of radio and television broadcasts. It brings together for the first time the major documents resulting from state and federal investigations as of the beginning of 1971. It reprints editorials, articles, and letters chosen to illustrate the amazing variety of opinions and arguments which sprang out of these events and the beliefs upon which these views are founded. It offers a selection of maps and photographs chosen to help the reader visualize the elements of space and time and so gain an extra dimension of comprehension.

The editors have sought to represent every viewpoint they have discovered in their study of thousands of documents. Some readers will find things here which will surprise or offend them. This is the inevitable result of the editors' attempt to include all available interpretations. Some readers may be led to examine their assumptions and conclusions more closely because of evidence and conclusions exposed here, evidence often incomplete or contradictory, and conclusions which seem to result from altogether different systems of reality. Students of writing, journalism, sociology, political science, history, and psychology may here find documents of interest not only to study but to stimulate further investigation.

To avoid the repetition of background material, some selections have been given in excerpts. Where this is done, omissions are indicated in the heading or by ellipses [. . .].

We gratefully acknowledge the help of many persons, especially Vice-President Ronald W. Roskens, Ronald S. Beer, and Sylvia L. Beal of Kent State University's administrative staff; Dean H. Keller and Alex Gildzen of the University Library's Department of Special Collections; the University News Service and its director, James J. Bruss; Dr. John C. Weiser of WKSU AM-FM; Dorothy Fuldheim of WEWS-TV, Cleveland; Loris Troyer, co-editor of the *Kent-Ravenna Record-Courier;* and Linda Casale.

Introduction

On May 4, 1970, at 12:24 P.M., in Kent, Portage County, Ohio, four Kent State University students were killed and nine were wounded by members of the Ohio National Guard. It was the first military volley aimed at a civilian crowd in the history of the United States of America.

The shots fired on the campus commons that day still echo in the divided American psyche, for this was one of the events by which a nation's citizens define and divide themselves. The question the editors of this collection have been asked most often is: "Are you going to be pro-student or pro-Guard?" Each of these commitments carries such a great symbolic intensity of meaning that the complex reality of the tragic affair at Kent is in danger of being lost, replaced by a vision of grand, schematically pure historical forces in opposition. "Pro-student" often means a passionate commitment to saintly, peace-loving, sexually honest, flower-power fighters for a better world against repression in all its forms. "Pro-Guard" often means a commitment, equally passionate, to national honor seen in terms of Washington praying at Valley Forge; Old Glory raised on Mount Surabachi; fascism defeated by men whose sacrificial devotion to a way of life based on God-given principles and sustained by hard work and decency is now threatened by a generation corrupted into immorality and even treachery by the enemies of all that is good in America.

Many seek to interpret the deaths thoughtfully on the basis of available evidence without yielding to the strong temptation of prejudgment, and so follow closely the evidence and comment in the news media.

A minimalist position is also heard. Usually offered in exhaustion, it denies grand meaning and emphasizes the horror of mere chance, an unpopular viewpoint in a nation dedicated to making history rather than suffering it. If the incursion into Cambodia had been announced on a Monday instead of a Thursday, there might have been student protests in Kent the next day, but they would have been on campus on a weekday, not in town on a beery Friday night. The damage to town property that produced the fear which prompted the calling of the Guard would not have taken place. And even after the Guard arrived, how could a handful of Guardsmen, firing without orders, have represented a way of life? Of the approximately 20,000 students on campus, only a few hundred were demonstrating, only about 1,000 were watching. Many students were at lunch. Many were on the commons because it is a natural crossing place between dormitories and classroom buildings. How could such a group have represented a whole generation?

But the events of May 4, though not symbolically neat, are not to be minimized, for, in an awful way, the Kent deaths had everything: the well-publicized generation gap; the new life-style of the young as expressed aggressively or casually in speech and personal appearance; the conflict over American involvement in Indo-China, over the power of the President, over the influence of the military, over the choice of working "within the system" or "smashing the state;" and the pervasive presence of the news media, with their ambiguous power to create news by reporting news. Like the killing of John Kennedy, of Robert Kennedy, of Martin Luther King, Jr., the killing of the Kent students was a public and personal shock, a shock that forced people to examine their deepest definitions of themselves as citizens and as mortals. The frequent invocation of basic national and religious faith to be found in this collection gives evidence of how crucial this event was to Americans. Many seemed driven to find a reason which would provide the security of truth, if not relief from shock and fear.

Fear to the point of panic was certainly one of the chief reactions to the weekend of May 1 through 4: the fear of a shopkeeper threatened with destruction of his business unless he displayed an Aldermaston peace symbol; the fear of a student who went home to find himself reviled by a formerly friendly neighborhood; the fear of a housewife in a supermarket at the sight of a group of hairy students swinging down the aisles; the fear of a teacher that Western humanism was being murdered; the fear that impelled thousands to cry out on radio open-line programs, in letters to the editor, in conversations obsessed with making sense out of the feared senselessness of death.

The campus of Kent State University would not have seemed the place for such death. Although not immune to the conflicts of the larger society, Kent had no reputation for political activism. The *Daily Kent Stater* regularly charged the student body with apathy. Some students countered that not to do as the *Stater* wished was not necessarily to be apathetic. The argument was one that concerned many campuses. But Kent did not seem likely to join Berkeley, Columbia, San Francisco State, and the other schools which had become known to the general public as trouble spots.

Founded as a normal school to train public school teachers in 1910, the college grew quickly but quietly. Required by law to enroll any Ohio high school graduate, it drew mostly from within the state, and was dedicated to the ideal of the state-supported college: that college study be available to any student who could prove his ability for it, regardless of his family's economic position. This ideal was deeply, even devoutly, felt to be a characteristic and important part of the American dream of self-realization and civic usefulness.

The school achieved university status in 1935. It had the typical enrollment drop during World War II, a post-war rise due partly to the GI bill, more veterans after Korea, and then, in the sixties, a steep rise. Estimated enrollment went from 5,500 in 1950, to 7,500 in 1960, to 21,000 in 1970. This growth is reflected by the school-grounds. The neo-classic buildings on the crest of a curving hill, looking down on the library centered in a spacious, wooded green, are Kent ca. 1940. The jumble of new, architecturally mixed buildings stretching far beyond the hilltop was built mostly after 1960. Between the two groups of buildings is the commons, one of the major open spaces of the campus, especially popular with students in the sunny days of spring and fall.

The students of 1970 were part of the post-war baby boom, children of parents who grew up in the depression and fought in the war and saw a college education as a necessity. The relationship of Kent State University to the city of Kent was changing. Kent was no longer a little town with a little university. Its population had grown from 4,500 in 1910 to 27,600 in 1970. The ratio of students to townsfolk was almost one to one. Many citizens were beginning to feel swamped and estranged. For instance, students now lived mostly in dormitories and apartments, not as roomers with Kent families and thus part of the civic community. More than one out of ten students was from out of state. The student often seemed to take for granted the kind of money the middle-aged had not had in their youth, and to have little respect for advice as to how they should spend it. There was no ignoring their often disturbing sexual attitudes. Workers in offices and industries in the Akron-Kent-Ravenna area moved into Kent and its surrounding housing developments. Often from outside of Ohio as well as from outside of Portage County, they had little family feeling for the University and its teachers and students.

By 1970 many students had as little feeling for adults in general. The Viet Nam war had exacerbated normal youthful idealism, self-awareness, and distrust of elders to a new intensity. Some students supported the war as a measure of their patriotic faith; others disliked the war but hoped that things in the nation would somehow improve; others worked for change within the political system; others called for violent destruction of that system.

The young were strong in numbers and had learned from the optimistic days of civil rights action in the sixties that they could influence the powerful and be powerful themselves. After the first teach-ins in 1965, their power was turned against a system seen to be less and less worthy of trust and respect. Their proof of this was the Viet Nam war, to them the embodiment of militarism, racism, oppression, dehumanization—everything hateful. For some the university was just another part of that system.

The variety of youthful feelings should be stressed. Like their elders the young can show concern and understanding, or prejudice and arrogance. They are capable of commitments ranging from chauvinistic violence to anarchic violence. It seems fair to say that the great majority of students do not wish to be the violent horde which the extreme right accuses them of being and the extreme left exhorts them to become. It also seems fair to say that they are dissatisfied with the war and all it embodies and would like to make changes.

When President Nixon announced on April 30 that American troops had entered Cambodia to destroy Communist sanctuaries and base camps, many students felt this to be another betrayal of their hopes for America. Kent State University was not unusual in being a scene of protest.

The University would have preferred to be known for its Ph.D. programs, its connection with the Cleveland Orchestra through Blossom Center, its library whose collection would soon be over a million volumes. It became best known for the events of May, 1970. This volume concerns itself with how these events are known and how they are understood. The extent to which existing belief influences the perception of events as well as the understanding of them has taken on new poignancy for the editors, as we feel it will for the reader. We have included news coverage of these events, responses to them by the public and the press, reports of the major investigative bodies, and responses to these reports.

As 1971 began, 22 of the 25 indicted by the State Grand Jury had been charged and were awaiting the opening of their trials—trials which might take months or years. No decision had been made on the possibility of calling a Federal Grand Jury.

To establish the facts of the Kent affair fully; to understand them rightly; to act on them justly—these are problems which deserve the thoughtful attention of Americans and their representatives in public life. It is the hope of the editors that this collection, which shows how difficult these problems are, may be of use to those who work to solve them.

Kent, Ohio
May 1-4, 1970

As the events in Kent during the first week of May, 1970, escalated, they were given wider coverage in national news media. In Portage County, Ohio, from whose citizens a state grand jury would later be chosen, the local sources of information were WKNT AM-FM, the Kent commercial radio station; WKSU AM-FM, the University radio station; the *Kent-Ravenna Record-Courier;* and the *Akron Beacon Journal.* The country as a whole learned of Kent from news service stories and photographs; radio and television broadcasts, especially the network coverage; and weekly news magazines. The responses (often fierce) of the county and country were largely prompted by these reports. Those responses helped to create further news, in which Kent and the nation interacted.

In this section, therefore, we include selected news coverage from both local and national sources. Many of the doubts and problems raised tentatively here were to be the subjects of intensive investigation later.

Kent-Ravenna Record-Courier, May 2, 1970.

7 Injured, Police Arrest 14 in Kent Disturbance

50 Windows Smashed in Business Places

By Ben Post

Five police officers and two students were injured when a crowd of approximately 500, mostly Kent State University students, swept through downtown Kent late Friday night and early today, taunting police and breaking store windows.

The injured policemen were: Sgt. Ross Jamerson, Tony Messina, and **Maj.** Roy Pemberton, all of the Portage County sheriff's department, and Sgts. Jack Rose, and Donald Lemons, of the Kent Police Department. Identification of the students was not available.

According to police reports, none of the injuries was serious, the worst being a dislocated shoulder suffered by a sheriff's deputy who was not identified.

Fourteen demonstrators were arrested and charged with disorderly conduct, police reported.

The first acts of violence flared at approximately 11:30 p.m. when a police cruiser on routine patrol was pelted with beer bottles and other debris as it cruised N. Water St.

Kent police then alerted the Portage County Sheriff's Department, State Highway patrol, Stow police and the Kent State University police.

The Stow police supplied four men to support the 21-man Kent police force. The sheriff's department called out 71 men to help quell the disturbance.

As the violence intensified, Mayor LeRoy Satrom ordered a state of civil emergency and established a curfew that went into effect at 1 a.m. Saturday until dawn. Police said the curfew also will be reestablished at 8 p.m. Saturday until dawn Sunday.

Kent Police Chief Roy Thompson said: "I just can't understand why a group would do what they did for no reason."

Thompson also said that it was "hard to understand why the university police couldn't give some assistance with their 36 men." The university did, however, supply university buses to the police department.

The weather, the chief said, was not a substantial factor in the disturbance which he said was instigated by a "bunch of agitators" and "subversive groups."

Damage to businesses near the intersection of N. Water and Main Sts. was confined primarily to the breaking of windows.

As the crowd moved through the downtown section, rocks, bottles and other debris were hurled through windows. Police said, however, that there was little looting.

Buildings where windows were broken included the City Bank of Kent, the Portage National Bank and the Captain Brady Restaurant, opposite the university campus.

Two small fires were reported by the Kent Fire Department during the disorders. According to fire reports, the department extinguished a fire in an "old shack" at the rear of 112 Portage St., and a burning pile of rubbish in the middle of N. Water St.

University police reported at least two persons arrested in connection with the breaking of windows at the ROTC building on campus.

Twelve sheriff's deputies were placed on a night patrol in Kent to enforce the curfew and prevent looting.

Using tear gas and riot formations, the police moved the crowd through the streets of Kent until the crowd, dissipating as it moved, was finally forced onto the university campus.

At E. Main and Lincoln St. a stand-off resulted between cat-calling students and police, who occasionally threw a barrage of tear gas into the crowd.

An unusual but potentially dangerous incident produced a calming effect on both the police and the crowd of students.

A car driven by Lee Manning, 25, 93 Manchester St., Akron, hit a truck scaffold at the intersection of E. Main and Linden Sts., where a Tree City Electric Co. crew was working on a malfunctioning traffic light.

Glen Kruger, S. R. 261, Kent, who was working on the light, was injured when the car hit the scaffold and he was taken to Robinson Memorial Hospital.

Another man, Blain Baldasare, 5117 Tappan Court, Ravenna, working with Kruger, was not injured, but was stranded on the traffic signal.

When police removed Baldasare, a cheer was heard from the dissident students, who were now less than 100. Except for a few disgruntled demonstrators, the crowd began to disperse.

Although the primary force of sheriff's deputies was removed from the area, a token force patrolled the perimeter of the university.

Mayor Satrom, tired from a long night, said early this morning he was "disturbed and disgusted" with what had happened and hoped that it would not be renewed this evening.

Kent-Ravenna Record-Courier, May 4, 1970 (the *Record-Courier*
did not publish on Sunday, May 3)

ROTC Building Gets Torch; Firemen Get Pelted

It was the second of three nights of disturbance on the Kent State University campus.

When the campus had finally been cleared of demonstrators Saturday night, 34 persons had been arrested, several were injured and the Army ROTC building had been burnt to the ground.

The tumultuous night of violence began with an 8 p.m. rally of some 800 students on the KSU Commons. Crowds of students migrated to the area and were rallied by the ringing of the Victory Bell.

Before students ever moved, three of the young protesters made their way around to all newsmen telling them they would "get it" if they took photographs of the demonstration. "We don't want to go to jail again," said the spokesmen for the three.

He threatened to kill three Record-Courier reporters.

A long-haired youth stood on top of the brick structure which holds the bell and told the students they had to rally the support of those students who were in the domitories.

The long line of blue jeans and long hair began to make its way toward Tri-Towers, a dormitory complex on the near southeast side of the campus.

The walk toward Tri-Towers was marked with chants and slogans and spray paint which was used to coat trees and buildings with revolutionary names.

They passed through Tri-Towers and someone triggered a fire alarm there.

Continuing on through Eastway Center, a four-dormitory center for freshman students, they picked up additional marchers and the crowd had swelled to some 1,200 demonstrators.

As they crested the hill between Johnson Hall and Taylor Hall which overlooks the Commons, a "down with ROTC" chant rose up from those at the head of the march.

Dissidents armed with stones began to rally at the Army ROTC building and began hurling the missiles at the building. Demonstrators ran to the building with sticks and began breaking in the windows.

A flare shot out from the crowd and landed on the roof of the building. The flare rolled off on the ground.

That arson attempt was unsuccessful. Two more dissidents, a boy and a girl, ran to the building throwing burning rags into a broken window.

The crowd cheered and waited for the fire to start. But soon the glow inside the building went out and a young man who looked inside announced that the fire had died.

A third attempt was made by a long-haired youth who touched a burning rag to the curtains inside the building. Flames shot up and another cheer rose from the crowd.

Police or firemen had still not arrived.

When firemen arrived, one of the Kent city firemen was attacked by dissidents who took the hose from him. They finally cut the hose in half. . . . the building still burning.

Kent city police accompanied by university police arrived on the scene and stood alongside the building waiting for the firemen to get a new hose.

The policeman, armed, masked and wearing riot helmets, were stoned by the dissidents.

Two firemen grabbed the hose and ran to end of the building. Before they even put water on the building, they sprayed a young demonstrator who was ready to throw something at them.

Police threw canisters of tear gas at the crowds, forcing them back onto the middle of the Commons. The police then forced them back farther by shooting the tear gas at them with tear gas guns.

The dissidents cheered, "Burn, baby, burn."

They set fire to a small shed in the far corner of the Commons. Then they left.

Marching to E. Main St., a group of about 450 destroyed signs, telephone booths and anything that appeared breakable in their way. Signs and other debris were strewn into the road. Cars were turned away as they approached the demonstrators.

As they marched, the demonstrators picked up stones and other missiles.

They later threw them at National Guard troops who roared down E. Main St. about 9:45.

After stoning the passing guard units, the demonstrators headed back to the center of campus, setting fire to the information booth near the university library. Parking meters in the lot also were destroyed, the demonstrators filling their pockets with the change that rolled out on the sidewalk. University lights were broken as the demonstrators weaved their way back toward the Administration Building.

The group assembled in the area between the Union and Lowry Hall where they were again hit with tear gas fired by police.

The students then regrouped on the far side of the Commons to watch the building burn.

Cheers went up as the flames broke through the roof of the building and many continued the old chant of "Burn, baby, burn."

Police fired a couple bursts of tear gas to keep the dissidents back.

Then the Guard moved in, slowly breaking the large groups into smaller groups.

"Ladies and gentlemen, go back to your dormitories. If you remain outside you will be arrested. We do not want to arrest you," they warned over bullhorns as they approached the groups.

The last large group of students was forced into Johnson Hall by a group of Guardsmen armed with rifles and other weapons.

Admitted to the University Health Center for treatment for tear gas were Mike Sparr, 21, of Twin Lakes, and Doreen Dranek, 21, of Hudson. Treated for cuts were, Stephen Williams, 19, of Manchester Hall, and Brad Sinicrope, 19, of McDowell Hall. Primo Funeri, 21, Glenmorris Apartments, was treated for bayonet lacerations of the hands and face. Funeri received an eight-inch cut on his right check and a deep stab wound on his leg.

At 1:30 a.m. Sunday it was a quiet campus again. But it was a campus junkyard of broken glass and stones.

In the center of the junkyard was the totally destroyed ROTC building.

Two views of the National Guard arriving on the KSU campus.
(*Photos on both pages:* Cleveland Plain Dealer)

ROTC building: burning Saturday night, May 2; and the next morning.

Kent-Ravenna Record-Courier, May 4, 1970.

2 Guardsmen, 1 Student Dead in KSU Violence

69 Arrested, 10 Injured in Riots

BULLETIN

Three were killed in a shooting confrontation on the Kent State University campus shortly after noon today. Robinson Memorial Hospital reported three of 14 gunshot victims brought to the hospital were dead. One report said the dead, all unidentified at presstime, included two National Guardsmen and one student. Law enforcement agencies sent an escort to Ravenna Arsenal for more ammunition.

R-C Staff Report

An atmosphere of tense foreboding hangs like a pall over Kent and Kent State University today after the campus was shaken Sunday night by another serious student-police confrontation which left 10 injured and 62 arrested.

Ohio National Guard troops still patrolled the campus after thousands of students defied a dusk-to-dawn curfew and confronted police and Guardsmen on the campus and in the streets last night.

Although demonstrations of any sort have been prohibited by a court order, a rally was scheduled for noon today on the university Commons by dissident students.

More than 800 National Guardsmen, supported by hundreds of area policemen, including State Highway Patrol units, county sheriff's deputies and city police, responded to the third night of civil disorders in Kent.

What began as a campus protest march escalated into a violent confrontation with police when an estimated 2,500 students staged a massive demonstration at the university.

The violence culminated two nights of civil disorder which included the breaking of windows in downtown Kent Friday night and the burning of an ROTC building on campus Saturday night.

Many of last night's demonstrators were embittered over the stationing of Guardsmen on campus after the Saturday night disorders.

This issue, compounded by the recent military move into Cambodia by U.S. troops, was probably the instigating factor, according to many students interviewed by Record-Courier staffers.

The protest began as a word-of-mouth campaign at the Student Union at 7 p.m. before moving to the campus Commons, the center of the university, where the main rally was held.

Hundreds of students became thousands as they formed at the Commons, called by the sound of the "victory bell," a large bell once used to report sports victories.

"Join us, Join us," they chanted. And many did. As they marched they shouted diatribes at police and the war. "One, two, three, four, we don't want this (blank) war," they cried.

Many of the students tried to restrain some of the demonstrators from over-reacting, yet two rocks were thrown through windows at Manchester Hall as the group passed.

The students, planning to emphasize their demands by marching on university President Robert I. White's house, were stopped by Guardsmen at Nixson Hall.

The Guardsmen fired a series of tear gas canisters into the crowd, scattering the demonstrators.

Regrouping back on the Commons, dissidents headed for the front campus and E. Main St. Although an on-campus curfew was not in effect (1 a.m. Monday), the city curfew was violated when they left the campus and began to march down E. Main St.

Advancing at first past the intersection of Lincoln and E. Main Sts., approximately a half a block, the group split into factions and retreated back to the intersection for lack of support.

There at 9:30 p.m. about 200 students sat down in the middle of E. Main St. near the intersection and began to taunt the Guardsmen and police. Other students waited close behind on campus.

Police and Guardsmen lined the streets and for an hour and 15 minutes the two groups faced each other, the police gripping clubs and the students mocking the officers and Guardsmen.

During that time many of the students tried to persuade the Guardsmen to come over to their side, shouting: "Come on, you're not pigs."

At 10:15 p.m. three students approached the police, asking for a conference. Speaking to Sgt. Joseph Myers, of the Kent Police Department, they requested time to present a list of demands to President White and Mayor LeRoy Satrom.

They said they did not want violence and would leave if these demands could be aired:

1. That the National Guard and police leave the campus by 1:30 p.m. Monday.

2. That ROTC be removed from campus.

3. That amnesty for all students arrested Friday and Saturday night be granted.

4. That approval be given to the demands made by black students earlier in the week, which included increased black enrollment, a new cultural center and more black faculty.

They also asked Myers if they could sit peacefully in the street until the 1 a.m. curfew and then be allowed 45 minutes for off-campus students to return home.

Myers told the dissidents that he would warn them if the police were to clear the area, but said the other demands, although a possibility, had to be considered by those concerned.

As the students turned to leave, after their conference with Myers, a National Guard major said an order was read earlier in the evening telling the demonstrators to disperse and that he was now going to make arrests.

As the Guard moved in, students ran south on S. Lincoln St., shouting obscenities and screaming at the police: "You lying pigs. You (blank) pigs."

A young man who fell during the initial charge was stabbed by a bayonet in the back and ran up the street bleeding. He was later taken to Robinson Memorial Hospital after collapsing in the kitchen of a house where he took shelter.

While the Guardsmen advanced, many students hid in houses and dorms. Three police helicopters, which had been surveying the scene with high intensity searchlights, circled the campus area continuously.

A Guardsman was injured when he was hit in the leg with a wrench as he advanced with the column of Guardsmen.

During the next two hours, students outside of their dorms were arrested for curfew violations. Some members of the press were also threatened by the National Guard. A photographer was threatened with confiscation of his equipment if "you take one more picture."

Many of the students took refuge in he Tri-Towers dormitory complex where they gathered in the "pit," a central meeting place for the three dormitories—Wright, Koonce and Leebrick.

According to reports, many students thought the National Guard would break in. The Guard investigated, but did not enter the building.

Rumors that 200 student agitators from Ohio State University were in Kent were groundless, according to many of the students. "There aren't any new faces," one said. Police maintained otherwise.

Kent-Ravenna Record-Courier, May 4, 1970. (Early in the press run, the following headline and bulletin were substituted for those reproduced above.)

4 Kent State Students Killed in Clash Today

BULLETIN

Four students were reported killed and possibly eleven others wounded in a shooting confrontation on the Kent State University campus shortly after noon today.

The students were shot in a clash with National Guardsmen and police during a campus rally.

Three of the students were dead on arrival at Robinson Memorial Hospital. The fourth died shortly after arrival at the hospital.

President Robert I. White today announced the closing of Kent State University for the remainder of the week. The president ordered all students to their rooms and said that transportation for the students' departure is being arranged. He said that efforts to reopen the university next week would be made.

It has also been learned that a search is on for a female sniper who is said to have started the shooting at Kent.

All businesses in Kent have been ordered closed by the National Guard and the city has been sealed off to outside transportation. All banks in Ravenna closed today.

From the *CBS Evening News with Walter Cronkite,* May 4, 1970.

CRONKITE: Good evening. Four students at Kent State University in Ohio are dead, two of them coeds. They were shot during protests against the American presence in Cambodia. Ike Pappas reports.

PAPPAS: A bell on the campus commons called students together again today for another rally. It should have been a warning signal for what was to follow. After two days of rioting over ROTC and Cambodia, the university had banned rallies and the National Guard stood by to enforce the ban.

MAN: Leave this area immediately. Leave this area immediately.

PAPPAS: The warning was issued several times but the students were angry and they stood defiant. Guards then were given the order to move out, but first the students were peppered with tear gas fired from rifle-like launchers.

In moments clouds of tear gas covered the center of the campus. The students fell back over a hill, answering the Guardsmen with rocks. Suddenly, from over the hill, there was rifle fire. Four students, two of them females, were shot to death. At least another dozen were wounded. Assistant Adjutant General Frederick Wenger said that snipers fired into the ranks of the troops, and the troops fired back. The students were angry. John Dramis was there.

DRAMIS: There were guards at the top of the hill, just gathered around, like a big circle, just gathered together. They never said anything. All at once, they just put their rifles up in the air, from what I could see on my side—they started shooting blanks, or that's what everybody said, they were shooting blanks. One kid standing by me said that a bullet came down and ricocheted by his leg, and everybody just started running and got real scared. I walked back up the hill, and there was four—I could see three kids laying in the driveway down there, with blood, and girl friends were standing over them, crying and everything, and everybody was saying they were shooting blanks, but one kid came up, told me he saw a kid get hit right through the head. I saw them bring the ambulance and they brought him away, and everybody said they had blanks, but some of them had real bullets. They just looked like they fired up in the air and I looked around and this guy's laying, dead.

PAPPAS: The National Guard suffered its injuries, too, today. Several men were hurt by thrown rocks—one suffered what appeared to be a heart attack.

This, then, was the climax of three days of rioting on the campus; the students, demanding that ROTC be removed from the campus, Saturday burned down the ROTC headquarters. But the shootings today have caused a shock wave of reaction, not only in this usually quiet college town but across the state. Governor James Rhodes called in the State Police and the National Guard to conduct investigations. The FBI was also called. The university closed its doors late this afternoon; the town of Kent was sealed. Officials feared for more disturbances tonight. Veterans of this kind of campus turbulence say they have never seen students angrier.

Ike Pappas, CBS NEWS, Kent, Ohio.

CRONKITE: The commander of the Ohio National Guard said that his men fired only after they ran out of tear gas and the students advanced on them.

From the *CBS Evening News with Walter Cronkite,* May 5, 1970.

CRONKITE: After the four Kent State students were shot to death yesterday by National Guardsmen, a Guard spokesman said that an Ohio highway patrol helicopter had spotted a sniper on a nearby building, but today a highway patrol official said there is nothing in the log about such an incident, and it would have been there if it had happened. For the story today on the Kent State campus, here is Ike Pappas.

PAPPAS: Today the Kent State campus, under virtual martial law, guarded by some 2,000 troops and police, was sealed to everyone, so it was quiet. Classes were suspended indefinitely but every now and again there was a reminder, such as the campus flag at half staff, of the tragedy of yesterday. The last of the students, most of them bewildered and angered over the killing of four of their classmates, packed their things and moved out. What movement there was came from investigators from the National Guard and the state police attempting to determine what happened on Taylor Hill ["Blanket Hill"] at 12:20 yesterday afternoon, when gunfire rang out.

National Guardmen opened fire with semi-automatic weapons. The Guard says 16 or 17 weapons fired some 35 rounds. Four were killed: two young men, William Schroeder of Lorain, Ohio, and Jeffrey Miller of Plainview, New York, and two young women, Sandy Lee Scheuer of Youngstown, Ohio, and Allison Krause of Pittsburgh, Pennsylvania. A dozen others were wounded. After the shooting one young man dipped a black flag of revolution in the blood and waved it about as a symbol of the students' anger and frustration.

One of the wounded, Douglas Wrentmore, spoke of the incident today. Some Guard commanders said that their men were threatened by a sniper; but the student said he saw no excuse for the shootings.

WRENTMORE: Well, as far as I can figure out, it seems to be almost completely unjustified.

PAPPAS: I didn't hear that. Did you say completely unjustified?

WRENTMORE: Yes.

PAPPAS: Can you elaborate a little bit on that.

WRENTMORE: Well, if there was a sniper, as some people say, he would have been on top of one of the buildings. He wouldn't have been shooting from the crowd. And they fired into the crowd, not at the top of the building at a sniper.

PAPPAS: Doug, what do you think about what's happened to Kent State, what's happened to you?

WRENTMORE: Well, I don't feel too bad really, 'cause I got out really lucky, but those kids that got killed, like, there's nothing you can do, you know. I don't know. I don't want to see it happen again, it's just such a bad thing.

PAPPAS: In the event the men would run out of gas again, and something like this would happen and they're being rushed by students, is there again this danger of being shot?

SYLVESTER DEL CORSO [Commander, Ohio National Guard]: Yes, when an individual's life is at stake, they're—troops are there to perform a mission, and there is certainly danger of an individual being shot. Not that we want to shoot anybody, but it's just inconceivable that an individual would attempt to rush a trooper with a bayonet and a loaded weapon and expect him not to do anything, to permit them to beat him up or kill him.

FRED KIRSCH [student]: The general claims that there was a sniper up in a building. Well, there wasn't any sniper in the crowd then, so why did they shoot into the crowd. They shot into the crowd. They didn't shoot over heads. Maybe some of the Guardsmen were shooting over heads, who knows. But they were coming at me, and the ground around me was being thrown up by—by bullets.

PAPPAS: The National Guard said the men fired because they were being threatened with rocks. "We consider rocks a lethal weapon," said one commander. Robert Schakne asked Guard General Robert Canterbury if he had a sniper report.

CANTERBURY: I do not know.

SCHAKNE: Now, general, I don't want to press the point too hard— these are difficult circumstances—but I'm sure many people will be asking what possible justification there can be for firing bullets into a crowd of people, many of whom may be innocent bystanders, if in fact they have not necessarily fired on your troops?

CANTERBURY: I think the only justification is where your own life is endangered.

PAPPAS: What the investigators have to determine, then, is whether indeed there was a sniper, and whether the Guard was justified in firing its weapons, or whether, as some people here believe, the Guard panicked under the pressure of a rock-throwing attack and fired its weapons indiscriminately into the crowd, killing four students.

Ike Pappas, CBS NEWS, at Kent, Ohio.

Time, May 18, 1970 (excerpt).

Kent State: Martyrdom That Shook the Country

It took half a century to transform Kent State from an obscure teachers college into the second largest university in Ohio, with 21,000 students and an impressive array of modern buildings on its main campus. But it took less than ten terrifying seconds last week to convert the traditionally conformist campus into a bloodstained symbol of the rising student rebellion against the Nixon Administration and the war in Southeast Asia. When National Guardsmen fired indiscriminately into a crowd of unarmed civilians, killing four students, the bullets wounded the nation.

Paradoxically, the turn toward violence at Kent State was not inspired by the war or politics. The first rocks thrown in anger were hurled through the muggy Friday night of May 1 by beery students who could not resist the urge to dance on a Kent street. Hundreds of students were drinking at the bull-and-beer spots that flourish in most college towns. Spirits were light. A crowd swarmed into the warm night, blocking busy North Water Street, responding to the rock beat.

"Get Out"

One irate motorist gunned his car's engine as if to drive through the dancers. Some students climbed atop the car, jumped on it, then led a chant: "One-two-three-four, we don't want your------war!" A drunk on a balcony hurled a bottle into the street—and suddenly the mood turned ugly. Students smashed the car's windows, set fires in trash cans, began to bash storefronts. Police were called. Kent Mayor LeRoy Satrom had ordered a curfew, but few students were aware of it. Police stormed into bars after midnight, turning up the lights, shouting "Get out!" Some 2,000 more students, many of whom had been watching the Knicks-Lakers basketball game on TV, were forced into the street. Police and sheriff's deputies pushed the youths back toward the campus, then fired tear gas to disperse them.

Saturday began quietly. Black student leaders, who had been demanding the admission next year of 5,000 more blacks to Kent State (it now has about 600), and leaders of the mounting antiwar sentiment on campus talked of joining forces. They got administrative approval to hold a rally that evening on the ten-acre Commons at the center of the campus. There, despite the presence of faculty members and student marshals, militant war protesters managed to take complete charge of a crowd of about 800, many still smarting from the conflict of the night before. They disrupted a dance in one university hall, then attacked the one-story Army ROTC building facing the Commons. They smashed windows and threw lighted railroad flares inside. The building caught fire. When firemen arrived, students threw rocks at them and cut their hoses with machetes until police interceded with tear gas. Without bothering to consult Kent State authorities, Mayor Satrom asked for help from the National Guard. Governor James Rhodes, still engaged in his tough—and ultimately unsuccessful—campaign for the Senate nomination, quickly ordered Guardsmen transferred from points of tension in a Teamster strike elsewhere in Ohio.

Within an hour, about 500 Guardsmen, already weary from three nights of duty, arrived with fully loaded M-1 semiautomatic rifles, pistols and tear gas. They were in time to help police block the students from charging into the downtown area. Students reacted by dousing trees with gasoline, then setting them afire. Order was restored before midnight. On Sunday, Governor Rhodes arrived in Kent. He made no attempt to seek the advice of Kent State President Robert I. White and told newsmen that campus troublemakers were "worse than Brown Shirts and Communists and vigilantes—they're the worst type of people that we harbor in America." He refused to close the campus, as Portage County Prosecutor Ronald Kane pleaded; instead, he declared a state of emergency and banned all demonstrations on the campus. Late that night, about 500 students defied the order and staged a sit-down on one of Kent's busiest intersections. Guardsmen, their number now grown to 900, moved into the face of a rock barrage to arrest 150 students.

"Our Campus"

On Monday, the campus seemed to calm down. In the bright sunshine, tired young Guardsmen flirted with leggy co-eds under the tall oaks and maples. Classes continued throughout the morning. But the ban against mass assemblies was still in effect, and some students decided to test it again. "We just couldn't believe they could tell us to leave," said one. "This is *our* campus." At high noon, youngsters began ringing the school's Victory Bell, normally used to celebrate a football triumph but rarely heard of late. About 1,000 students, some nervous but many joking, gathered on the Commons. Another 2,000 ringed the walks and buildings to watch.

From their staging area the burned-out ROTC building, officers in two Jeeps rolled across the grass to address the students with bullhorns: "Evacuate the Commons area. You have no right to assemble." Back came shouts of "Pigs off campus! We don't want your war." Students raised middle fingers. The Jeeps pulled back. Two skirmish lines of Guardsmen, wearing helmets and gas masks, stepped away from the staging area and began firing tear-gas canisters at the crowd. The Guardsmen moved about 100 yards toward the assembly and fired gas again. A few students picked up canisters and threw them back, but they fell short of the troops. The mists of stinging gas split the crowd. Some students fled toward Johnson Hall, a men's dormitory, and were blocked by the L-shaped building. Others ran between Johnson and nearby Taylor Hall.

Leaderless

A formation of fewer than 100 Guardsmen—a mixed group including men from the 107th Armored Cavalry Regiment based in neighboring Ravenna, and others from a Wooster company of the 145th Infantry Regiment—pursued fleeing students between the two buildings. The troopers soon found themselves facing a fence and flanked by rock-throwing students, who rarely got close enough to hit anyone. Occasionally one managed to toss a gas canister back near the troops, while delighted spectators, watching from the hilltop, windows of buildings and the roof of another men's dorm, cheered. Many demonstrators were laughing.

Then the outnumbered and partially encircled contingent of Guardsmen ran out of tear gas. Suddenly they seemed frightened. They began retreating up the hill toward Taylor Hall, most of them walking backward to keep their eyes on the threatening students below. The crowd on the hilltop consisted almost entirely of onlookers rather than rock throwers. The tight circle of retreating Guardsmen contained officers and noncoms from both regiments, but no single designated leader. With them in civilian clothes was Brigadier General Robert Canterbury, the ranking officer on the campus, who said later: "I was there—but I was not in command of any unit." Some of the troops held their rifles pointed skyward. Several times a few of them turned, pointed their M-1s threateningly at the crowd, and continued their retreat.

When the compact formation reached the top of the hill, some Guardsmen knelt quickly and aimed at the students who were hurling rocks from below. A handful of demonstrators kept moving toward the troops. Other Guardsmen stood behind the kneeling troops, pointing their rifles down the hill. A few aimed over the students' heads. Several witnesses later claimed that an officer brought his baton down in a sweeping signal. Said Jim Minard, a sophomore from Warren, Ohio: "I was harassing this officer. I threw a stone at him, and he pointed a .45-caliber pistol at me. He was brandishing a swagger stick. He turned away. He was holding his baton in the air, and the moment he dropped it, they fired." Within seconds, a sickening staccato of rifle fire signaled the transformation of a once-placid campus into the site of an historic American tragedy.

Like a Firing Squad

"They are shooting blanks—they are shooting blanks," thought Kent State Journalism Professor Charles Brill, who nevertheless crouched behind a pillar. "Then I heard a chipping sound and a ping, and I thought, 'My God, this is for real.'" An Army veteran who saw action in Korea, Brill was certain that the Guardsmen had not fired randomly out of individual panic. "They were organized," he said. "It was not scattered. They all waited and they all pointed their rifles at the same time. It looked like a firing squad." The shooting stopped—as if on signal. Minutes later, the Guardsmen assumed parade-rest positions, apparently to signal the crowd that the fusillade would not be resumed unless the Guardsmen were threatened again. "I felt like I'd just had an order to clean up a latrine," recalled one Guardsman in the firing unit. "You do what you're told to do."

The campus was suddenly still. Horrified students flung themselves to the ground, ran for cover behind buildings and parked cars, or just stood stunned. Then screams broke out. "My God, they're killing us!" one girl cried. They were. A river of blood ran from the head of one boy, saturating his school books. One youth held a cloth against the abdomen of another, futilely trying to check the bleeding. Guardsmen made no move to help the victims. The troops were still both frightened and threatening. After ambulances had taken away the dead and wounded, more students gathered. Geology Professor Glenn Frank, an ex-Marine, ran up to talk to officers. He came back sobbing. "If we don't get out of here right now," he reported, "the Guard is going to clear us out any way they can—they mean *any* way."

In that brief volley, four young people—none of whom was a protest leader or even a radical—were killed. Ten students were wounded, three seriously. One of them, Dean Kahler of Canton, Ohio, is paralyzed below his waist by a spinal wound.

The Fatalities

WILLIAM K. SCHROEDER, 19, a psychology major from Lorain, Ohio, was the second-ranking student in Kent State's Army ROTC unit. A friend recalled that he was "angry and upset" that the ROTC building had been burned down. A former Eagle Scout, high school basketball and track standout, he was the image of the clean-cut, academically conscientious Middle American boy. He apparently was only a spectator at the Monday rally. Even so, he illustrates the fact that youth's sentiment is shifting too rapidly to permit any student to be neatly tabbed. "My son was very opposed to the Viet Nam War," said William Schroeder's mother, "and his feelings against the war were growing."

SANDRA LEE SCHEUER, 20, a junior from Youngstown, Ohio, was walking to a class in speech therapy (her major) when she was caught in the Guardsmen's fire. A bubbly girl and an honor student, Sandy seemed too gregarious and full of laughter to take much interest in politics or protest. Although she sympathized with the peace movement, she did not join her college friends when they went to work for Senator Eugene McCarthy's presidential campaign. "Sandy lived for what everyone else lived for—to find someone to love and someone who loved her," said her best friend, Eileen Feldman.

JEFFREY GLENN MILLER, 20, a transfer student from Michigan State, where he found fraternity life a lot of "adolescent nonsense," was no militant activist either. But he did call his mother in Plainview, N.Y., to say that he felt he had to join the demonstrations. He wore his hair long, liked bell-bottoms, love beads and rock music. A psychology major, he was, according to acquaintances, "a great believer in love." "I know it sounds like a mother," said Mrs. Elaine Miller, "but Jeff didn't want to go to war, not because he'd be hurt, but because he might have to hurt someone else."

ALLISON KRAUSE, 19, a quiet, almond-eyed beauty, was more of a listener than a talker; she never preached about her deeply held views. She opposed the war, and with her boy friend, Barry Levine, was among the spectators caught in the rifle fire. An honor student interested in the history of art, she believed in protest but not in violence. She had placed a flower in a Guardsman's rifle at Kent State and said softly: "Flowers are better than bullets." "Is dissent a crime?" asked Allison Krause's father. "Is this a reason for killing her? Have we come to such a state in this country that a young girl has to be shot because she disagrees deeply with the actions of her Government?" . . .

Newsweek, May 18, 1970 (excerpt).

"My God! They're Killing Us"

Kent State University, in the rolling green hills of northeastern Ohio, seems the very model of a modern, Middle American university. Until last year, the most vicious outbreak of violence there was a 1958 panty raid launched against two women's dormitories, which resulted in the prompt dismissal of 29 students. Recently, the radical spirit had begun to drift over the 790-acre campus—but only a fraction of the school's 19,000 students was affected. Antiwar rallies attracted no more than 300 people at best, and even the appearance of Jerry Rubin of the Chicago Seven drew only about 1,000. . . .

. . . With the [ROTC] building in ruins and the townspeople in an angry uproar, a request was made by Mayor Leroy Satrom that Gov. James Rhodes call in the National Guard. "If these anarchists get away with it here," said a lifelong Kent resident, "no campus in the country is safe."

The governor was eager to oblige. Having made campus disorder a key issue in his hard campaign for the U.S. Senate, Rhodes quickly ordered in men from the 107th Armored Cavalry Regiment and the 145th Infantry Battalion, declared martial law—and then showed up himself to set the tone in a public address. Attributing the violence to students "worse than the 'brown-shirt' and the Communist element and also the night-riders in the vigilantes . . . the worst type of people that we harbor in America," the governor pledged: "We are going to eradicate the problem . . . It's over with in Ohio."

Orders

Off the podium, said a reliable source, Rhodes all but took personal command of the guardsmen. Without consulting top guard officials or the university administration, he reportedly ordered that all campus assemblies—peaceful or otherwise—be broken up and said the troops would remain on campus twelve months a year if necessary. "There was no discussion," an insider informed NEWSWEEK, "because it wouldn't have done any good. The governor had made up his mind."

The guardsmen were already tired and tense, having been brought in from five days on duty in the Cleveland area during the wildcat Teamsters strike. Though many were young and some were even Kent State students, most of the troopers seemed to share the antipathy to student protests characteristic of small-town Ohio. They got through Sunday with no serious incident. But with the start of classes on Monday, the scene was set for a fatal confrontation. . . .

In the aftermath, Ohio guard brass obdurately defended the conduct of their men. They quickly whisked away the troops who had fired the fatal rounds and then tried to explain what had happened. First they contended that the volley had not been ordered but that it was fired in response to a sniper's bullet; next day they were forced to admit they had no real evidence of any such sniping. However, there was an unaccounted for bullet hole in a metal sculpture outside Taylor Hall that some felt was consistent with a sniper shot from a rooftop; and more mystery was added with reports that a bullet wound suffered by one victim, as well as some shell casings on campus, did not match the ammunition authorized for the guard.

Ultimately, guard commanders rested their case on what seemed an extraordinary Ohio National Guard regulation that permits each individual soldier to shoot when he feels his life is endangered. "I am satisfied that these troops felt that their lives were in danger," said General Canterbury, 55, who was in charge of the troops. "I felt I could have been killed out there . . . Considering the size of the rocks and the proximity of those throwing them, lives were in danger . . . Hell, they were 3 feet behind us . . . I do think, however, that under normal conditions, an officer would give the order to fire."

"Bastards"

Some guardsmen on campus evidenced little if any regret over the killings. "It's about time we showed the bastards who's in charge," said one. And many of the townspeople of Kent shared the same sentiment. "You can't really help but kind of think they've been asking for it and finally got it," said a motel clerk. What did the troops who did the actual firing think? "They didn't go to Kent State to kill anyone," cried the wife of one of the men who fired at the students. "I know he'd rather have stayed home and mowed the lawn. He told me so. He told me they didn't fire those shots to scare the students off. He told me they fired those shots because they knew the students were coming after them, coming for their guns. People are calling my husband a murderer; my husband is not a murderer. He was afraid."

Even granting the genuine fear felt by the guardsmen, disturbing questions persisted about their behavior during the episode. The guard insisted that the men fired as they were about to be "overrun" by the students. But if the troops were so closely surrounded, how was it that nobody closer than 75 feet away was hit? And if the rocks and bricks presented such overwhelming danger, how did the troops avoid even one injury serious enough to require hospital treatment?

If the danger was not quite as great as first portrayed, why could not the detachment's cadre of officers—a top-heavy group of four or five captains, and Brigadier General Canterbury himself—keep the men under control. A 22-year-old drama student named James Minard charged that he saw an officer give the command to fire. "This lieutenant had his arm raised and carried a baton," Minard said. "When the baton came down, they fired. I was apparently the only one who saw it; nobody believed me." A well-connected guard source flatly told NEWSWEEK's James Jones and Jon Lowell: "There had to be some kind of preliminary order."

Spark?

Ohio's Democratic Sen. Stephen Young said in Washington that he had learned the firing was actually touched off by a nervous guardsman whose rifle went off when he was hit by a tear-gas canister or rock. Other observers wondered whether a student photographer, armed while on assignment for the university and the police, might have provided the spark—although an initial police check indicated his gun had not been fired.

As a spring rain washed the bloodstains from the campus, Kent State president Robert L. White ordered the university closed (for the rest of the quarter, it developed), and asked for a high-level investigation of the entire affair. After a visit by six Kent students, President Nixon announced that such an inquiry would be conducted by the Justice Department. The guard itself and the Ohio state police are also investigating the shootings. But even before the evidence was in, 1,000 Kent State faculty members rendered a verdict of their own. Prevented from meeting on the campus, they crowded into a nearby Akron Unitarian church and passed this resolution: "We hold the guardsmen, acting under orders and under severe psychological pressures, less responsible for the massacre than are Governor Rhodes and Adjutant General [Sylvester] Del Corso, whose inflammatory statements produced these pressures."

"Do More"

Beyond that there was little left but to bury the dead. In New York City, nearly 5,000 mourners joined the family of Jeffrey Miller at services addressed by Dr. Benjamin Spock, who declared that the Kent State killings "may do more to end the war in Vietnam than all the rest of us have been able to do." . . .

FOUR STUDENTS KILLED IN ANTI-NIXON RIOT: DEATH OF A CAMPUS BUM

Daily Sketch (London), May 5, 1970

THREE ARE DEAD, 12 SHOT IN BATTLE AT KENT STATE

Youngstown (Ohio) Vindicator, May 4, 1970

3 Dead, 15 Wounded in Rioting at KSU

Canton (Ohio) Repository, May 4, 1970

GUARDSMEN KILL 4 STUDENTS DURING RALLY AT OHIO COLLEGE

Detroit Free Press, May 5, 1970

РАССТРЕЛЯНЫ В КЕНТЕ (THE EXECUTED IN KENT)

Izvestia, May 19, 1970

Quattro studenti uccisi nell'Ohio durante una manifestazione contro la guerra (FOUR STUDENTS KILLED IN OHIO DURING AN ANTI-WAR DEMONSTRATION)

Corrierre della Sera (Milan), May 5, 1970

4 DEAD, 11 WOUNDED AS GUARD FIRES INTO RIOTERS AT KSU

Akron Beacon Journal, May 4, 1970

4 killed in student protest

Times (London), May 5, 1970

ПОЗОР И ТРАГЕДИЯ АМЕРИКЕ; ФОТОГРАФИИ ОБВИНЯЮТ; ПРЕСТУПЛЕНИЕ В КЕНТЕ ОСТАЕТСЯ БЕЗНАКАЗАННЫМ; КОНГРЕСС ПРОТИВ БЕЛОГО ДОМА (SHAME AND TRAGEDY IN AMERICA; THE PHOTOGRAPHS ACCUSE; THE CRIME IN KENT REMAINS UNPUNISHED; CONGRESS OPPOSED TO WHITE HOUSE)

Izvestia, May 16, 1970

KENT PROTESTOR REPORTED KILLED

Cleveland Press, May 4, 1970

2

Reactions

The shock of the events of May 4 provoked immediate response. This section presents a selection of reactions by professional writers, public men, and members of the public at large. It is divided into four sections: news, rumors, editorial comments, and letters. This division is more convenient than absolute, since statements in one area often gave rise to counter-statements in others, but we feel it is generally just.

NEWS

The antagonisms underlying the shootings at Kent State did not end with the events themselves but seemed to gain in virulence during the succeeding days and weeks. While memorial services were being held throughout the nation in honor of "The Kent State Four" and two students killed at Jackson State College, Mississippi, on May 15, the nation continued to be racked by confrontations and protests.

At the national level, President Nixon attempted to cool matters by issuing a statement on May 5 and by holding a press conference the evening of May 8 to explain once again his rationale for the Cambodian invasion. Critics of the President seemed to give more weight, however, to the widely quoted remarks he had made informally to a group of Pentagon workers on May 1: "You know, you see these bums, you know, blowing up the campuses. Listen, the boys on the college campuses are the luckiest people in the world—going to the greatest universities—and here they are burning up the books, storming around about this issue, I mean—you name it. Get rid of the war and there'll be another one. And then, out there, we got kids who are just doing their duty, and I've seen them: they stand tall and they're proud."

Senator Edward M. Kennedy (Dem., Mass.), who was later to open his home for a benefit raising money for the Kent State Medical Fund, denounced on May 5 the killings by drawing a parallel with recently reported atrocities in Viet Nam: "Who of us, seeing American troops in Ohio fire wildly into a crowd of students, does not also see My Lai, with its defenseless Vietnamese civilians cut down by American troops?"

Within the administration itself protest occurred when a young official of the Health, Education, and Welfare Department resigned his position, citing the repression of youth as his reason; and Secretary of the Interior Walter Hickel wrote a personal letter (quickly leaked to the press) charging that administration policies seemed "to lack concern for the attitude of a great mass of Americans—our young people."

Vice-President Spiro T. Agnew, whose recent attacks on the academic community and on the press had inflamed liberals, struck a balance during the aftermath. On May 8, while taping an interview for David Frost's television show, he was reported as agreeing that the Guard may have committed murder, "but not in the first degree." Some days later the Vice-President questioned the motivations of protesting students: "I think a lot of these students were out on a typical Spring lark."

Across the land, university students engaged in a massive strike which the Urban Research Corporation, reporting in late June, attributed chiefly to the Kent killings. The report identified 760 (or one-third of the nation's) campuses as participating in strike activities, and added that the 100 strikes per day for four days following the deaths were "unprecedented in our history." Furthermore, between 40,000 and 100,000 young people gathered in Washington, D.C., on May 9 to protest the war and killings.

But the student reaction was met by at least as powerful an impulse on the part of thousands of Americans who, weary of years of campus turbulence, rose to the defense of their apparently threatened nation, leaders, and way of life. The most striking counter-demonstration occurred on Friday, May 8, when thousands of construction workers, many wearing "hard hats," paraded with flags and banners in New York City. The banners carried by the marchers—who occasionally clashed violently with unsympathetic onlookers—proclaimed hostility toward Mayor John V. Lindsay, who had had city flags lowered to half-mast in tribute to the slain students, and support for Nixon's policies.

In Ohio, while Governor Rhodes remained silent on the events of early May, attempts were made in the press, the courts, and the legislature to fix responsibility and prevent repetition of the disaster. The sharpest verbal exchange occurring in the first week after the killings was that between Ohio National Guard General Del Corso and United States Senator Stephen Young. Del Corso, replying to Senator Young's criticism of the Guard, called the Senator "a senile old liar," to which Senator Young responded by saying, among other things, that "my father told me, 'Never get into a spraying contest with a skunk.'" At the state level, the legislature moved to curb unrest by passing in June a campus disturbance bill (Ohio House Bill 1219) laying down stern procedures to be invoked against any university personnel who might interrupt the functioning of universities. As the summer went on, law suits were filed (some by the ACLU) to protest the "wrongful deaths," and the dormitory search conducted by the county prosecutor after the campus had closed down.

The most widely read journalistic investigation of the Kent incidents was conducted by a team of reporters from the Knight Newspapers, who on May 24 published their results under the title, "Kent State: the Search for Understanding." This 30,000-word document, which found both Guardsmen and students responsible for the tragedy, anticipated both in its thoroughness and its conclusions the "Scranton Commission Report" released months later.

In Kent, the town and University sought to restore order and improve communications. While hundreds of meetings were being held, often in private homes, to foster dialogue between University personnel and townspeople, the University acted to complete the quarter's work with its student body scattered over the state and country. The term's work was finished through various means: class meetings were held in professors' homes; local TV and radio stations gave air time for lectures; faculty drove tens and sometimes hundreds of miles to meet with students; and, most importantly, the mails were used in an attempt to complete what had seemed an inpossible task. Among other things which spurred the University on were the responses of students who felt suddenly lost and uprooted. A student's letter to the University ended with a sentence which was widely publicized: "I want to come home to Kent."

Although no official ceremony was held by the city or the University, a memorial service occurred on June 3, when Robert Shaw came to Kent to conduct a performance of the Cherubini *Requiem* in memory of the dead at Kent and Jackson State. Many of the performers and audience, both groups drawn from the University and town, wept at the conclusion.

As committees and commissions began their work to probe the causes of what happened at Kent, the University tightened security and communications. On June 13, seniors returned to campus for graduation, and on June 22, the summer sessions began with a slight drop in enrollment, with a certain tension, but without incident. On September 28, the University began its fall quarter (the enrollment was slightly higher than the year before) with a memorial service arranged by and for its students.

KSU President White's Comment at a Press Conference after the Shootings

I hear lunacy on the one side and frightening repressions on the other and I don't hear from that traditional center position that says: "Let us discuss fully and without limits and let us come to a decision and a conclusion within orderly processes which are in themselves subject to orderly change."

Resolution Passed by the KSU Faculty Senate, May 5, 1970

We the faculty of Kent State University, hereby affirming our belief that the faculty and students of a university constitute an indivisible community dedicated to the same ideals, and therefore regarding the deprivation of the life and liberty of any member of that community as our common deprivation, do strongly condemn the fatal shooting of four KSU students and the wounding of ten others by National Guardsmen on May 4, 1970. We hold the Guardsmen, acting under orders and under severe psychological pressures, less responsible for the massacre than are Governor Rhodes and Adjutant General Sylvester Del Corso, whose inflammatory indoctrination produced those pressures. We deplore the prolonged and unduly provocative military presence on the campus not only because we regard the use of massive military force against unarmed students as inappropriate in itself, but because it symbolizes the rule of force in our society and international life. We regard student protest against this rule of force as their moral prerogative. We profoundly regret the failure of the Governor and other civil officers to understand the complexity and variety of the issues motivating our students, to comprehend the diversity of the students involved, and to adjust flexibly and humanely to their morally based unrest.

In this moment of grief, we pledge that in the future we shall not teach in circumstances which are likely to lead to the death and wounding of our students. We cannot keep the civil authorities from assuming control of our campus. But we can—and do—refuse to teach in a climate that is inimical to the safety of our students and to the principles of academic freedom. We pledge ourselves to a thorough consideration of the relationship between the University and the military establishment.

Finally, we protest the abridgment of our academic and civil liberties. While in no manner sanctioning violence to person and property by protestants, we find the massive peace-time imposition of martial law unconscionable. Not only were four members of our community deprived of life without due process, but all persons in our academic as well as local community have been subjected to abridgment of their rights to assemble and to move about.

We urge all our fellow citizens to consider the condition and the direction of our country: Why is there such hatred of dissident students? Why is there such intolerance of nonconformity? We respectfully but emphatically remind all that, especially under times of strain, Constitutional guarantees must be preserved and abided by and all universities must not only be allowed but be encouraged to perform their historic task of presenting and examining all points of view.

RESOLVED THAT: the faculty of Kent State University condemns the use of force, violence, arson, and civil disturbance by any member of the university community; student freedom carries with it student responsibility for mature action, and to this end the faculty encourages an expression of cooperation and constructive effort on the part of all students to improve the total university; the faculty is convinced that we cannot view this tragic violence as a phenomenon separate from the violence in which the American government is involved in Southeast Asia. Our government's participation in the unpopular and apparently interminable war in Vietnam is chiefly responsible for the frustration and anger which is increasingly apparent among university students.

From an unpublished article.

Non-Commercial Radio Serves a University in Crisis

By John C. Weiser
Professor of Speech, KSU

. . . [T]he guardsmen turned and retreated several times. Then a "crack" was heard. This has been described by all reports as a shot. This was the controversial "sniper shot," but no one, even after several months, was or is able to define what this was, whether a firecracker, a rifle or pistol shot from some unknown source, or some other noise. The origin of this noise is still unknown. At this point, however, the guard unit on the south end of Taylor Hall seemed to turn in unison and face the crowd, many of the guardsmen dropping to a kneeling firing position. Within one second after the "shot" the guard opened fire on the crowd. Two WKSU-FM reporters on the scene, reporting via their walkie-talkies, indicated the guard did not seem to pick out any individuals. Some guardsmen shot into the ground, others into the air, and still others directly at the crowd. Ambulances were on the scene in moments. They had been parked on the campus on a standby basis. At this time another WKSU reporter radioed to the station, "I'm sick —I'm coming back." . . .

On Tuesday, May 5, WKSU-FM began its broadcast day at 9:00 A.M. One of the most heartwarming responses to the station's broadcasts began on that day, and continued for the next four days. People in the surrounding area, specifically in Kent, Ravenna, and Akron, called the station opening their homes to students who could not get home or had no place to go. Other callers offered transportation for up to a distance of 200 miles. In brief, the people in the community responded with compassion to the plight of students forced to leave the university without their clothes or belongings. Most left with just a few items, or just the "clothes on their backs." The station received over 200 calls from 82 different families, and the list of names and telephone numbers of those offering help got longer as each of the five days passed, and the station continued to broadcast their names. . . .

Resolution Passed by the KSU Faculty Senate, May 14, 1970.

We, the faculty senate of Kent State University, having experienced the reality of violence in a most tragic way, hereby affirm our commitment to peace in the world and on the campus. Having seen our students slain and wounded, we feel compelled to speak out against the use of violent means on behalf of any cause, no matter how noble.

We have seen how the language of violence and hate leads to destruction and death. We have seen how the metaphorical burning of a building leads to the actual burning of a building and how that, in turn, leads to grief. Finally, we have seen how this chain of violence can threaten the very existence of a great university.

Students today dream of a world ruled by love, not hate. They dream of a world in which all men are brothers. We honor them for their dream. It is ours, too, as it has been the noblest dream of all men everywhere. But, sobered by the violence that has stained our campus, we beg them to consider that the peace and love they yearn for cannot be won by violence and hate.

Emerson told us long ago that the end pre-exists in the means. This law of life applies not only to professors and politicians and generals, but to students as well. None of us is exempt. Unless all of us—young and old alike—renounce violence and hate we will all be doomed endlessly to repeat the failures of the past.

From an *Associated Press Release*, May 5, 1970.

President Nixon says he hopes the fatal shootings of four students at Kent State University in Ohio will convince the nation's universities that while they protect the right of peaceful protest, they must stand "just as strongly against the resort to violence. . . ."

Vice President Spiro T. Agnew said, meanwhile, that he views the killing of the four students and the wounding of 11 others by National Guardsmen as proof that his criticism of violent demonstrations and revolutionary politics has been justified.

Nixon, in a statement on the shootings, said, "This should remind us all once again that when dissent turns to violence, it invites tragedy."

"It is my hope that this tragic and unfortunate incident will strengthen the determination of all the nation's campuses, administrators, faculty and students alike, to stand firmly for the right which exists in this country of peaceful dissent and just as strongly against the resort to violence as a means of such expression," he said. . . .

Agnew said the Kent State violence had been "predictable and avoidable." He said the events of the day make self-evident the truth of his repeated attacks against militant dissent.

From the *Cleveland* (Ohio) *Plain Dealer,* May 5, 1970.

2 Troopers' Collapse Led to False Reports

By Carl Kovac

KENT—The collapse of two Ohio National Guardsmen before the echoes of shots that killed four young persons at Kent State University died out yesterday gave rise to widespread rumors that two troopers had been slain in an exchange of gunfire on the strife-ridden campus.

It was not until several hours later that it was confirmed that those killed by gunfire were students, two of them coeds.

The two guardsmen, Dennis Brackenridge, 28, and William Heisler, 26, were taken to Robinson Memorial Hospital in nearby Ravenna.

Both were said by hospital officials to be suffering from shock apparently brought about by the battle with students. . . .

From the *CBC Sunday Magazine,* May 10, 1970;
Guardsmen Interviewed on May 5.

GUARDSMAN 1: Nobody cares about us. All they care about is them poor kids up there that got killed. They can throw rocks at us and we're supposed to stand there and they're pebble-throwers just harassing us. . . .

GUARDSMAN 2: I was so scared Saturday night I was gonna get it, it was pitiful. We went on top of that hill when that fire was down there—I never been so scared in all my life. . . .

GUARDSMAN 1: I feel it's about time one of 'em got it like that. . . . I don't like to see anybody get killed, but I mean, we come up here and these people all they do is stand around and give you a peace sign, throw rocks at you and harass you and call you dirty names, wanna know who's sleeping with your wife—ain't none of their business in the first place. I mean, I don't like to be here, I'm losing money at work. . . .

GUARDSMAN 3: I wouldn't shoot anybody. I don't even load my weapon. . . . Why would I want to shoot innocent kids?

From the *Chicago Daily News,* May 11, 1970.

'V' Sign for Peace at Kent Services

By Lynn Langway

WASHINGTON—There were no clenched fists when they came together, the young and the leaders, to memorialize the four slain students of Kent State University.

No fists—only the "V" of peace, the bowed heads of two famous widows, and the voice of one, Mrs. Martin Luther King Jr., raised sweetly Friday night in the crowded Washington church.

"As He died to make men holy let us live to make men free," Mrs. King sang to the 2,000 or more in the New York Avenue Presbyterian Church. Many sang with her, but Mrs. Robert F. Kennedy lowered her head silently during "The Battle Hymn of the Republic," the hymn that had so often eulogized her husband.

"You are here tonight to warn the nation and tired reactionary men that you will not accept an inheritance of evil," Coretta King told the hushed audience of students, many crying quietly, and senators, congressmen and one Nixon Cabinet member, Labor Sec. George P. Shultz.

"I did not have the privilege of knowing these four students, but perhaps they knew my husband. . . . Because they lived, our people and our attitudes have been changed, and their deaths are not in vain.

"Peace . . . shall be their luminous memorial. The greatest memorial we can make to them is to reaffirm our commitment to making our society, our nation and the world just, peaceful and loving," she said, and the students, many with camper packs on their backs, responded with a standing ovation.

Applause rang out again for Sen. Edward Kennedy, who said that "hopefully, their deaths can strengthen in us the resolve to take down these walls which now separate our people from each other and the purposes of this nation."

Then, with a catch in his voice, the young senator prayed: "Dear God, our prayer tonight is a simple one. Help us, dear God, this war must end."

Kent State student Martin Kurta read a statement from the parents of the four, shot by National Guardsmen Monday on their Ohio campus.

"We thank you for making our grief your own," it said.

"There is only one fitting memorial to the fallen. It is for the living to stop the killing . . . on the battlefields of Asia, in any part of the world, on any street corner . . . or any university or college campus . . . or on the Ellipse in Washington, D.C."

Then the students, led by folksinger Judy Collins in "Where Have All the Flowers Gone," filed out of the church and into the streets with lighted candles.

They walked to the iron railing that curves in front of the Ellipse, where they will gather again Saturday, and they left their candles there, flickering on the fence.

Through the lilac bushes, and the fountains, and the floodlights, and haloed by the candles, was the White House, several hundred feet away.

From the *New York Daily News*, May 13, 1970.

Says Kent Killings Made Guards Weep

Wooster, Ohio, May 12 (UPI)—An Ohio National Guard sergeant said today he saw guardsmen "throw down their weapons and start to bawl" following the confrontation at Kent State University in which four students were shot to death.

"They didn't want to shoot," said Sgt. Richard A. Parker of Wooster, a member of Co. A, 145th Infantry. "After it happened I saw guys run back from the hill, throw down their weapons and start to bawl.

"None of the guys up there wanted to fire. Most of the guys were scared. And nothing scared them more than going to face those students. Some of them were facing friends and relatives."

From an *Associated Press Release*, May 15, 1970

KENT (AP)—Authorities say a search of Kent State University's 3,316 dormitory rooms after the campus was closed May 4 following the shooting deaths of four students turned up a shotgun, a damaged pistol and many knives.

Non-students had occupied some of the rooms.

Some sources claim there was sniper fire before National Guardsmen opened fire during the campus anti-war demonstration in which the four died. It has not been determined whether the four played any role in the protest.

Portage County Prosecutor Ronald Kane, displaying the items Friday, said they were taken during the dormitory search by the State Patrol. He said the "facts will speak for themselves."

Exhibited for newsmen in the campus gymnasium were a .20-gauge single shot shotgun and a damaged weapon described as a .25-caliber pistol, scores of knives ranging from machetes to penknives, five air pistols, four slingshots, 10 blank-firing starters' pistols, five marijuana plants growing in pint-size milk cartons and a laundry bag containing pornographic pictures.

Quantities of pills and capsules also were displayed. Officials said the drugs ranged from hallucinogens to vitamin pills and antibiotics.

Also confiscated were a baton twirler's torch baton and carrying case, a bottle labeled benzine, the burned-out stubs of a highway flare, and a rock wrapped in red cloth.

"It appears to me that some of the students were obviously not here to get an education," said Kane. . . .

Excerpts from the *Akron Beacon Journal,* May 24, 1970.

Kent State: The Search for Understanding

Three weeks ago in Kent, three to five dozen bullets killed four young persons, wounded nine and plunged the nation into the most divisive controversy so far in this decade.

The four students who were slain were unarmed and had harmed no one. The National Guardsmen who shot them were tired and hungry and many had been hit by stones.

While a nation quarreled and chose up sides, more than 400 college campuses closed down and President Nixon set a cutoff date for U. S. warfare in Cambodia, the issue that led to the fatal confrontation at Kent State University on May 4.

Overtones of the affair suggest that the four fatal shots at Kent State may have been part of the first heavy volley fired by a nation now at war with its young.

Obviously, violent protest is no longer a monopoly of traditionally liberal universities like the University of California at Berkeley, Wisconsin and Harvard. The mood of young rebellion now runs so deep that it convulses even conservative campuses.

The killings at Kent State could have happened anywhere. The gulf between the generations seems to have spread so wide that there is now room for violence almost anywhere.

An examination of Kent State during the weekend of May 1–4 is a study in escalation—broken windows, burned buildings and rocks on one side, matched by tear gas, bayonets and bullets on the other.

There were special ingredients in the mix at Kent, notably a governor who reacted to confrontation with heat instead of light.

But most of the ingredients are widespread in America:

Hundreds of students deeply resentful of the Indochinese war.

A well-meaning university administration which seems aloof to many of its charges.

A townful of small businessmen who are suspicious of beards and easily frightened by rumors.

A handful of young radicals who have given up on peaceful dissent.

Add to this a National Guard ill-led and ill-equipped to cope with a young unruly mob, and you have a situation in which two boys and two girls are killed, all before they grew old enough to even vote.

A team of Beacon Journal and other Knight Newspapers reporters spent two weeks investigating the case. They interviewed more than 400 students, National Guardsmen, public officials and townspeople, examined photographs and studied official reports.

The evidence they found prompts these conclusions:

The four victims did nothing that justified their deaths. They threw no rocks nor were they politically radical.

No sniper fired at the National Guard. No investigative agency has yet found any evidence sufficient to support such a theory.

The guardsmen fired without orders to do so. Some aimed deliberately at students; others fired in panic or in follow-the-leader style.

It was not necessary to kill or wound any students. The Guardsmen had several other options which they did not exercise, including firing warning shots or marching safely away.

There is no evidence to support suggestions by university and city officials that four members of the Students for a Democratic Society (SDS) planned and directed the trouble.

No reasonable excuse could be found for three violent and illegal acts by the students—breaking downtown store windows, burning the university ROTC building and throwing rocks at the Guardsmen before the shooting. All these created turmoil and ill feeling.

The prime and immediate cause of the trouble was President Nixon's decision to invade Cambodia. Kent State, a basically conservative campus, has not generally been violent in the past. . . .

Older than the Republic itself, laden with tradition, the National Guard is a remarkable institution: A citizens army, a militia of townspeople ready to be called to arms in defense of the nation.

Made up of people from all walks of life—teachers, milk men, mechanics, farmers, insurance men—the Guard could exist only in a democracy. No institution, not the jury system, mass education, nor the right to worship, is more a part of America.

But despite its tradition, the Guard, as it was after the black riots in Detroit and Newark in 1967, is under severe criticism.

On a brilliant Spring afternoon 20 days ago, a small group of Ohio National Guardsmen, hot, tired, angry and afraid, opened fire on demonstrators at Kent State University and killed four young students.

Sen. Edward M. Kennedy (D., Mass.) said that the killings were the home-front equivalent of the My Lai massacre. He asked: "Who of us, seeing American troops in Ohio fire wildly into a crowd of students, does not also see My Lai, with its defenseless Vietnamese civilians cut down by American troops?'"

Sen. Stephen M. Young (D., Ohio,) a long-time Guard critic, says that the Guardsmen at Kent State University were "trigger-happy" and that the four students were "murdered."

He says that the Guard officer who "held his arm aloft and then pulled it down" as a signal to fire "should be investigated" for murder —as should the two senior Guard commanders, Maj. Gen. Sylvester T. Del Corso, the adjutant general, and Brig. Gen. Robert Canterbury, assistant adjutant general.

Vice President Spiro T. Agnew says that the Guardsmen may be guilty of murder, although the Vice President, who like Kennedy and Young, speaks with no detailed information on what occurred, adds, "not first-degree murder."

Agnew says "there was no premeditation but apparently an over-action in the threat of danger."

America's students called the killings at Kent State a massacre.

Whether it was massacre or murder or whether—as many Guardsmen later claimed—there was no choice but to fire is the subject of federal and state investigations.

The team of Beacon Journal and other Knight Newspapers reporters examining the incident found evidence to support these conclusions about the Guard:

Gov. James A. Rhodes, who has called out the Guard at least 40 times in the last two years, was responsible for the order that the Guard was to break up any assembly at Kent, peaceful or otherwise.

Gen. Del Corso champions the special Ohio Guard rule allowing Guardsmen to carry live rounds in the weapons.

Gen. Canterbury exercised no control over the men on the hill under his command—the men who eventually fired.

The Guard, despite increased training in the last three years, still has no effective anti-riot equipment and no meaningful anti-riot training. Its equipment was limited to antiquated tear-gas canisters and the M-1—a killer weapon with tremendous velocity and range.

Some Guardsmen aimed shots at students or groups of students. Most fired wildly, as if by impulse or reflex.

The Guard, in firing at the students, violated its regulations which stress "restraint" and "minimum application of force."

In escalating from tear gas to bullets, the Guardsmen ignored several suggested intermediate steps which federal manuals say must be used before soldiers fire their weapons.

Guard officers failed to inform students, faculty or the Kent administration that they had live ammunition in their weapons, although a 1968 statement by Del Corso said this was to be done as part of crowd-control strategy.

The Guardsmen violated the most important regulation of all: Avoid death. . . .

A Pentagon spokesman says there is no doubt within Pentagon circles that the Ohio Guardsmen did not perform at a level of the active Army.

Full-time soldiers, a Pentagon colonel says, would have carried rounds in their ammunition pouches, not their weapons, and would have loaded—and fired, if it came to that—only at the command of an officer. This would have caused the soldiers to think before they fired, he says, precluding instinctive firing.

The 60 or so Guardsmen on Kent's "Blanket Hill," once a favorite student necking spot, were not, for the large part, soldiers at all, but civilians—farmers, public relations men, a truck driver, a milk man, factory workers, businessmen.

They were equipped with World War II and Korea-vintage rifles—M-1s—which were designed for combat, not riot control, and which have an immense power (a maximum range of 3,450 yards), a power which most Guardsmen simply do not comprehend.

For their work, foot soldiers earn $12.80 a day. At Kent, Guard officials say that 46 of them were injured, three of them requiring hospitalization. Two had teeth knocked out.

In the days after the shooting, Guardsmen would ritualistically walk back to the shooting site, and many would touch the bullet holes in a tree and a steel sculpture with their fingers. . . .

A Guard chaplain, Capt. John Simons, of the 107th Armored Cavalry regiment, says simply of the M-1s and the Guard's antiquated gas canisters which students simply tossed back: "There's gas and bullets and nothing in between."

"The killings never should have happened," says Simons, who married into an Army family and who has what amounts to almost a love for the Guard. . . .

Many of the Guardsmen are from towns such as Ravenna, 20 miles east of Akron, and Orrville and Wooster, 25 miles to the southwest.

Indeed, all of G Troop of the 107th Armored Cavalry Regiment—whose members were responsible for most of the firing—are from Ravenna.

A Guard officer says, "If you had to categorize them, the 107th would be composed of men from a rural background."

Many of the Guardsmen were strongly critical of the student demonstrations. Says 1st Lt. Roy W. Dew of G Troop of the 107th: "I feel it had to come to an end sometime. These kids just don't understand. They're 19–20–21-year-old kids and they just want to run the country."

Capt. Raymond J. Srp, of Cleveland, commander of G Troop of the 107th, laments: "People don't want to be told. They want to talk."

Certainly the Guardsmen were vexed at being called to duty—first to ride shotgun on trucks because of a wildcat Teamster strike, and then to guard Kent State University. . . .

And Gen. Del Corso, in a newspaper interview in September, 1968, said he had seen more action in Ohio in the Summer of 1968 than he had seen since World War II. . . .

Canterbury and Del Corso are correct, of course, when they say that Ohio Guardsmen have the right, according to Guard regulations, to fire if they believe their lives are in danger. Ohio Guard regulations say: "I will fire when required to save my life or when returning fire."

Yet, even protected by that regulation, the Ohio Guardsmen violated a number of other rules when they fired including the policy that Del Corso laid down in April 1968.

For even if there was a sniper, as the Guard has sometimes claimed, the Guard fired indiscriminately into the students. Some Guardsmen, Knight Newspapers learned, fired aimed shots at students, or at least groups of students. But many simply fired wildly, as if by impulse or reflex. . . .

Ron Steel, 18, a Kent freshman, said: "I just stood there and thought to myself that surely they must be shooting blanks to scare the crowd off. Then I saw the bullets kicking up the dirt in front of me. I just turned and ran."

Why did the Guard fire?

Overwhelming evidence upholds the contentions of Canterbury and Maj. Harry D. Jones, who was acting commander of the 145th and 107th troops on the hill, that there was no order to fire.

Capt. John Simons, the 107th chaplain, who interviewed a number of Guardsmen who fired, says, "I think they were angry, they were scared, and that something caused them to fire. What, I don't know."

Importantly, neither of the two commanders of the companies that fired, Capt. John E. Martin of Company A 145th Infantry and Capt. Srp of G Troop, believed their lives were in danger.

"I was right in the middle of it (the Guard formation)," Srp says.

Yet, the Guardsmen, hot, weary, angered by verbal harassment and rock barrages, vexed at being called from their civilian jobs, some of them angry at student demonstrators, turned and in the space of 13 seconds, fired what the Guard says were 35 rounds (this actual count, however, may run as high as 60, authoritative sources say) from their M-1 rifles.

Certainly there were a number of alternatives available to the Guard short of discharging their weapons into the milling students without warning.

The federal government, for example, has laid down six escalating "rules of engagement" for federal troops. The intent of regulations is clear: To avoid death. They are:

Show of Force, or the massing of enough troops to demonstrate to a crowd that it is overpowered.

Employment of riot-control formations to disperse crowds while allowing the crowd a clear exit as the troops advance.

Use of water—fire hoses or water cannons.

Use of riot control agents, that is, tear or pepper gas.

Fire by selected marksmen at definite, specific targets.

Full firepower, with the rounds being directed low to wound, and not to kill. Clearly, the Ohio National Guard did not follow some of these rules of engagement. They moved out, for example, with only some 100-plus men, and had only about 65 men on the hill when the shooting occurred, even though it is estimated that the students on and around Blanket Hill numbered 2,000 to 3,000 when the Guard moved on them.

The Guard weapons, M-1s, are combat weapons, and can kill even at up to their maximum range of 3,450 yards—almost two miles.

This, then, was the guard at Kent State: ill-trained, and ill-equipped for this particular job, possessing no desire to be there.

Since the incident, guard officials have searched for evidence that they were fired upon by a sniper, and that this triggered the shooting.

No evidence of a sniper has yet been found. Neither is there evidence to support the claims of Ohio Sen. Young that a Guard officer "held his arm aloft and then pulled it down" as a signal to fire.

The only arm that was raised, films and still photographs show, was that of Maj. Jones, who beat on Guardsmen's helmets to make them stop firing. . . .

County prosecutor Ronald J. Kane displayed the dormitory search findings, drawn from the possessions of 7,500 students, at a much-publicized news conference.

They included two typical hunting weapons, a .22 caliber rifle and a shotgun; about 60 knives; three slingshots and several BB guns.

The police, who had no search warrant, also confiscated several hashish pipes, six growing marijuana plants and a yellow button saying, "Dare to Struggle, Dare to Win."

After the long straggling line of troops descended the 149 feet to the western base of "blanket hill," "nobody talked about it," said Mike Chizmadia, a Guardsman from Orrville.

"Some threw down their weapons, and started to bawl," said Pfc. Richard A. Parker, a Wooster policeman. He had been an "innocent bystander," standing at the corner of Johnson Hall when the firing began. "Wow! I ran, too. Everybody did," he said.

In the days to follow, most Guardsmen were extremely reluctant to discuss publicly the shooting. Again and again, they adamantly refused. Some said they feared they would be activated and sent to Vietnam if they talked about what happened. . . .

"There was tremendous hostility, tremendous anger. Absolutely unbelievable," said Dr. Seymour H. Baron, chairman of the Psychology Department, a professor who taught a 600-student lecture course.

"The girls were crying. Some of the boys started crying. They told me they'd rather die right here, now, than in Vietnam. It terrified me. They were defiant as hell."

Dr. Baron, a balding, bearded man, half-ran from the students congregating on the hill across the barren no-man's land of the commons to the line of Guards.

"And I saw a captain and I said, "Where is your commanding officer?" And he pointed to the man in the suit. "That's the General.'"

Gen. Canterbury, wearing a single-breasted dark brown suit suitable for the board of the trustees of the Kiwanis Club in Columbus to which he belonged, again ordered the students to disperse.

He spoke softly.

"I said, 'General, for Christ's sake. I beg of you. There is going to be a slaughter. Tell your men to put down their guns. For heavens sakes, do something.'"

"And the General said, 'I've got to do my job. Take this man away.' Those were his exact words."

And Dr. Baron, fear in his throat, returned to the students, now sitting on the grass, and he made a speech from a bullhorn.

"You've got to survive! I don't want you to die! It won't help! You're going to get a bullet in the belly if you stay."

Glenn W. Frank, 43, a white-haired, crewcut associate professor of Geology, who thought he had heard "ladyfinger firecrackers" over a bowl of soup at the Student Union 30 minutes before, crossed no-man's land.

He pleaded with Canterbury, now firmly in command, a General whom he would later overhear telephoning his superiors in Columbus, at the gym headquarters.

"He was trying to get his orders rescinded," said Dr. Frank.

At that chaotic moment on the Commons, though, Frank pleaded for time. Time. Time.

Capt. Ron Snyder stood listening. He quoted the General. " 'They're going to have to find out what law and order is all about.' "

In the 35 minutes after the shooting, Maj. Donald Manly, of the Ohio Highway Patrol, had bolstered his force from 30 to 181.

They stood in formation in their Smokey Bear hats, gripping 22-inch long wooden clubs, their revolvers holstered.

"Give us time to get them out," Frank pleaded.

"I'll give you five minutes," said the General.

"Take all the time you need," said Maj. Manly.

And Frank, emotionally torn apart, now crying openly, raced back to the slope of "Blanket Hill," and he begged.

"We've got to leave or we'll be slaughtered," he said. He believed it. Kent State University had ceased to function. It was closed.

"Almost beyond reality they got up and started to leave," said Frank. He was so weak he could hardly walk.

He couldn't see because of the tears in his eyes.

Across the no-man's land of the Commons, a grass gulf of perhaps 40 yards and 40 years, Guard Capt. William Reinhard, a Lutheran pastor from Cleveland, tried to comfort a perplexed and overwrought young man with an M-1 rifle, a weapon of death.

Reinhard spoke of Ecclesiastes. "A time to weep," he said. "A time to mourn. This is the time."

And the sound of the G-sharp faded. The victory bell again hung motionless. There was no victory.

A Comment by KSU President Robert White, from "For Your Information" (Internal KSU Communications Pamphlet), Week of May 24, 1970.

Out of it all I see a Kent State University which is going to add to itself a role—a role which will be national and even international, a role which will be truly unique among all other institutions. One might put it somewhat like this: This is where it happened; this is where it ends and shall never happen again. Dedications to the study of nonviolence, dedications to the development of peace, dedications to the study of every development of community problems and matters of that sort.

In summary, this University is not done by any means. We are all at work and out of it will eventually come a better Kent State University, one which will genuinely and honestly attract the allegiance of its alumni, its students and its faculty.

From the *CBS Evening News with Walter Cronkite,* June 4, 1970.

CRONKITE: One month ago today four Kent State University students died in a fusillade of National Guard gunfire. Their deaths served as a rallying cause for the protest against the war, triggered widespread campus disorders, and led to the first nationwide student strike in U.S. history. Ike Pappas revisited the Ohio school for a report on what has happened since May 4th.

(MUSIC)

PAPPAS: "Eternal rest grant them, O Lord, and let perpetual light shine upon them." Words from a requiem mass last night in a church just off the Kent campus, a mass for the four who died and symbolic of the grief that came to many in this community.

(MUSIC)

Except for a few bullet-holes here and there, like the one in the steel sculpture in front of Taylor Hall, there are very few visual reminders of what happened here a month ago. In fact, there was only one other reminder. At the base of Blanket Hill, over which the demonstrators retreated as the National Guard advanced, there is a bell, in front of which flowers have been placed. It stands now as a makeshift memorial to those who died.

The university has been closed since that day. Only this week were a few seniors and graduate students allowed to return to complete their work. Kent will reopen, but there is continuing fear of more violence when all of the students return. There are more than thirty groups looking into what happened at Kent and what to do about it. This is one of the most important, a commission trying to find ways to reopen the university peacefully, using some experimental approaches.

MAN: So we'll let them in . . . What do you think of this recommendation?

PAPPAS: Here the commission is, through a sort of play-acting, being shown how faculty and student peace marshals could be trained to minimize future trouble. But many students say they will not tolerate more trouble. For many students, like these physical education majors meeting at lunch to discuss their problem, the primary concern is to get the school open so that they can get their degrees and then go on to jobs.

MAN: I think if anything happens after this, you'll find the heart—the 95 percent who happen to be silent aren't going to be silent any more. I think that they'll be there and they'll be able to be counted on to help, because nobody wants to see Kent State close down forever.

BIOLOGY PROFESSOR: Australopithecus also probably existed here, but Australopithecus was more wide-ranging.

PAPPAS: A biology class in the professor's living room, one of many makeshift ways that students at Kent are trying to complete their work. Some professors are even driving cross-country to hold classes with students who live outside Ohio. The vast majority of students and faculty want the university reopened, but some students on the left insist that reforms must come first.

CRAIG MORGAN: If students come back on campus and they see there's been no effort to re-evaluate the role of ROTC, there's been no effort to disarm the campus police, etcetera, etcetera, etcetera, in other words, what we're trying to do is just business as usual, things are not going to go on as business as usual, no matter how many repressive measures you make. You're going to have to disarm the police. You're going to have to re-evaluate ROTC. You're going to have to consider a university senate. You're going to have to do all the measures possible to establish a feeling of a university community rather than trying to make it a Kent Police State University.

PAPPAS: A major problem for the university is hostility in the town of Kent itself brought on by student vandalism in demonstrations prior to the shootings. City Councilman Dal Hardesty.

HARDESTY: We're afraid of getting our houses burned, for one thing. We're afraid of seeing the community being blown up—destroyed, which it could be, which I think had the National Guard not gone up that hill a half hour later, or had they gone up a half hour later than when they did, I don't think this city block would be here now.

PAPPAS: A search of student dormitories immediately following the shootings added greatly to the community's unrest. According to a state police list, searchers found some dangerous weapons and drugs, which they displayed for the press. But some faculty members, students, and the Kent chapter of the American Civil Liberties Union charged that the display was a publicity stunt by the police and the county prosecutor and that press and television reports created the impression that Kent students were preparing for violent conflict.

CARL MOORE: Some of the items he had on the table were World War II-relic knives, guns which were inoperative, antihistamine tablets, syringes, which I've heard from another individual was in a girl's room because she played a nurse in a play and had it there. But this was exhibited as the kind of material you find in a college classroom. This will have a scare effect on the community, and that's too bad that it will have, but it will have.

PAPPAS: The community is scared and angry. The Ohio Assembly this week passed a bill that would require students or faculty arrested in a demonstration to be automatically suspended before they had a hearing or trial.

MAN: I believe the tool of summary suspension for the short period of time is vital to maintaining discipline at our state universities.

PAPPAS: The National Guard claims to have received more than ten thousand letters since the shooting. Over nine thousand of them have been favorable to the action of the Guardsmen.

Has there been any change in policy? For instance, are the men still carrying live ammunition?

LT. COL. JOSEPH McCANN: Yes, they are.

PAPPAS: There's been no . . .

McCANN: No change in policy at all.

PAPPAS: Do you think that might be warranted, perhaps?

McCANN: What, a change in policy? I don't see why.

MORGAN: If I ever see National Guardsmen raise, you know, a rifle and fire it—and aim it into a crowd, I don't think that I can personally be responsible for what I may do to that National Guardsman.

PAPPAS: Some think that day will never come, and moderates like Professor Harris Dante are attempting to play down the prospect of violence when Kent State reopens.

DANTE: We do have sort of a unity here, and I'm optimistic that we won't have any more violence. It will be almost a desecration to commit any more violence in this place.

(MUSIC)

PAPPAS: The chorus for the requiem mass last night was made up of university administrators, students, faculty, and townsfolk. It was a symbolic coming together of the community. Much more difficult will be the real unification that must take place if Kent is to open and stay open. If this can be done, no more symbolic memorials will be needed, for peace will be memorial enough.

Ike Pappas, CBS NEWS, Kent.

KSU Commencement Address by Dr. Harris Dante, President, Faculty Senate, June 13, 1970.

The tragedy has been doubly hard to bear because no state university in Ohio had taken more significant steps to prevent disruption. Some of the programs we have such as the Human Relations Center, Afro-American Studies Program, Faculty and Student Senates are high on the list of demands at other institutions.

Moreover, other institutions had higher property damage, more injuries to law enforcement officers and so on. I offer this as a statement of fact, not as an excuse, nor with any idea of mitigating the seriousness of what occurred. In my judgement we do not deserve what happened.

The university academic community cannot be judged as one would judge a business or even a public school system. We are committed to the three-fold task of teaching, research and public service. This is our tradition and our heritage and it represents the common purpose and ideal of the international academic community. . . .

It is because a university is basically decent and dedicated to reason that it is particularly vulnerable. We need to recognize how fragile it really is and how easy it is to attack it and destroy it. The university today is caught between contending forces in our troubled society, yet, the university as an institution cannot be all things to all men.

Moreover, in a time when the bill of rights would have tough sledding in the public opinion polls and even in legislative chambers, the university must remain a sanctuary of freedom and of free but responsible expression. Any successful educational system attempts to civilize man, to make him more rational and to increase his wisdom.

Thus the university cannot as an institution give in to those forces that would have it espouse one cause against another because this would only diminish the search for truth, and the pressure for the just cause of today may be replaced by the evil cause of tomorrow. Nevertheless, the university must remain a forum for the study and expression for unpopular ideas and minority views. . . .

From the *Akron Beacon Journal,* July 15, 1970.

"Campus Peace When War Ends"—Ted Kennedy

WASHINGTON (AP)—A presidential commission aimed at pacifying the nation's campuses was told today it will not succeed until the Vietnam war is ended.

"It may well be," said Sen. Edward M. Kennedy, "that the only line in the commission's report that will have any real meaning for our colleges and universities is the line that reads: 'This war must end.' "

The Massachusetts Democrat and Senate Republican Leader Hugh Scott were among the six witnesses called at the opening hearing of the President's Commission on Campus Unrest.

The others were San Francisco State President S. I. Hayakawa, University of Michigan President Robben Fleming, National Student Association President Charles Palmer and Otis Cochrane, president of the Black American Law Student Union. . . .

Kennedy deplored "the violence and various confrontations that have become the hallmark of too many campus demonstrations." He said:

"No amount of . . . commitment . . . can . . . justify the wanton acts we have seen on campuses."

But "the most destructive campus violence has not been student violence. It has been official violence—the official violence of the National Guard at Kent State, the official violence of the Highway Patrol at Jackson State."

From the *Daily Kent Stater*, October 1, 1970.

Disruptions Now a Crime

By Jim Quilligan

This summer the 108th Ohio General Assembly heard the drumming of violence on the state's campuses. In reaction, they passed Amended House Bill 1219, aimed at dampening the desire for participating in "disruptive" activities and stiffening the punishments for such acts.

One section of the bill, Section 2923.16, has been added to the Criminal Code of The State of Ohio. This section, known as "Offenses Against Society," creates a new crime: "disruption." Disruption is considered a misdemeanor. Persons convicted of this crime will be subject to criminal penalties.

A first offense could entail a $100 fine and one month in jail. The maximum sentence for a second conviction is $500 and six months imprisonment.

No person in circumstances "which create a substantial risk of disrupting the orderly conduct of lawful activities at a college or university" is allowed to enter a campus or campus buildings without permission. Under the same circumstances, no one may refuse to leave a building or area "upon the request of proper authority." No individual may violate rules dictated by the Board of Trustees or by the university president concerning curfew, assembly or campus access.

No person is permitted to encourage another person to "violate any restriction upon access to a campus." No one may urge another to refuse to leave a college campus or building.

No person may disrupt the orderly conduct of a college or university. No one is permitted to "engage in conduct which threatens or involves serious injury" to individuals or college property.

Section 3345.23 of the Ohio Revised Code now provides that if any student, faculty member, staff member or employee is arrested for one of the following crimes he may be suspended by the university:

Maiming or disfiguring a person.

Intentional shooting, cutting or stabbing.

Assault and battery and making menacing threats.

Assault and battery upon law enforcement officers and firemen.

Arson.

Manufacture, distribution and possession of firearms.

Burning property of another.

Attempt to burn property.

Malicious injury to property.

Intentional injury or damage to public or private property.

Malicious destruction of property.

Injury to or committing nuisance in buildings.

Destruction of public utility fixtures.

Carrying of firearm or similar weapon.

Carrying other concealed weapons.

Interference with authorized persons at emergency scenes.

Second degree riot.

First degree riot.

Inciting to riot.

Campus disruption.

Any person arrested appears before a hearing official, appointed by the Ohio Board of Regents. The hearing must take place no later than 5 days after the arrest.

The job of the hearing official is not to judge the case, but to decide how severe the punishment must be. Punishments range from "strict disciplinary probation" to suspension from the university.

A person is considered "under suspension" until he is acquitted or convicted. The suspension may be appealed within 20 days at the County Court of Common Pleas.

A new "State of Emergency" section, 3345.26, has also been added to the Revised Code. The board of trustees or the president of the college may "declare a state of emergency when there is a clear and present danger of disruption" of normal, orderly campus activities.

The board and the president have the power to impose a curfew and curtail access to university property. In addition, they have the right to restrict assemblies of more than five persons.

"Ohio House Bill 1219," one faculty member said recently, "hangs over the head of every individual on campus . . . from faculty, to maintenance, to students. It includes just everybody."

From the *Daily Kent Stater*, September 29, 1970.

Abernathy: "Get on the Case"

Five thousand people packed into Memorial Gym last night to attend the memorial service for the four students slain May 4 by Ohio National Guardsmen here.

Sheila Barton, winner of the 1970 Peace Speech contest, singer Phil Ochs, Ira Sandperl, leader of the California Institute for the Study of Non-violence and Rev. Ralph David Abernathy, chairman of the Southern Christian Leadership Conference, joined Tom Grace and Dean Kahler, both injured in the fatal confrontation, on the speakers' platform.

The speakers and nearly 2,000 students held a candlelight march from the gym to Taylor Hall, scene of the fatal shooting.

More than a dozen draft cards were burned during a short ceremony on the hill behind Taylor.

Kahler, permanently confined to a wheelchair after being shot in the spine, rolled to the center of the platform at the end of the list of speakers. "I'm glad to be alive and here to speak to you tonight," said the former freshman Health-Physical Education major.

"I hope to be back on this campus to study in January," Kahler said. "It has been a long fight, but it's all over now and I'm going to be all right."

"I don't hate that National Guardsman who shot me," he went on, "but I don't agree with the people who sent him here."

Kahler related that he has no belief in violence and would like to see more young people become conscientious objectors to all forms of violence.

Kahler had been preceded to the podium by Rev. Abernathy, who renewed his call for people to take up the cause of non-violence and put down war, racism, and exploitation of humanity.

"Once when I was with Dr. Martin Luther King," Abernathy said, "he told me that if he were to die, we should not let our grief end in mourning, but should be thankful for the ideals for decency, freedom, and peace, and rededicate ourselves to the achievement of those goals."

"The proper way to mourn the passing of the lives of the four who died here and of the countless others who have died in the struggle for nonviolence," he said, "is no longer to afford the luxury of being a 'silent majority', but to 'get on the case'."

"It is the state, the government, that is violent," Abernathy went on, "not the masses of people who protest—supposedly justified because of the right wing's atmosphere of fear. We must make it clear as to who perpetrates the real violence."

Sandperl, an enthusiastic elf of a man, said that "only revolutionary non-violence will get us out of this century alive." He said that Gandhi was the greatest thing to happen to the world in this century. He was the only revolutionary of the century. Lenin was "only a policeman, while Gandhi attempted to build a counter-culture."

"We must organize and come together," Sandperl said, "for the war in Viet Nam has come home, to our streets and our hearts, and we must stop it. Those four were murdered the day the advisors were okayed in Viet Nam."

Grace, on crutches, spoke of the hypocrisy of the university that exists in R.O.T.C., war research in the Liquid Crystals Institute, and the repressive violence in police training on the campus.

"There are four people dead on this campus," Grace said, "and all the university has done is to double security forces. There have been narcotics arrests here, this year, repressing the counter-culture students have tried to build."

On the steps of Taylor Hall, while burning draft cards lighted his face, Tim Butz, head of the Vets Against the War in Vietnam, spoke to the crowd through the cold drizzle. "I hope you all understand that these burning draft cards are the only flames that should engulf Kent State now," said the 18-month veteran of the Asian war. "No more buildings must ever be burned. We have too much to lose for that. We have lost too much already."

Think Week began earlier in the day when President Robert I. White, Faculty Senate chairman Martin Nurmi and student body president Craig Morgan addressed a convocation on the Commons. Called by the victory bell that hailed students to the fatal confrontation in May, 3000 stayed through a cold downpour to listen. Nearly 400 pledged to join Morgan and Nurmi in a 24-hour fast to cement their pledge of nonviolence.

"We have been brought here to this place by the Kent problem," said Morgan. "The nation and the world are watching. If we don't care we will join the generation of silent Americans and will deserve any fate which we receive."

RUMORS

Written communications alone do not give a full awareness of the extreme violence of some responses to the deaths at Kent. For obvious reasons, most of these responses never reached print, either because newspapers and magazines wouldn't print them, or because many people, having expressed their emotions and ideas in conversation, did not write letters or did not believe such letters would be printed.

Resulting often from real panic, and leading often to more panic, such statements have a place in this collection. Every statement given here was heard in varying forms by one or both of the editors.

One [or two, or three] Guardsmen were killed by the students but their bodies were smuggled away because the authorities are leftists [or afraid to antagonize the students].

President Nixon [or the CIA] gave orders to have some students killed because of fear of the youth culture's political force [or because of jealousy of the youth culture's sexual liberation].

When the bodies of the slain students were examined at the hospital, they were found to be so riddled by venereal disease [or drugs, or both] that the students would have died soon anyway.

SDS members were converging on Kent from all over the country to burn it to the ground as the signal for a Communist revolution [said both in approval and in disapproval].

It is deeply meaningful that three of the four dead students were Jewish.

Ohio students are patriotic; the out-of-state students make all the trouble.

The older faculty is patriotic; the teaching fellows make all the trouble.

Students are forced to read un-American history and pornographic literature by faculty members who are traitors [or dupes, or sex-fiends, or homosexuals, or atheists].

The leftist news media tried to create sympathy for the slain students by printing high school portraits, not photos showing that they had become hippies.

The state was going to take over the University and turn it into a mental institution.

The University should be blown up and started over with real Americans.

The University will be moved to another town to be chosen for its loyalty to American ideals.

National Guardsmen forced coeds to perform sexual acts.

All the Guardsmen were members of the Ku Klux Klan, the John Birch Society, or both.

Students were stockpiling weapons for a take-over of the University when the fall term began [said both in approval and in disapproval].

EDITORIAL COMMENTARY

Editorials, columns, and articles commenting on the Kent affair are reproduced in this section. Three poems of a polemical nature are also given places here.

From the *Kent-Ravenna Record-Courier,* May 4, 1970.

Universities Must Oust Hooligans

Ohio will no longer tolerate its state universities being used as sanctuaries by lawbreaking hooligans who destroy, terrorize and burn and then seek protection in the academic community.

That was the major message of Gov. James Rhodes, who visited Kent

Sunday morning and termed the rioting in Kent as the worst the state has suffered.

Gov. Rhodes proposed two major pieces of legislation that he will push for in the next assembly—one making it a felony to throw a projectile at a police officer, the other requiring an automatic and permanent suspension for anyone convicted of any crime arising out of campus violence.

In essence, the Governor stated that the days of the "go easy" policy toward campus law breakers is over, and they can expect their violence to be met with every law enforcement tool the state has at its disposal.

Amen to that, for Kent in the past three days has had its fill of these violence-prone toughs who use legitimate causes, such as a drive for peace, as vehicles to allow them to riot and disrupt.

The acts of violence in Kent and on campus during the past two days are so serious as to merit the sternest repression: store windows broken and store owners threatened; a campus building burned, fire hoses cut and firemen and policemen pelted with bricks, stones and bottles.

We are pleased, however, to hear from state authorities that for the most part students aren't that way. The great majority—all but the very few—are on our campuses to get an education and become the leaders of tomorrow.

It is our job to protect and encourage them.

As for peaceful and legitimate protests, we're all for them and, in fact, encourage them. Students—in fact, any groups—get their ideas across effectively that way. As for violence, destruction and rioting, we don't believe that our country can tolerate them.

A Statement from Dorothy Fuldheim, News Analyst, WEWS-TV, Cleveland, Ohio, December 8, 1970.

A few weeks before the fatal day when four students were killed on the Kent State University campus I had thrown Jerry Rubin off of my show for his bad manners and his obscenity. I was hailed as a Joan of Arc and everywhere I went I was patted on the back and received hundreds of letters, flowers, wine, telegrams, etc. But on that fatal day when I returned from Kent and went on the air and expressed my deep feeling that the killings were unwarranted, that no Guardsmen had been wounded, sent to the hospital or killed, that the killing of the students was therefore inexplicable and that the whole tragic event was an aberration of the American spirit, I became a villain.

I pointed out that an American who is accused of a crime is given an opportunity to defend himself in court. But these students who had been shot down had not been asked what their philosophy or intentions were. It is true that students did engage in destruction—they burned the ROTC building and they created disturbances in the town. For this it would have been legitimate to arrest them as anyone who disturbs the peace is arrested. But the slaughter occurred not in the town but on the campus.

As an American who believes in fair play I felt that the students had been the victims of some sort of hysteria on the part of the National Guard. Further, I said I was deeply agitated that such an occurrence could take place on a university campus and that the student movement now had their martyrs.

It seemed to me that my statements were a legitimate appraisal of what had taken place, but not to my viewers. We were deluged with calls, hundreds of them. Some threatened to kill me. All insisted on talking to me personally. It was apparently no longer the message but the messenger who was being attacked. This time, not hundreds, but thousands of letters came in. Seventy-five percent at least criticized my stand vehemently and even savagely. I was accused of being emotional and that what we needed were a few more of these killings and that the students should be taught a lesson, etc. There was even a petition signed by some of the townspeople to get me off of the air. Many reluctantly said they would never listen to me again.

In my 24 years on television, nothing that I ever said drew such an avalanche of disapproval and some of it couched in savage and brutal words. I admit to being emotional about this matter, but I am still bewildered at the intensity of the feeling against the students and the support of the shooting by the National Guard who undoubtedly were unnerved by the whole bizarre situation.

From the *Lorain* (Ohio) *Journal,* May 5, 1970.

Outrage at Kent State

William Schroeder of Lorain was an All American boy—a splendid student and a fine athlete—and he was one of the innocent victims of the student riots and National Guard shootings at Kent State University yesterday.

The one hope left is that the death of this outstanding youth and three other students might somehow, someway bring us to our senses.

What President Nixon, Vice President Spiro Agnew, Gov. Rhodes and all other government leaders do not understand or appreciate is the deep resentment and frustration felt by so many college students from coast to coast, in private schools and in state universities.

They don't understand that there are two kinds of protesters—the small militant, crazy Weatherman faction that wants to tear down, burn down and bring down the government and the vast majority of students who just want us to know they detest the war and want it stopped now.

You must be able to differentiate and separate the honest protesters from the wild-eyed radicals.

You must be able to prevent the radicalization of all the good, young demonstrators by using restraint in handling the demonstrations. We cannot allow the radicals to make us overreact.

For every shot you fire, for every kid you beat up, you radicalize thousands of moderates on every campus.

It is about time we all understood the mood of the campus. The young people are against the war in Vietnam and they have a right to protest.

They don't have a right to burn down, destroy, shoot, loot or beat up. And those radicals that do, when you find them, should be arrested and tried in a court of law.

But understand, once and for all, they are frustrated. They have heard their President say he has a secret way to end the war, which he won't disclose, and they see him instead expanding the Vietnam War into Cambodia. This has triggered a general wave of discontent on virtually every college campus, including moderate, middle America schools like Wooster, Kenyon, Ohio State and Denison.

It has needlessly spawned violence, shootings and killings on the Kent State campus in a "get tough" confrontation between excited students and green Guardsmen.

The melancholy tragedy at Kent State cries for a complete and impartial investigation—of who did what and why. . . .

—Irving Leibowitz, Editor

From the *Port Huron* (Mich.) *Times Herald,* May 5, 1970.

Liberal Paper Distorts Truth

Of the Kent State University tragedy we have this to say:

We extend our deepest sympathy to the parents and relatives of the dead and injured students and of the young national guardsmen who were injured or stricken in the confrontation at Kent.

Kent University has a student body of some 23,000. There were some 500 of these involved in the fatal fracas Monday.

Said the liberal Detroit Free Press today, "What is unmistakable, though, is that the right of peaceful dissent is being suppressed. . . ."

We are at a loss to understand how the demonstration at Kent could be called "peaceful." The guardsmen—and we believe they are just as honest as the students—said that a shot was fired at them. It is on the record that rocks and other missiles were thrown at them. It is a fact, too, that the interior of a college building was firebombed and that the students pelted university and private enterprise buildings with rocks and other missiles.

Do these and other incidents testify to "unmistakable . . . right of peaceful dissent"?

It was almost inevitable that a publication which supported Mr. Nixon in his campaign but has consistently attacked him since would blame him for what happened at Kent. It was to be expected, and to quote it, "Now the angry response to President Nixon's Cambodian decision, etc."

In one paragraph the Free Press calls the Kent incident "peaceful dissent." In the next, it says mildly that the violence is wrong.

The editorial in that newspaper is titled, "The Search for 'Order' Has Reaped Its Reward."

As nearly as we can figure out, that newspaper is advocating revolution. Read and re-read carefully, that is all that can be deduced from its contents. . . .

From the *Dayton* (Ohio) *Daily News,* May 5, 1970.

Why Didn't We Learn?

By Jim Fain

The tragedy yesterday at *Kent State* is first of all a subject for mourning. It seems so stupid and unnecessary. But after we have wept for the needless wastage of young lives, we need to ask ourselves whether there was any way of avoiding what happened.

Many adult Americans find the unrest on campus an unfathomable mystery. Parents have worked all their lives to give youngsters opportunities they themselves were denied. Now, with the world as their oyster, the kids seem intent on destroying it.

So the reflex response of many adults is to favor repressing any kind of demonstration or rebellion, however peaceful, with whatever force is available. Any opinion poll will show you that this is mainly what the people think. In election years, politicians and office-holders are inordinately sensitive to what people think.

Yet it also is true that the country has been undergoing the wave of campus rebellion for more than three years now and that those who have studied it thoroughly have learned some practical things about how to meet it with a minimum of disruption, a low level of violence, if any, and without bloodshed.

Columbia and San Francisco State proved, for example, that a student body that is largely hostile to the small band of radicals now to be found on almost any campus will tend to sympathize with the radicals if the radicals can find some way to provoke the police and the authorities into over-reacting.

In all forms of confrontation and conflict management, police and troops have learned that the wisest course is to give student moderates an opportunity to handle student radicals and to find ways for troops to stay out, if possible, while that process takes place.

If everything else fails and the police and military do have to intervene, then they must do so in maximum force. The intervention must be overwhelming so as to discourage anyone from attempting to combat it.

None of these lessons has been applied in the recent series of campus disturbances in Ohio.

At Miami, a largely peaceful group of demonstrators occupied an ROTC building, which they were not harming. Obviously, they could not be allowed to remain there indefinitely, but it would have been a simple matter to obtain a court injunction, giving individual students time to reflect on whether they wanted to deliberately defy the law.

Instead, the police moved in with tear gas and dogs. The State Highway patrol operated with considerable restraint, but the police overkill created much sympathy for the demonstrators, who initially were a tiny percentage of the campus.

At Ohio State, the student provocation was even less and the reaction of the Columbus police and National Guardsmen was even greater. No buildings were invaded and the only excuse for police intervention into a peaceful parade came when someone blocked a campus entrance.

After that, tear and pepper gas were fired indiscriminately and the next morning, a small band of guardsmen felt called upon to gas and disperse a group of fewer than 200 students who were sitting or standing quietly on the Oval.

Throughout the OSU troubles, the police and guard seemed to be the primary aggressors, until finally toward the end of the week, a truce of sorts was arranged. Until then, a lot of innocent bystanders and even people in their dormitory or fraternity house rooms were being gassed.

At Kent State, the problem was different. Here student radicals burned a building, seemingly with no provocation.

Then the guard moved in, but not in numbers sufficient to squelch any thought of resistance. By this time, a lot of guardsmen had been used around the state. And a lot of animosity had been built up by police actions on other campuses.

The result was a blood-letting, and I believe a needless one. We may never know exactly how it started. The National Guard claims a student sniper fired first. Most of the kids seem to think otherwise. Undoubtedly, the guardsmen were being pelted with rocks.

In any event, Guard procedures call for no volley-type fire at a civilian crowd and there never has been any such fire in American history until yesterday at Kent State university in Ohio. In firing to quell disturbances, guardsmen are supposed to await orders from the senior officer present and to aim low so as to disable, rather than kill. There is no evidence that this procedure was followed.

I have no brief for student revolutionaries, but the way to handle them is not to kill innocent kids on college campuses.

I also believe the tragedy at Kent State came about partly because of what happened at Miami and Ohio State. In all three highly different situations, police reactions were unfortunate. At Ohio State and Kent, the guard also handled itself badly.

At Kent, where things obviously were more dangerous from the beginning, the troops went in without sufficient numbers and apparently without adequate planning or training.

Controlling and channeling protest is a complex, tough business, but we have learned a good bit about it in this country in the last few years. Few of those lessons were applied in Ohio these last two weeks.

The key decision to load their rifles with live ammunition is one that ought to be studied carefully.

It did not help, either, that we were in the middle of a political campaign in which the governor of the state was promising "no MITs or Berkeleys in Ohio." We have had no MITs or Berkeleys in Ohio, but we have had Kent State and that is something no other state has had.

From the *Wall Street Journal,* May 6, 1970.

Tragedy at Kent State

A tragedy like the one at Kent State University leaves a drained and empty feeling. There is much that can be said, but one is left wondering if any of it has real meaning.

The first thing to confront is the ghastliness of the act of National Guardsmen shooting into a crowd of students, leaving four of them dead. Perhaps there may have been a rooftop sniper; it at least seems likely the Guardsmen thought there was. But neither this nor the excuses of weariness and panic detract from the utter brutishness of firing at random into a crowd.

This ghastliness must be confronted especially by those of us who have repeatedly warned that appealing political decisions to the streets is a risky tactic that will inevitably lead to grief. We must make it clear to those who will listen that we are absolutely heartfelt in deploring the tragic consequences against which we have so often warned.

That need not mean, though, that we must abdicate repeating that the warning still applies. One of the most touching things about the Kent State episode is the report that when the firing started students assumed blank bullets were being used. Coming as it does after the students had indulged themselves with arson and after the authorities had explicitly declared martial law, this assumption casts a painful poignancy on the sense of game-playing that permeates so many of these student uprisings. Somehow the students are convinced that whatever they do nothing tragic will happen to them.

How should they know otherwise, with their experience embracing only a few cloistered years in what is still, despite its current passions, a singularly cloistered nation? Nothing in their limited experience or tentative learning prepares them to understand the deadly serious facts—that mobs bring repression, for example, or even that when you throw rocks at armed men eventually some of them will either panic or turn inhuman. Somehow this ought not be too much for a 20-year-old mind to grasp, but it is also true the failing is not only theirs but ours—those of us who ought to have some grasp of history's lessons, some duty to communicate them to youth, and also of course some wit to guard adequately against predictable breakdowns and excesses in suppressing violence.

Somehow the trends of our times have made a tragedy like this one inevitable at some point or another, and this makes it hard to lay any ultimate blame on anyone at Kent State. Perhaps these trends are pure fate, beyond control (that drained and empty feeling again). But surely they must be powerfully affected by responsible men, political leaders, editors, educators and so on. Those who have set the prevailing tone among this group have failed. We as a nation have not managed our affairs prudently, and we have been equally imprudent in our reaction to mistakes. There is a lurching around, a tendency to think in one absolute or another, that betrays a loss of leadership and self-confidence.

So after the tragedy at Kent State, the question to ask is not whether the blame lies here or there, not where the absolute can be found. The appropriate question is whether it is possible to give either rebellious students and those who must confront them a better notion of how to perform where there are no absolutes. And if responsible persons are to help others toward the needed sense of perspective and balance, the first thing they must do is get a good grip on that sense for themselves.

From *Newsday* (Long Island, N.Y.), May 6, 1970.

The Deadly Dramatists

Confrontation is a process of high drama. Like the children's game of cops and robbers it offers heroic roles and a chance to improvise bravado. But when it is played out in the streets of a city or on a college campus the spectacle can be deadly.

So long as the National Guardsmen on the campus of Kent State University in Ohio withheld their fire, the drama was intact. The militant students played their roles against splendid props, long lines of guardsmen and clouds of tear gas. But behind the gas masks were other young Americans. They held in their hands lethal props and they obviously were unsure of their roles. The result was a deadly improvisation that ended the tableau. Gross reality is the enemy of drama, and a bullet is the epitome of verisimilitude. The nation was shocked by the deaths of the four young men and women at Kent State. But why? Other young persons have died during violent confrontations, and the violence has not abated. Thus, further deaths were predictable, perhaps inevitable. Yet the occurrence itself is traumatic, a whiplash in the face.

Perhaps this is because too many people are playing let's pretend. The scenario of confrontation isn't supposed to include real bullets and real blood. It is supposed to be stirring and noble, a pageant demonstrating conscience and concern in a setting of burning ROTC buildings and tear gas. The intrusion of death was shocking. It was as if a passion play had ended with a real crucifixion.

Of course there is reason for protest. The course of the war in Indochina demands demonstrations of conscience and concern. But why must the protest be cheapened by excess, by the decline into the shoddy drama of violence by a mob? Reason cannot coexist with violence. Yet too many students attempt to appeal for reason with acts of violence. It won't work.

Albert Einstein once observed that people who respond to martial music do their thinking with their spinal columns. The students would undoubtedly reject martial music. Its spinal appeal is too obvious. Instead, they too often embrace the stimulation offered by drama, by costume, gesture and slogan. A mob is a fine match for a military band in its ability to charge the emotions.

The regiment being piped into battle and the mob charging itself for "confrontation" have much in common. They often produce the same end product: a casualty list.

From the *Chicago* (Ill.) *Tribune,* May 6, 1970.

Are the Universities Worth Saving?

American universities have been politicized by revolutionaries to such an extent that it is a serious question whether they can be saved. It is a serious question whether some of them are worth saving, particularly those which have suspended classes in support of student demonstrations and strikes for reasons which have nothing to do with the function of a university. . . .

Many campuses have been so disrupted by violence, including the fire-bombing of buildings, that it would be almost impossible to continue normal academic work. Most of the institutions that have closed, however, have done so because their faculties are overwhelmingly in sympathy with the student revolutionaries. Thirty-five university presidents have encouraged the mounting campus madness by signing a telegram urging President Nixon to terminate all military operations in southeast Asia immediately.

Universities as such have no business meddling in foreign policy or political affairs of any kind. Faculty members and students, like all Americans, have a constitutional right to dissent, to protest, to petition for a redress of grievances, but not to disrupt universities or turn them into centers for revolutionary action programs.

Students are affected by the draft, and it is a legitimate grievance. But if there were no war in Viet Nam and no draft the campus revolution would not end. Mark Rudd, organizer of disturbances which almost destroyed Columbia university in 1968, used the word "bull" in confessing that the pretended grievances were manufactured.

The plight of the universities was brought upon them by a failure of academic responsibility, which is a corollary of academic freedom. After the riotous events at Berkeley in 1964, when the administration refused to condemn the seizure of Sproul hall, Prof. Sidney Hook of New York predicted that American higher education would never be the same again. He was right. Violence soon spread across the nation, encouraged by the cowardice or the sympathy of faculties and weak-kneed submission by administrations.

President Nixon warned Columbia university two years ago that if "student violence is either rewarded or goes unpunished then the administration will have guaranteed a new crisis on its own campus and invited student coups on other campuses all over the country." Mr. Nixon's prescience, like Prof. Hook's, has been confirmed by events. It is possible that vigorous and courageous leadership could save the universities, but time for action is running out. Soon they will not be worth saving.

From the *New York Post*, May 6, 1970.

A Drama of Blood (& Corn)

By Emil Milne

It was only play acting, but the stark realism sent chills up the spines of the young spectators.

It was a shocking scene when five machinegun-wielding "soldiers" marched eight student "prisoners" bound together with ropes out the front doors of NYU's Loeb Student Center in Washington Square.

"If you try to escape you'll be shot," a tall, lanky soldier warned the prisoners.

"Pig!" one of the students snarled back at him.

Suddenly, machineguns beat out their tattoo of death and the prisoners, blood-splattered, dropped to the ground. An alert soldier who spotted one of the victims taking too long to die delivered the coup de grace with a bullet in the head.

Thus ended the "Kent State Massacre," presented by the Guerrilla Theater in front of the student center yesterday. The production was witnessed by nearly 1000 high school students who marched to the NYU downtown campus from Union Square. . . .

From the *Washington* (D.C.) *Post,* May 6, 1970.

The Aftermath of Kent State

It is almost beyond belief that the ultimate tragedy in the opposition of young people to the war in Vietnam came in the heartland of America. But there, on the placid campus of Kent State, shots were fired and four students died. The other campus tragedies of recent years happened at places like Spartanburg where the racial instincts of the Old South held sway or on the coasts where the climate has long been regarded as more hospitable for political militancy and disruption. Thus they could be brushed aside as aberrations by some Americans. But Kent State cannot be brushed aside. It is in the great center of the country where those who disregarded the earlier incidents have argued that reason and moderation reign and where that great mass of silent students dwell. Yet it is there that four students died Monday afternoon. The country will be a long time getting over this. . . .

From the *New York Times,* May 6, 1970.

Death on the Campus

The four students, including two women, killed by M-1 bullets fired by Ohio National Guardsmen, did not die on their campus because they were known to be committing acts of violence or engaging in illegal dissent. They were victims of panic, ineptness or worse on the part of National Guard officers and soldiers with loaded weapons—almost as if Kent, Ohio, were Parrot's Beak, Cambodia.

Many students at Kent State University had indeed been demonstrating with inexcusable violence against expansion of the Vietnam war. The National Guard had been called in after an Army R.O.T.C. building had been burned down. Rocks and vile names were thrown at Guardsmen; Guardsmen laid down a tear-gas barrage against the provocative students. But shooting the students down? According to a New York Times reporter standing ten feet away from one of the students who was killed, there was no audible or visible gunfire until the National Guardsmen set to.

The State of Ohio has an obligation thoroughly to investigate this tragedy and tell the American people how and why these four students were killed—and if there is criminal responsibility. The statements by National Guard officials reveal at the very least a gross lack of control of the men under their command. Do individual guardsmen have an option to fire without orders? Are Guardsmen allowed to fire point-blank into crowds without warning or warning shots? Did these Guardsmen and their commanders fail to carry out guidelines issued by the Pentagon on civil disturbances and riot control?

The deplorably unfeeling statement by the President of the United States—through an intermediary—certainly does not provide either any answer or any comfort—nor does it show any compassion or even understanding. Mr. Nixon says that the needless deaths "should remind us all once again that when dissent turns to violence it invites tragedy," which of course is true but turns this tragedy upside down by placing the blame on the victims instead of the killers. The way this dreadful incident has been handled could hardly have been better calculated to drive the mass of moderate students—the great majority—over to the side of the alienated. It is nothing short of a disaster for the United States, and it is doubly tragic that the President does not seem to realize that this is so.

From the *Georgia State* (University) *Signal,* May 7, 1970.

Freedom to Die

Last Monday, four Kent State University students were shot to death during a campus demonstration in Kent, Ohio, against President Richard Nixon's decision to send troops into Cambodia and to resume the bombing of North Vietnam.

Four young people were killed because they had the courage to stand up against the policies of government with which they were opposed. They lay dead now, eleven of their friends wounded.

Four young people were killed by National Guard troops which were called to the campus to maintain order.

Four young people were killed much like other youths have been slain in the communist countries of the world when dissent disrupts the orderly status quo, countries which are run as a police state.

How far will our society go to stifle freedom of speech and the freedom of assembly?

How free are we now to state our opinions, be they assenting or dissenting?

If the events at Kent State are an indication of the future, may God help us all.

From the *Cleveland* (Ohio) *Press,* May 7, 1970.

Kent State—Tragic Symptom

By Don Robertson

God knows, it would be easy—and abundantly cheap—to take a rigid moral position on the hideous tragedy that took place three days ago at Kent State University.

If you oppose the war and feel that this country is beyond redemption, you can say: We are a nation of brutal cowards who shoot down unarmed kids.

If you belong to Nixon's silent majority and feel that everything would be fine if only the kids stopped rocking the boat, you can say: Those punks got what they deserved, and it is about time somebody took care of them.

But the thing is, both sides are wrong. The truth of the situation has eluded them, and their confusion has bred violence—Ghastly, psychotic, animalistic blood-letting that is symptomatic of a nation wracked with the most agonizing dilemma in its history. And, clearly, it is no longer one nation, and the "United" in United States is a mockery. . . .

If one word can be used to sum up what happened, it is dehumanization. Both sides apparently think that the situation can only be solved by employing all the varieties of violence. As a result, we have slaughters—at My Lai and Kent State—and a bunch of idiots block Euclid Ave. and scrawl dirty words on a student union wall.

When Nixon ordered the invasion of Cambodia, he compounded the violence. Apparently it is not enough that 40,000 Americans already have been killed in Southeast Asia. Now they are dying on a green and lovely Ohio campus. (And one was an ROTC cadet.) There is an answer to this, and it is called sanity. But maybe the time has passed for sanity.

From the *Cleveland* (Ohio) *Plain Dealer,* May 7, 1970.

KSU Story One-Sided in TV Reports

By William Hickey
Television-Radio Editor

The events of the past few days at Kent State University and elsewhere, tragic enough in themselves, created still further tragedy in that they brought out the worst in a number of local and network broadcast news departments.

Try as I may, I cannot recall [anything] that so distorted the reason and objectivity of television and radio news teams as did the deplorable incident on the Kent State campus. Never has one side of a story been so graphically illustrated, while the other has been so completely ignored or discounted.

This is not to suggest that the print media, both here and across the nation, was above reproach in handling of the story, but at least a great deal more attention was given to varied facets of the confrontation between students and members of the National Guard than was heard over the electronic counterparts.

It was a case of emotion winning the day and reason be damned. Unfortunately, that attitude was displayed time and time again. This is the ultimate disservice to the community, for in a time of highly charged feelings the last thing needed is additional fuel.

Dorothy Fuldheim, long one of the city's leading news analysts, hosted a special broadcast Monday evening on WEWS-TV after returning from a trip to the scene of action and reason played a little or no part in it.

The program was unworthy of Miss Fuldheim, who never quite managed to get her emotions under control. It should never have been aired for, taken in substance it was a blatant assault on the National Guard, with no regard for the particular circumstances its members faced that fateful day.

However, Miss Fuldheim's single-mindedness of purpose paled in comparison when placed alongside the National Broadcasting Co.'s Huntley-Brinkley Report of Tuesday evening.

NBC-TV News has too many skilled and talented people on its payroll to push a half-hour of such one-sidedness upon a nation of viewers as it did with that piece of programming.

To make matters worse, the program was a technological horror. The lip sync was completely off and served only to make it all the more ominous.

David Brinkley, who has never mastered the fine art of concealing emotion despite his long tenure in front of television cameras, was nothing less than a disgrace.

Posturing, glaring, letting the world know exactly where he stood on that situation out in Ohio, left him no time to be a newsman.

He was too busy acting.

Watching these and several other shows, one gathered the impression that a troop of National Guardsmen invaded the campus without cause, provoked the students into a protest action and then fired into their ranks at will.

The cheapest moment of the Huntley-Brinkley Report came when the NBC-TV cameras rested upon the father of one of the slain students. The man, understandably near hysteria, made a number of irrational charges against the government and the condition the country was in, labeling it a totalitarian state.

While it was heart-wrenching to watch and all one's prayers and sympathies were extended to the father, that piece of film was totally dishonest and begged for rebuttal.

It is incumbent upon the news media, broadcast and otherwise, to investigate and understand both sides of a particular situation before it takes up a crusade in defense of what it knows not.

Certain facts should have been brought off with great emphasis, such as the demolition of downtown Kent of Friday evening; the total destruction of the ROTC Building Saturday evening; and that a state of martial law was in force.

If those points were stressed, the average viewer could better understand why the Guard was there in the first place, for as far as I know, nice college kids don't demolish towns and building. Radical types do, however, and some protection was needed for the town's citizens, as well as the students themselves.

Perhaps, if NBC-TV had interviewed and shown a number of former members of police departments, who are now condemned to live the remainder of their lives as vegetables, because they were struck in the head by rocks, that would have allowed the average viewer to better understand the nervousness and discomfort of the Guardsmen.

NBC-TV could have done any number of things to put the tragedy at Kent into proper focus.

However, to its undying discredit, it chose not to.

As a result, Vice President Agnew could present that 30 minutes of film as evidence to any court in the world to prove without doubt that the broadcast news media is biased.

From the *New York Times*, May 7, 1970.

In the Nation: The Dead at Kent State

By Tom Wicker

WASHINGTON, May 6—It was obtuse and heartless for President Nixon to say of the dead at Kent State only that "when dissent turns to violence it invites tragedy." It was indecent for Spiro Agnew to call this awful event "predictable and avoidable," then to go on with one of his standard denunciations of students, as if he and the President, pledged as they are to "bring us together," had not instead done as much as anyone to drive us into conflict. No one has less right than they to "murder the mankind" of these senseless deaths with "grave truths" about violence and dissent.

Mr. Agnew's sustained and inflammatory assault on some young

Americans could have had no other purpose, and no other result, than to set generation against generation and class against class for the calculated political purposes of the Nixon Administration. Mr. Nixon's blurted condemnation of "bums" on the campus is all the more culpable for apparently having been spontaneous and from the heart, a true revelation of his inmost feelings.

But there is more to it than the spirit of fear and vengeance and repression—that spirit exemplified by the use on a tense college campus of tired and frightened National Guardsmen with live rounds in their weapons and discretionary orders to return fire.

Even this piece of insanity might not have left the dead at Kent State had it not been for Mr. Nixon's monumental blunder in reversing the whole course of what he had said was his Vietnamese policy with the invasion of Cambodia and the reopening of the bombing of North Vietnam. That is real violence. And any President less swayed by generals, less awed by the myopic political hardline of John Mitchell, less fixed in the outdated attitudes of cold war days, could not have failed to have foreseen that re-escalation would set off an explosion of anger and despair and bitterness—hence violence and counterviolence, rebellion and repression.

It may be argued by those politicians and commentators as concerned as Mr. Nixon about manhood, humiliation and American vanity that, even had he known his people well enough to expect the reaction he is getting, he still would have had no choice but to act in the national interest, as he saw it. But none will be able to explain what interest is worth having pushed so many of the educated and concerned of a whole generation into hatred and mistrust of their own Government; and who can say how the future can be protected abroad if a nation must club and shoot its children in the streets and on the campus?

What, in fact, has re-escalation gained us? A chilly diplomatic reaction, for one thing, including quite possibly a setback to the nuclear arms limitation talks. For another, the most severe Congressional reaction in decades against the exercise of Presidential powers.

The Administration itself is divided and wounded at the top, with Mr. Nixon—like Lyndon Johnson only two years ago—suddenly unable or unwilling to travel among his own people. Secretary of State Rogers is shown either to know little of what is happening or to have minimal policy influence; Secretary of Defense Laird was apparently overruled and—worse—uninformed about what his own bombers were doing. Is it an accident that these two, with Robert Finch among the ablest men in the Administration, now join Mr. Finch in the kind of public embarrassment to which he has had to become inured?

On the battlefield itself, no supreme Communist headquarters has been found, although its presence had been advertised as if it were

Hitler's bunker. In fact, not many Communist troops of any kind have been found, according to reporters on the scene, although captured rice tonnage mounts daily and the body count is predictably inflated. Destruction is wholesale, of course, but mostly of Cambodian towns and farms, not of Vietcong or North Vietnamese soldiers.

Begging the Question

To cap this futility with absurdity, Mr. Nixon now pledges to let the invaders go no further into Cambodia than eighteen miles from the border, a guarantee which if honored makes the rest of that sizable country a real sanctuary easily reached; and he further promises to pull the troops out within eight weeks, a period that probably can be survived by an enemy that has been fighting for more than twenty years. These public restrictions beg the question what the invasion can accomplish.

Whatever the answer, the dead at Kent State are far too high a price for it. Like the dead in Cambodia and Vietnam, they can be buried; but somehow the nation has to go on living with itself. Mr. Hickel's courageous letter to the President shows that even within the Administration, Mr. Nixon and Mr. Agnew have only made that harder to do.

From the *Grand Rapids* (Mich.) *Press,* May 7, 1970.

When Dissent Turns to Violence

Whatever may be said of President Nixon's decision to send American forces into Cambodia, there can be no quarrel with his comment that the fatal shooting of four Kent State University students "should remind us all once again that when dissent turns to violence, it invites tragedy."

Whether or not the killings were due to trigger-happy enforcers of the law, these facts remain: Students massed in dissent against still deeper American involvement in the bloody quagmire of Southeast Asia, understandably distraught at a far-off conflict that threatened to disrupt their lives; they tangled with Ohio National Guardsmen, exchanging barrages of tear gas canisters for barrages of rocks. Then came the shots and the tragedy of four young lives snuffed out.

Who can say from this distance what it was that triggered the shooting? A firecracker prank, a taunting jest, a rock striking some exposed part of the body? When dissent turns to violence, the fuse is lit for the tragedy which shames us all.

Peaceful dissent is our right as Americans. But the President has spoken wisely in cautioning that we must stand as strongly against the resort to violence as we stand for the right of peaceful dissent.

From the *Cleveland* (Ohio) *Plain Dealer,* May 8, 1970.

The Sanity of Sports

By Chuck Heaton

This has been a difficult week for at least one sports columnist.

A daughter home from Kent State University at a time when she normally would be worrying about semester examinations makes the tragedy on that campus even closer and more real. Her deep feelings about the war in Vietnam and the sad event on her campus gives her family new thoughts on a confused subject. . . .

With the status of such staples as motherhood, the flag and even apple pie now in doubt, sports are something to hang on to.

They just even may be able to help in this troubled situation. It was only last fall that Mayor Lindsay and many others credited the surprising surge of the Mets to the National League pennant and a World Series victory with aiding in keeping things quiet in tense New York City.

Perhaps these athletic contests—on all levels—and the people involved, will continue to be of some importance in maintaining a degree of sanity and order in a nation where violence off the field seems to be gaining the upper hand.

From *Newsday* (Long Island, N.Y.), May 8, 1970.

About Jeffrey Miller

Jeffrey Miller came to rest yesterday in the ripening green of middle spring. He was 20 years old, in the middle spring of manhood, employed as a student at Kent State University in Ohio. Almost no one had heard of him last Sunday. Yet in his name, and in that of three other Kent State students, campuses are afire across the country, young people march and cry their agony, and a troubled nation trembles. Who was Jeffrey Miller of Plainview, Long Island, New York? A former teacher, Sidney Firestone, offers on today's letters page a partial definition: "He did not believe in violence. He was not even an 'activist.' He was no threat to your 'fatigued' National Guardsmen, who 'lost their heads' and shot him and his schoolmates, in cold blood. HE WAS NO 'BUM', Mr. Nixon!"

A friend, Jeff Weingarten, offers a slightly different perspective in a second letter: "Like many of us, though, he left for college confused, seeking answers, and trying to legitimize his own existence . . . College, radicalism—they were all games he played trying to get a perspective on life . . . Yes, he would demonstrate and might even hurl some verbal abuse; BUT NO PHYSICAL VIOLENCE." . . .

The picture of Jeffrey that emerges so far from the public record fits neatly into the recollections of his teacher and his friend. His books, for example, included "Lost Horizon," which is about a world that never was; "The Catcher in the Rye," which is about growing up in a wrong-sized world; "Inherit the Wind," which is about a contest between ignorance and knowledge; and "The Sun Also Rises," which is about impotence, courage and a number of other things. This is a tried and sturdy list that has lighted many a search before Jeffrey Miller's. It is not a revolutionary's bookshelf. . . .

From the *Eastern New Mexico University Chase*, May 8, 1970.

Killings Radicalize Nation

In one tragic day this week the Ohio National Guard created millions more radicals in this country than any extremist group has ever succeeded in doing.

In one fateful afternoon, guardsmen acting in the holy name of "law and order" shot to death four of our fellow students at Kent State University.

No one really knows what the guardsmen were thinking. Perhaps they thought their efforts would transform KSU into a quiet retreat of academic pursuit. Whether the Guard's motives were survival or blind rage, the miscalculation was disastrous. . . .

In the future, when people talk about radicalizing and destructive forces in this country, they're going to be talking about how the National Guard one day blasted into oblivion a precious part of our nation.

Violence against anyone is tragic and self perpetuating. The question now is, "Who will be the next victim?"

From the *Denison University Denisonian* (Ohio), May 8, 1970.

Black Cloud: The New Niggers

By Gail Garcia

Black people have been systematically murdered by the system in America for hundreds of years. The most recent examples are invasions of many black communities across the nation: i.e. Oakland, Chicago, Columbus, etc.

There has been no great furor about these murders, except in Black communities. The conscience of this great moral nation has not been pricked.

It now seems that the system has a brand new set of niggers—radical white students, often called effete impudent snobs. These students oppose the war in Southeast Asia.

President Richard M. Nixon has invaded Cambodia. This means more imperialism American style—making Southeast Asia safe for democracy, killing of a few million Asians in the process. Establishing American industry, and more draftees.

So the students protest against the system, and at Kent State four were killed and everyone gets uptight. The new niggers.

It is now clear that America is fast becoming a militaristic fascist state. First to go were the Indians, then come the Blacks, the Mexican-Americans, the Puerto Ricans, the radical white students—who is next?

The American military-industrial complex still grinds on. The system still functions wiping all opposition out of its path. It reeks of Nazi Germany.

And everyone is uptight because four were killed at Kent State, four straight members of the academic community, four white students. And the fair college on the hill still functions, how ironic. . . .

Full-page Advertisement from the *Cleveland* (Ohio) *Plain Dealer,*
May 9, 1970.

Dear Mom and Dad,

Your silence is killing me. You were silent when they sent me to Vietnam. You didn't protest when they sent me into Cambodia. Now they're killing me on campus. Can you remain silent? Appeal to your congress. Now. Before it's too late.

Committee of Concerned Students and Faculty, and Staff of Case Western Reserve University Law School, Medical School, School of Applied Social Sciences, Dental School, Nursing School.

From the *New York Times,* May 9, 1970.

Violence on the Right

The assaults by construction workers on students in downtown Manhattan yesterday were a tragic reflection of the polarization brought by the Vietnam war, campus turbulence, racial tensions and an Administration-fostered mood of political repression. Even more, the clashes in the financial district and at City Hall were a frightening lesson in the ease with which right-wing vigilantism finds in left-wing extremism an excuse for pushing aside constituted authority and enforcing its own brutal form of injustice.

The youngsters who massed in Wall Street with the declared purpose of shutting down the Stock Exchange were scarcely operating in the spirit of the "day of reflection" Mayor Lindsay had urged as a tribute to the four students killed by National Guard bullets at Kent State University. But there was no use of force until the helmeted building tradesmen marched onto the scene and initiated their own reign of terror.

The hardhats, long scornful of excesses by privileged longhairs on campus, were obviously delighted at the opportunity to pour out their hatred on the students and any who dared to raise a voice in their defense. From that it was a swift jump to City Hall for a direct-action display of their venom against the Mayor, the most articulate spokesman in public life for the right to dissent and for adult understanding of college youth's frustrations.

The police, badly outnumbered in Wall Street, were even more seriously short of men at City Hall. The result was a shambles in which the rampaging unionists beat students, smashed windows and cowed city officials into ordering the American flag back to full staff, thus canceling the half-staff memorial to the Kent State dead originally decreed by the Mayor. Not one construction worker was arrested at any stage of this civic humiliation.

The building tradesmen, of course, are in the forefront of those who deplore crime in the street and the decay of law and order. They have now joined the revolutionaries and bombthrowers on the left in demonstrating that anarchy is fast becoming a mode of political expression. Unless the peril in that trend becomes universally recognized, no one's liberty will be safe. American democracy can survive only in a climate of reason built on respect for law.

Victor Riesel (Syndicated Columnist), May 9, 1970.
Courtesy Publishers-Hall Syndicate.

WASHINGTON—It is the fashion of revolutionists to cry for blood. And cry they did at Kent State U. which many an observer would have you believe is a panty-raid enclave, where strollers down the tree-lined campus worship their wrestling team. And when the blood came, it came to children of working people who sought uncostly education ($642 a year) for their youngsters.

But Kent State U. is no movie set for an old Jack Oakie film. There are those of us who would hop off at Akron, drive the 10 miles and observe the SDS Weatherman faction—Mark Rudd, Bernardine Dohrn and comrades—scream, literally, for blood, for murder, for revolt, for the leveling of its buildings to wind-blown ashes, and for armed rebellion. For some time now Kent State U. has been the target for the SDS Ohio region and the Akron communes.

It's all in the record. There is the SDS pamphlet, written in the ancient argot of old Czarist era terrorists which shouts: "The war is on at Kent State." It was written by two SDS regional staff people. It was distributed from a table set before the auditorium on April 28, 1969. It lay among publications of the Peking Chinese, the early rifle-toting Progressive Labor Party, and other "splinters." This pamphlet begins with today's nihilist father image, as did the old Russian literature. The paragraph under "the war is on" is a quotation from Mao. "Then follows a report of weeks of intense struggle" on the college grounds—epecially to "raise the political consciousness of thousands on the campus, while the pig-thug Administration has responded with swift and heavy repression."

Intelligence sources have been reporting Kent State U. as the target for years. And why?

No one has bothered to look at the SDS "demands" at Kent. There are four points—indeed significant. And this quadripartite program should be the pivotal point of any objective probe—preferably by a Congressional select committee whose report should be unimpeachable to the reasonable.

Note what the SDS shouted for on this bucolic campus. (1) The elimination of the ROTC. This demand is standard neo-anarchist operating procedure. (2) "End Project Themis Grant to the Liquid Crystals Institute."

Do note that there are but two such institutes in our land. One is on Kent State campus. Its objective is to develop "liquid crystal detectors." These crystals are extremely sensitive to heat. They are used in mechanisms to detect campfires in jungle areas and in some instances to detect body heat at long range. This is of vital strategic use by our troops in Southeast Asia seeking hidden Viet Cong and North Vietnamese forces either encamped or set to spring an ambush. In recent years, Project Themis has funded some two-score anti-insurgency scientific projects for the Department of Defense.

Third point in the SDS tactical schedule is a demand for the abolishment of the Law Enforcement School. This trains students for police careers. And fourth, Abolish the Northeast Ohio Crime Laboratory used for swift identification of rioters as well as criminals.

Obviously the SDS is out after more than the radicalization of a quiet campus where in the spring young men's fancies turned to panty raids.

Let's pass over for a moment the looting, the burning, the attacks on banks, the assault on firefighters and the destruction of inventories of small businessmen which hit Kent U. last week. Let's go back some years when the SDS's national self-appointed female revolutionist, Bernardine Dohrn, created herself in the image of a young Russian woman who almost 100 years ago became the sole survivor of a band of bomb-making terrorists who even then worked with electrical gadgets.

"Bernardine," who sees herself as a latterday "La Passionara," is one of several National SDS leaders. It is she who targeted Kent State U. for quite a while. Then on April 28, 1969, she spoke to a student crowd in Williams Hall. At one point during the discussion which followed her speech she became agitated, lost her cool, rushed to the rostrum, grabbed the microphone and shouted that she could murder for self-defense, an eye and ear witness has reported under sworn testimony, and could murder for revenge. She stopped. And she added "in a sense." Well, what sense?

A week later, on May 6, almost exactly a year before the awesomely tragic shooting of four students, the SDS helped whip up a rally. Joyce Cecora, reportedly an important SDS speaker, bluntly called for the use of arms to end "the repressive action of the administration."

"They used guns at Cornell and they got what they wanted," said this young woman now typical of the new fraternity of violence. "It will come to that here!"

On Feb. 27, 1969, this same Joyce Cecora had said that, unless the administration gave way, the SDS would burn and level the campus (according to sworn testimony in federal reports).

Blood, now rotting the earth of Kent's lovely campus, did not spill accidentally. That soil was tilled—furrowed by the clanging iron words of the toughest band of nihilists this land has known. Virtually all of them are outsiders. Virtually all of them chose Kent State because it is what it is, a source of strength for American forces, a source of learning for the children of working people, a spot in middle America.

The SDS has been crying for blood. It knows, for its leaders are deeply read, what can happen when any military in any land shoot down children of America's middle class. It identifies. It cries out. It can shake governments.

In the "right on" argot, let's cool it. Men of structure must go to the scene and search the record.

I have criss-crossed this land a hundred times. I know America will listen to an appeal to reason. It is time there be more reason or there will be more blood.

And it is time for the young men and women to appeal for that reason. The SDS is not their world—or it would be fighting for true peace and not be the explosive advocate of a provincial Mao Tse-tung.

Comment by Professor Dennis Duffy, University of Toronto, interviewed on the *CBC Sunday Magazine,* May 10, 1970.

. . . I think something like Kent State, following the Cambodian action, showed that in a real sense, many ways in which Americans have always viewed their country are simply unreal; that in fact they have seen the canons of liberal democracy progressively eroded, so that on the one hand you have a President who says, well, I don't care how the nation feels, we're going into Cambodia; on the other hand you have response of the politically frustrated which comes out in the form of actions that are not allowable—you can't allow people to go throwing rocks—but at which point the establishment responds by shooting them down. And it's just one impact after another of people doing these seemingly unreal things but that are extremely real but that have changed the tenor of American life and committed America to a course whose ultimate end I don't think anyone can conceive right now.

From the Garrettsville, Ohio, edition of *Town and Country Trader,* May 13, 1970.

> ### *Wake Up!! Mr. and Mrs. America*
> ### *"Let the Silent Majority Be Heard"*
> ### *Put an End to . . .*

Punkism, hooliganism, cowardism, hippyism, agitatorism, draft dodgerism, communism, and tolerance for those who refuse to obey and enforce the laws that protect our Citizenry! STOP: The undermining of our great Democracy!

TAKE ACTION NOW!! [Suggested actions include]

Visit your college children often—make surprise visits—"See them in Action!" Is your child in college misbehaving? (If you question all parents of Kent State University students as to whether their student was involved in the last violent episode, the standard answer would be "No, it's the other bad students"!)

Enforce existing laws—(Make direct arrests) of all persons desecrating the "Stars & Stripes" which is our "Symbol of Freedom."

Back Governor Rhodes and General Del Corso and our National Guard for their actions at Kent State University. Remember—millions of dollars in property damage, irreparable damage was done to the community and citizens were terrorized before the National Guard entered the picture. . . .

Paid for by Citizens of the College Community.

From the *Wall Street Journal,* May 14, 1970.

The Cultural Conflict

In this editorial office as in many others, the shootings at Kent State University caused a voluminous outpouring of letters from readers. We were impressed by their number, but even more surprised at the uncommonly venomous anti-student tone of many of them. The rise of such feelings prompts us to think a bit more about the problem of escalating cultural conflict in America.

Only the more rational letters have been included in the sampling printed elsewhere on this page. The less rational letters tended to denounce students in sweeping terms as "cavemen," "parasites" and "sneering, jeering, wild-eyed slobs." Such ugly sentiments in reaction to the militancy of the young—itself hardly immune to ugliness—are perhaps the starkest reminders yet of the cultural problem: Beyond any concrete issue, a large segment of domestic conflict has developed into an argument over the way people think of themselves and how they should live.

Realizing that political revolution is out of the question in the U.S. right now, many of the young instead espouse "cultural revolution." The problems of America, they contend, lie in the values of its people, who are materialistic, racist, imperialist, and violent. A proper response lies in creating a "counter culture" based on different values. This, of course, is far easier to accomplish than a political or economic revolution. One need only change one's attitudes and perhaps one's "style of life." And people still are free to do this in America.

We do not care to repeat here our own criticisms of the cultural revolutionaries, who, we believe, are at best guilty of shallow insight. For the moment, we are more concerned with the notion that, absurd as it often can appear, cultural conflict is potentially every bit as volatile as conflict over more substantial issues. Here, for example is a Chicago advertising salesman commenting on student militants in a news magazine roundup of last week's events:

"I'm getting to feel like I'd actually enjoy going out and shooting some of these people. I'm just so god damned mad. They're trying to destroy everything I've worked for—for myself, my wife and my children."

One can point out that the ad salesman is being ridiculous. Some of the cultural revolutionaries may engage in bombings and such from time to time, but most of them are neither ready nor able to launch a widespread destruction campaign. The ad salesman and a lot of other people feel threatened mostly by the questions the revolutionaries raise, rather than their acts. And it can be suggested plausibly that their murderous thoughts stem mostly from insecurity, the fear that the cultural revolutionaries may actually be on to something. . . .

From the *East Side* (N.Y.) *News*, May 15, 1970.

Parents' Prayer Today

By Lillian Waller

Dear God: Give us strength to withstand the slaughter of our children. They are killed because they sympathize with their fellow students who refuse to accept the massacre of innocent men, women and children in other lands and who refuse to be trained to continue such massacres. The shooting of our children at Kent State University was deliberate murder by the order of those who resent the disobedience to their authority; that authority by sadists who have the power to extinguish the lives of the young by a command or stroke of a pen.

Dear God: Give us strength to tolerate the stupidity and the inhumanity of our leaders who were elected to protect our children in accordance with the Bill of Rights and the United States Constitution. . . .

From the *Berkeley* (Calif.) *Tribe,* May 8–16, 1970.

. . . The authorities hoped to fragment the 20,000 angry students (there are 20,000 students at KSU and everyone of them was angry), lest they begin to make that anger collective. That anger won't go away easy. That's why the University is closed indefinitely.

In addition, authorities attempted to stop the outflow of any information. All phones within 30 miles were disconnected for at least 12 hours. A phone company repairman remarked, "The lines are needed for police emergencies." Thousands more troops and Highway police were brought in quickly. Kent and the nearby towns of Stow, Strongsville, and Twinsburg were sealed off under martial law. School children and factory workers were sent home. The killings had been swift. The subsequent massive attempt to cover up, silence and prevent any protest of those killings was equally swift.

Tuesday morning the Kent campus and the surrounding city were deserted. Students who lived on campus were forced to leave. There was an injunction against anyone entering the area. However, a number of students living off campus remained. Despite heavy campus surveillance, a university storage barn in a somewhat remote area of the campus was hit by fire, causing $6000 damage.

There are many factors which make it difficult to piece together this conspiracy. Many look to the Governor of the State, who was running for Senator in the primary election the next day. What about the Guard? Why were they so gentle on the Teamsters? Were they tired from six days of duty? Who gave the orders? This is all unclear.

What is clear, however, is that the KSU massacre fits the pattern of increasing repression at home. Because the US is losing the war in Vietnam, it must run a tight ship at home. The connection between protests against the war and the course of the war itself is inextricable, and this was certainly true at KSU. The US has declared war on black people for many years now. The massacre at Kent State may signal its declaration of war against young people.

Here at KSU, 20,000 sons and daughters of Middle Amerika have been thrust into the belly of the warring monster. For some it will be an unforgettable, yet momentary, exposure, but for others (quite a few thousand others) it will be the beginning of a struggle to destroy that monster.

From the *Detroit* (Mich.) *Free Press,* May 16, 1970.

Universities Must Retain Freedom to Be "Irrelevant"

For those among us who love the university and cherish the spirit of free inquiry for which it stands, this has become a season of infinite sadness. More and more universities are becoming battlegrounds or empty camps in the wake of the killings at Kent State. And while name-calling from Washington, the inept use of force and the widening of the Indochina war are partly to blame, it is now also a time for student dissidents to search their own hearts.

A dangerous psychology of protest is spreading this spring. It is becoming easier and easier to demonstrate for less coherent reasons, to play at guerilla theater and adolescent war games with ever more use of violence and risk of tragedy. The more that happens, the more it tears apart the university and subverts the very ideals and victories the students claim to seek. . . .

To a great degree, the protests have been impelled by the students' conviction that they and the university must be "relevant" to the society outside. But in some ways the university was never meant to be relevant. Its very irrelevance was cherished. Its freedom from outside pressures loosed the minds within to search where they would for truth. The student tested other men's wisdom and disciplined his own mind, and somehow in that stretch and interplay he found the only thing a university ever had to give: Not the answers, but the critical spirit and the intellectual tools to begin the lifelong task of looking for them.

Now that view of the university seems hopelessly antique, like the scribblings of the Latin scholars of medieval Paris or Bologna. In some ways, and good ones, our children have irrevocably changed the shape of the university. But in the end they will also have to rediscover the cloister.

Every society must have its free and quiet place for scholars and visionaries, where men can trace their roots and dream their futures and think thoughts to shake the world. That is what the university is about. That is what the young dissenters must, even in their righteous passion, hold forever in mind. There are some prices that are too high to pay for any goal, and the destruction of the free university is one of them.

From the *Afro-American Newspaper* (Baltimore, Md.), May 16, 1970

Kent Tragedy In Focus

The Ohio National Guard has demonstrated again that our civilian soldiers still have not attained the professional level of military conduct and detachment to control domestic outbreaks without resorting to unnecessary force.

Because of that, four students at Kent University in Ohio died when guardsmen opened fire on them, apparently without having been fired upon and definitely without required orders for such a situation.

From Detroit, to Watts to Newark studies have shown that our civilian soldiers are prone to panic or deliberately resort to unnecessary force under pressure. Detroit was an example of costly errors by the guardsmen and a professional job in the same situation by regular soldiers.

Most discussions of the shortcomings of the guardsmen emphasize their lack of training and experience. That is part of the trouble but may not be the most important negative aspect.

It begins to look more and more as if the guardsmen are too civilianized, too prone to be affected by prevalent moods in the country, too emotionally involved in behalf of or against those in the turbulence they must curb. They simply are not detached enough.

In racial confrontations the predominately-white guardsmen have shown repeatedly their proneness to take sides, despite statements denying this.

Now there is reason to fear that the rhetoric against student demonstrations is creating a mood which encourages, or at the least excuses, unnecessary force being used to put down these incidents.

This is but another law and order step in the swing to the right. First, blacks, then students and next the silent majority.

If all this seems to be straying from the question of shortcomings in the national guard, the point is that our civilian soldiers are listening more to the prevailing mood than to professional military dictates. They have consistently proven themselves to be too civilianized to respond otherwise.

From the *Pittston* (Pa.) *Sunday Dispatch*, May 17, 1970.

Idle Minds Can Be Tools Of Devil

The country is still stirring with student protests.

Violence is gaining as the TV screens show. There's more to it than appears on the surface. The tragic death of four Kent State University students recently was shocking. Now it develops that a search of **girls** and boys dormitories at Kent uncovered hundreds of knives, marijuana equipment and dozens of offensive weapons. Why did the student body of Kent have all this in their dormitory rooms?

How degenerate can some students get in these lush days for college students who have all the blessings of living in a prosperous, luxurious United States? They should tour the poverty areas, see those who do without but never raise their hands or weapons against a fellowman. Too much luxurious living—can give it a bad taste. A little suffering and sacrifice builds character.

Far too many of our young have indicated a lack of individual character. There are many good minds among the young. Something to develop. They are the ones we hope will carry on the American traditions and continue to advance this country—a country built on the character, effort and sacrifice of so many millions in the past.

From an article by Bob Malone in *The Great Speckled Bird* (Atlanta, Ga.), May 18, 1970.

Kent State created for the first time a widespread realization that Amerika cannot achieve its present goals unless it is willing to kill its own children. That is a sobering thought, at least momentarily. Amerika has never shrunk from genocide before when somebody was standing in the way of something it wanted—like land, money or empire—but this time it's different: *these kids are white.* As a gauge of Amerikan racism, Kent State recalls the public reaction to the triple murder of Chaney, Goodman and Schwerner in Mississippi several years ago, after dozens of deaths had passed unnoticed. The fact that even Nixon felt the shock waves indicates how profoundly it jarred the national psyche, for few Americans are more isolated from the public mood than he. . . .

From *The Nation,* May 25, 1970.

After Kent

The shooting on the Kent University campus has been compared to the Boston Massacre. Actually, on a scale of atrocity, Kent ranks higher. The Boston event has been distorted in school history books. The British soldiers were under attack at close quarters; their commander, Captain Preston, intervened forcibly at the first shot, and John Adams himself successfully defended the accused. The Kent massacre seems to have lacked any justification whatsoever, and the age of the victims adds to its horror. Despite differences of degree, however, there is a psycho-political similarity between the killings of 1770 and of 1970. In both cases the timing of the event, the pent-up frustrations, the passions that were ready to explode, produced sequels out of proportion to the casualties. Kent may not be Boston, but it too marks a turning point.

Student agitation used to be confined to a band on the East Coast and another on the West, with a broad, largely unstirred population in between. The moral implications of the Vietnamese War have now penetrated to the universities of the "heartland"—Kent, Ohio State, Kansas, Kentucky and others, and to South Carolina. What is happening now is no longer a Berkeley or an Ivy League affair.

From the *Canton* (Ohio) *Repository*, May 28, 1970.

The FBI and the Professors

To use an expression they surely are familiar with, it appears that some Kent State University professors are getting "uptight" because the Federal Bureau of Investigation has dared to ask some questions about them.

It would seem that the professors, most of whom are reported to be in the English, speech and sociology departments, are indignant that they and their students should be asked to answer the FBI's questions.

They are speaking of the FBI inquiry in terms of "witch-hunt," "McCarthyism" and "climate of hysteria."

They go further and charge that such questioning violates "the right of free expression in the classroom."

It is not hard to understand the behavior of the radical students when one considers that they are subjected to the influence of professors and instructors who think like this.

Where do they get the idea that they are any more immune to questioning by the federal authority than the average citizen? What makes them think that the classroom is hallowed ground?

Perhaps they are getting edgy because they fear they may have to answer to the public for what they have been saying in those classrooms. If they are not fearful of this, why should they be afraid for the FBI to investigate?

After all the name of the federal agency contains the word "investigation." That is its business. The agency and its members are held in high repute by most Americans, with the exception of those who would advocate overthrow of our government.

Certainly most citizens would far rather believe the FBI than a few instructors or professors whose conduct had led them to be investigated. . . .

It is doubtful if the taxpayers of this state or any other wish to spend their dollars supporting the teaching of rebellion and revolution.

The implication that the professors should be exempt from the queries of the FBI hardly seems a democratic concept. It sounds more like special privilege—one which the average nonspecial-privilege American should find very offensive.

It has been reported that one high KSU official even ordered that no further class lists be given to the FBI unless a court order was obtained. This example of lack of cooperation with our Department of Justice seems intended to thwart rather than assist the cause of justice.

Some of those who reside and practice their profession on college and university campuses may think the academic community is sacrosanct. There are many more Americans, who financially support the professors in their work, that disagree.

From *The Voice of Americanism*'s Pamphlet No. 135.

Who Killed Whom at Kent State University

By W. S. McBirnie

What Kent Townspeople Say

The residents of Kent, Ohio, with little disagreement, believe that the Guard *had* to be summoned. They bitterly resent the property destruction the students have caused in Kent, and while they are saddened by the student deaths, they believe death was inevitable on a campus so beset with violence. One resident expressed it this way:

> These kids were ready to burn everything. If you would have had townspeople with guns out on their roofs to protect their property, you would have had a lot more than four dead. (*Indianapolis Star*, May 9, 1970)

In a letter to the "Mothers of Servicemen," in South Pasadena, a resident of Kent makes the following comment.

> It is terrible to live in Kent, a once beautiful and peaceful city, as sirens, cycles and shouts keep you awake every night. For over five years Kent people have had to stay out of their own town in night season. KSU should have been closed long ago. (Photostatic copy of letter referred to is in the files of the VOA.)

Today Kent University is closed, some 19,000 students have had their education disrupted, perhaps ended because of the riots. No one, except the communists and the nihilists, can take any satisfaction from the event. Competent observers know that Kent was a prime target of the SDS for months. The news media however has laid the entire blame for the unfortunate incident on the National Guard. The media could have put the tragedy at Kent into proper focus if they had so desired. Why are they so unwilling to relate the real causes of the disturbances?

Who is Really to Blame?

The National Guard has been called "murderers," a libelous state-ment. The real murderers are those radical students and faculty mem-bers who whip a disinterested crowd into a raging mob. They are the ones who advocate revolution and anarchy. They should be held ac-countable for all the heartache and destruction that has been caused. They are the "merchants of violence."

But back of all the radical faculty and students stands the *communist conspiracy* whose knowing or unknowing tools they are. . . .

From *The Daily Kent Stater*, September 30, 1970.

Visitor Discovers "a Rare Kind of Beauty" in Kent

By James A. Michener

When I first saw Kent this summer, I was impressed by the beauty of the town, the stateliness of the trees, the subtle manner in which in certain areas the urban areas blended in with the rural. The lake dis-tricts fascinated me, and I spent long hours jogging and hiking along the back streets, where the charm of the town manifested itself.

As for the two main streets, Highways 59 and 43, the less said about them, the better. They failed completely to live up to the beauty of the rest of the city and ought to have a major face-lift right away. The rail-road? The crossings? The interminable traffic jams? I am a visitor and prudence warns me to shut up.

But it was the university complex that stunned me with its vitality and appropriateness. Kent State is the only university I have visited in the last six years which has enough space. Residents of this town and this university cannot appreciate what a boon they have in the rolling landscape surrounding the university and giving it character. I could name a dozen great American universities, and every foreign one, who would envy Kent its spaciousness. Students who attend classes here live in the midst of a rare kind of beauty, a kind that is missing elsewhere.

And the buildings which have been planted on the hills are not bad, either. I grew to like the yellow brick, the sprawling manner in which certain new buildings hug their terrain. Even the old ones, along the semicircle, had a stubborn charm; and while I do not go for skyscrapers on a university campus—finding them antithetical to the spirit of a col-lege—if you're going to have them, I think Kent's are tasteful, well-de-signed and utilitarian. They're a lot better than what I've seen on other campuses.

My work, naturally, has taken me around Taylor Hall a good deal, and I would judge it to be one of the most handsome academic build-ings erected anywhere in the United States within the last decade. It has a touch of class.

I was quite astounded by one aspect of the university: the peripatetic quality of the student body. I don't think I have yet met a student who came here as a freshman and graduated with an M.A. Everybody is either from somewhere else or is headed somewhere else. And when I meet a junior, I automatically ask ". . . Where did you transfer from?" This is a striking development of recent years and one which alters the nature of university life as I used to know it. The good aspect is that it keeps Kent from being parochial; its danger is that it prevents the building of a cohesive school spirit such as I knew in the more unified institutions I attended.

Let me correct myself. I did meet a young man the other day who started at Kent in 1954 and is still more or less here, working on his M.A. But in the interim he has been to so many different schools in so many different states that I looked at him in wonder, trying to decipher how he could have withstood so much shifting about. He did not consider it strange.

I am at Kent because last spring when troubles overtook this campus the significance reached far beyond Ohio. At last count, 760 American colleges and universities shut down as a result of what happened here. Consequently, this beautiful campus in this attractive town is a bellwether for American education, and all of us who wish the university well as it begins a new term do so not only because Kent itself is a pretty good school, but because it symbolizes so much for all of us. You are part of us now, whether we wish to have it that way or not.

My major disappointment in Kent—in fact, I'd say my only one—is that I have failed so far to meet that brilliant young man or woman who is interested not in politics, not in the slums of Cleveland, but in subjects like Herodotus, or Darwin's theory of the origin of the species, or the paintings of Watteau, or Beethoven in his centennial year, or the architecture of Le Corbusier, or the role of James Wilson in the writing of the Constitution. Universities have traditionally been the home of young people who get steamed up over the historical considerations of mankind, and it is disturbing not to meet students who are so agitated.

I am convinced that the future governance of this world, and all its dependencies, will rest in the hands of people who are now grappling with these timeless problems of justice, form, the relation of man to his environment, the nature of truth, the character of a good government.

Half of what we need to know we learn from contemporary situations, and in this respect some Kent students are doing a whale of a job. But the other half, and I believe the more important, we learn from the contemplation of the same problems that excited Plato and Charlemagne and Suleiman the Magnificent and Thomas Jefferson.

Therefore, I hope that in the remainder of my days in this exciting spot I shall see the Kent Flashes roll up a big victory and meet some student who says "I am on fire with what Gustave Flaubert has to say about writing," or "Have you heard the late masses of Palestrina?" Because I believe that that's what a university ought to be for the bulk of its students.

From the *Ladies' Home Journal*, October, 1970.

Life Story

By Erich Segal

On May 3, 1970, Allison Krause, a freshman at Kent State University in Ohio, telephoned her father and mother in Pittsburgh, Pennsylvania, and reassured them that she was not involved in any of the radical activity that had disrupted her campus. In fact, though she disapproved of the Vietnam War, Allison strongly opposed any sort of violent protest. She concluded the conversation by telling her parents, "Everything's all right." Twenty-four hours later, she was shot to death by an Ohio National Guardsman.

By now this is ancient history. We've gone on to newer tragedies. Then why, with the fall semester upon us, when even those on campus seem to be looking forward and not back, do I once again bring up the name of Allison Krause?

Because too many have already forgotten. And too few really know why she died.

At the risk of being repetitious—and the greater risk of discussing things that most of us would just as soon forget—I would like to offer my own explanation of the meaning of Allison Krause's death. This is merely my opinion, of course, and everyone has a perfect right to disagree. But as an inducement for you to read on, I promise not to shout accusations at anyone. In fact, I promise not to shout.

Allison Krause lived in Pittsburgh with her father, a manager of material for a Westinghouse plant, her mother, a bookkeeper for a furniture store, and her 15-year-old sister Laurie. During one of her high school summers, Allison did volunteer work at St. Elizabeth's Hospital. At Kent State she was thinking about majoring in fine arts. She was a very gentle girl who would often walk around the campus with her pet kitten in her arms. During her freshman year at Kent, she fell in love. It had all the symptoms of the classic campus romance, but merely to see Allison at this time evoked something wonderful in her friends. Said a Kent junior, "Allison had a boyfriend, Barry, from New York and they were always together. I remember them one night in J.B.'s when the James Gang was still playing there. They were sitting on the floor holding hands, smiling at each other. They looked so happy."

I think Allison needs no more introduction than this. If I have made her sound like a nice, normal girl, it is because I think it is important to realize that she was just that. In all fairness, however, I should recount the now legendary "flower incident," which, beautiful gesture though it was, has been exploited and blown terribly out of proportion in order to make Allison something of a saint or a martyr, which she was not. She was just a victim.

It seems that during the last full day of her life, Allison walked up to one of the National Guardsmen who had been sent in to calm the Kent State campus. She placed a flower in the barrel of the soldier's rifle and said, "Flowers are better than bullets." It is not reported what the Guardsman answered.

What the Russian poet Yevgeny Yevtushenko said *is* reported. He published a poem in *Pravda* emphasizing the political lesson to be learned from Allison's death:

> Don't give a gift of flowers to a state
>   where truth is punished.
> The response of such a state is cynical and cruel.

But the poet himself was being rather cynical and cruel—and hypocritical. He exploited Allison's death to castigate our country for something of which his own is ten times more guilty: a systematic repression of dissent, which the Soviet novelist Solzhenitsyn has recently called "spiritual murder."

This is why I myself do not emphasize Allison's "flower gesture." The inherent drama in it distracts us from the true reason for her death, which has absolutely nothing to do with her objection to the war, or with her gentle and pacific statement to the Guardsman. And still less with the punishment of truth. Let me tell you in the simplest possible terms why Allison Krause was killed.

Allison Krause was killed because she happened to be in the line of fire when the National Guard began to shoot.

That is the real reason. And the only reason.

We must remember that all four students killed at Kent State— Allison, William Schroeder, Sandy Lee Scheuer and Jeffrey G. Miller —were innocent bystanders. The troops had been called because radicals had put the campus in turmoil, but none of the victims was in *any* way involved with the disturbances. None belonged to the S.D.S. or the Weathermen; ironically, Bill Schroeder was a member of ROTC— and an Eagle Scout. Not one of them was even old enough to be a voting Republican or Democrat!

The meaning of the deaths of Allison, Sandy, Jeffrey and Bill is that they had no meaning. And yet even this is not the real tragedy of Kent State.

The real tragedy is that some people think they *deserved* to die.

And when I say some people, I mean many people: townfolk in Kent, citizens of Ohio, Americans all over the land. A great many people thought—and said straight out to the press and on TV—that the deaths at Kent State were justified.

"They deserved it."

"They had it coming."

Some even went as far as to suggest that "all the rebels be shot," which I suppose meant gunning down every single student at Kent. Or maybe all students. (It was an emotional time and many emotional things were said.)

These sentiments were, by and large, expressed by men of good will. What were they saying? What were they talking about? Clearly, the topic was crime and punishment, and they obviously felt that the crimes committed by the students deserved the death penalty. The death penalty. Now you don't have to be a lawyer to realize that very few offenses nowadays warrant capital punishment. In fact, many states are abolishing capital punishment completely. (Though some 500 condemned murderers are in U.S. prisons, not one has been executed in the last three years.) Nonetheless, people all across America considered the deaths at Kent State not only justified but desirable. Please note I said "death," not "murder" or some other inflammatory term, because I am in no position to question the legality of the Guard's actions.

And for the moment, that is beside the point. For the moment the point is Allison Krause.

On May 4th, Allison was walking across the campus with her boyfriend Barry Levine. They came to the area where the confrontation between Guardsmen and students was about to erupt into violence. The students were taunting and goading the Guard. Allison completely disapproved of this sort of thing and wanted no part of it. But she had wandered there and, as one of her friends later explained, "She just stopped to look around and see what was happening." Barry described the rest:

"She was right next to me. We were starting to walk away from the Guardsmen when I heard the gunfire. She fell and I pulled her behind a car. A few others fell around us.

"When I looked up there were kids on the ground covered with blood.

"Allison was struck in the side and I could see blood coming out. She was still breathing, but she didn't say anything."

I wonder if in those moments between her wounding and her death Allison understood "what was happening." Barry says she didn't speak. But if she could have, what could she have said?

That is all there is to the death of Allison Krause. She was a nice girl and a good daughter. She rejoiced in her love for Barry not merely for its own sake, but for her father and mother, who would be pleased that Barry was also Jewish.

If this really is all there is, then why did people say "they had it coming"?

Of course, you will hasten to tell me that anybody who said that the Kent students had it coming didn't mean—*could not have meant*—Allison Krause.

Or, in fact, the other three who died with her, who were equally blameless, who all led equally mundane, innocent, *nice* lives. I agree. The people who said the deaths were justified did not know Allison or Sandy or Jeff or Bill. Not at all.

But you see, *that* is the real tragedy of Kent State.

And it is the tragedy of our times.

For if the good folk in nearby Ohio towns do not understand Kent State, how will they understand Jackson State, or Augusta, much less what happened in the far-off little village of My-Lai?

I bring up Allison Krause again because hers is the face of America. She was a cute coed who loved her boyfriend, her father, her mother and her kitten and who felt, because she could answer for herself, that she could assure her parents that *everything* was all right. Can any of us believe that now?

If we are so confused that we cannot distinguish a campus from a battlefield, if Kent and Khe Sanh look the same (an ex-G.I. present made this precise comparison), then we had better stop and look around and see what is happening.

Wait, you say, isn't that precisely what Allison did the moment before she . . . before the . . . before . . .?

Yes. A moment before the bullets, Allison "just stopped to look around to see what was happening."

Maybe if *we* had, she wouldn't have had to.

Poem by Yevgeny Yevtushenko in *Pravda,* May 18, 1970.
(Translated by Michael A. Rogers, Russian Instructor,
Kent State University.)

Flowers and Bullets

(As a memory to the student of Kent State University, Allison Krause, murdered during the protest demonstration against the U.S. war in Southeast Asia)

Original text in Russian by Soviet poet Yevgeny Yevtushenko, *Pravda,* May 18, 1970.

> He who loves flowers
>   Naturally is not liked by
>   the bullets.
> Bullets are jealous ladies.

Can one really expect kindness from them?
Nineteen-year-old Allison
    Krause,
You were murdered because
You loved flowers.
It was—
An expression of purest hopes
In the instant
    When defenseless as the thin
    pulse of conscience
You placed a flower
    In the barrel of the
    mute and brutal Guardian
    of the Establishment.
And you said:
    "Flowers are better than
    bullets."
Don't give a gift of flowers to a
    state where the truth is punished.
The response of such a state is
    cynical and cruel,
And that's what the response
    was to you,
    Allison Krause,
A bullet that pushed the flower back.
Let all the apple trees of the
    world
    be dressed not in white
    but in mourning!
Ah, how sweet the lilac smells
    But you do not feel anything.
As the President said about
    you,
    You are a "bum."
Every dead person is a bum,
    But this is not his fault.
You lie on the grass
    With a candy stick in your
    cheek.
You will not dress yourself in
    new clothes,
You will not read new books.
You were a student.
    You studied fine arts
But there is another art—
    It is bloody and terrible.

In this hangman's art there also
    probably
    Are geniuses.
Who was Hitler?
    A Cubist of new gas
    chambers.
In the name of all flowers
    I curse your creations,
You architects of lies,
    Conductors of murders.
Mothers of the world moan:
    "O, God, O, God."
And fortune tellers are afraid
    To foretell the future.
At this moment, death is dancing
    rock and roll
    on the bones in
    Vietnam
        and Cambodia,
And what stage
    Will death find tomorrow to
    perform in?
Rise up, girls of Tokyo,
    Boys of Rome,
Rise up, flowers,
    Against the common evil enemy,
Blow together on all the
    dandelions of the world—
Oh what a great storm there
    will be!
Flowers, gather for war!
    Punish the oppressors!
One tulip after another
    One daisy after another
Bursting forth in anger
    From tidy flowerbeds
Stuff the throats of all hypocrites
    with the earthy roots.
You, jasmine, clog
    the propellors of the destroyers.
You, the nettles, stick firmly to
    the lenses
    covering the gunsights.
Get up, lilies of the Ganges
    And the lotus of the Nile—
And block the props of

airplanes,
Pregnant with the death of
children.
Roses, don't be proud when
they sell you
For more
Although it is pleasant to touch the
girls' tender cheeks
Pierce
The gas tanks
Of the bombers,
Grow your thorns longer
And sharper
Against them you cannot rise
up only with flowers.
Their stems are too fragile
Their petals are a poor
armor
But a Vietnamese girl—the same
age as Allison—
took in her hands a rifle,
An armed flower of
The wrath of the people.
Even if flowers rise,
Then no use to play
hide-and-seek with
History,
Young America,
Tie up the hands of the
murderers.
Grow
Grow
The escalation of truth
Against the escalation of lies
that trample the life of
the people.
Flowers, gather for war!
Defend the beautiful.
Flood the highways and byways
Like the menacing flow of an
army,
And into the columns of people and
flowers
Rise up, murdered Allison Krause,
Like the immortelle of the epoch—
The thorny flower of protest.

Excerpts from poem by E. Merrill Root in *American Opinion*,
October, 1970.

American Hard Hats

They are the men who build into the sky
Thin mountain-nets of steel where the winds cry
Like vain invisible wolves. At work, they walk
Girders so high that clouds, like misty chalk,
Are almost neighbors. Firm and nonchalant,
They tread the dangerous heights, cohabitant
With sun and wind—and death at the foot's end.
In their stern world they do not condescend
To dizziness or fear: If so, they plunge
Downward, to lie a shattered bloody sponge.
They do and build. Erected toward the stars,
Their handiwork, set in earth's granite scars,
Blossoms in steel and stone, cement and glass,
Superb and steadfast though the years harass.
So they say *Yes* to life and set man's will
Strong, where the sprawling earth was void and nil.
·   ·   ·   ·   ·   ·   ·   ·   ·   ·   ·   ·   ·

But in the streets below their heady danger,
A new breed comes—the alien and the stranger
And the betrayer. There the American flag
Torn from its staff, a scorned and dirtied rag,
Is passed from hand to hand and rent to bits.
"Tear it up, kill it!" a young girl screams, "See, it's
Dead! The flag's dead!" And in another mob,
A Yippie strikes a match and lets flame throb
Up the brave folds. And one sets muddy feet
On the prone banner trampled in the street.
Mass-produced Robinson Crusoes on a binge,
Shaggy and rank as Crusoe's goats, life's fringe
Of impotence, they froth and seethe and shriek
Obscenities that fairly drip and reek.
A mob, dishevelled and recalcitrant,
Usurps the streets, to bicker and to slant
The high flag downward to half-mast, to mourn
"The Kent State Four." They vent indecent scorn
On all the Hard Hats love. They tear and spit
On the innocent flag that's our land's symbol: it
Is like a fair girl fouled by jackals. So
America (they think) finds overthrow.
But on this day, rising in anger, see
The Hard Hats in their thousands, militantly,

Throng New York's streets—spontaneous, passionate—
At last a *Yes* to love, a *No* to hate.
They part the noisy brawlers. High and proud,
They bear the Flag safe from the bawdy crowd.
They carry, too, their tools—and brawn. They cleave
The screaming mob, who only half-believe—
Many are dupes, with whom a few conspire.
The mob, foul-armed with stones and sleeping fire
Encased in glass, too used to cowardly
Tolerance, are amazed at what they see—
Men, *men* at last, the resolute Hard Hats come
Like Charlemagne's Paladins of Millennium.

Deep in their hearts they know: "This Flag is mine—
And should be yours. It is an outward sign
Of all our inward love. We set it there—
Beautiful rainbow in the stormy air.
.   .   .   .

You choose your way. And if you must dissever
America from Americans, on *your* heads
Be all the warfare that the country dreads—
The wounded and the dead. On *you* war lies.
God helping us, we can do no otherwise."
.   .   .   .

Poem by Lloyd Mills in *The Human Issue* (KSU Literary Magazine),
Fall 1970.

5 4 70

Where were you when the olive-drab conscience of
America turned and fired?
Does it matter where?
For this was everywhere
everywhere we closed our hearts in steel
steeled our hearts and fired our blind bullets
into hearts and heads
refracted in lineated light over the world as heat
climbed the screens' trembling adrenalin graph
out of our minds.

Reprise and reprisal, reprise and reprisal . . .
as the Average views
through America's eye his own eye,
an eye for an eye,

while the spirit's juggler rules for the land,
if x then y————

Our steel has smashed all syllogism into dust
overprized and inflated
has torn the ligament and lung of logic
shattered the bone and torn the heart.
America's a scream.

"...And in the Ever-widening Jungle War, U.S. Troops
Pushed Forward, Inflicting Heavy Casualties"

Above: Reprinted by permission of Hugh Haynie and the Louisville (Ky.)
Courier-Journal. *Below: Reprinted by permission of Pat Oliphant and the*
Los Angeles Times Syndicate © 1970 the Denver Post.

MAKE WAY FOR A PATRIOT

LETTERS

To write a letter to the editor is to place oneself in a self-selected minority, but letter writers, editors, and readers act and react on the assumption that a letter represents the opinion of more than one writer.

The volume of mail received by the press was so great that often whole pages of newspapers from New York to California were given over to the controversy.

By the end of July, Ohio Governor James A. Rhodes had received more mail on the killings than on any other event of his eight years in office. Chief Aide John McElroy said that of about 6,000 letters, representing about 15,000 citizens, 85 per cent judged that the National Guard acted correctly, and that the majority said more students should have been shot. Those who disagreed often wrote that the establishment wasn't listening to the young.

General Del Corso of the Ohio National Guard stated that his office received 7,000 pieces of mail commending the Guard and 433 disapproving. This is the greatest amount of mail ever received by the Ohio National Guard on one topic.

Letters to University president Robert I. White and to the University administration totaled nearly 5,000 by the end of 1970. An administrative assistant claimed that disproportionate numbers of letters condemning the University came from Florida, Texas, and California. The often passionate need to praise or blame or suggest courses for the future resulted in a collection of great interest. A few writers vehemently linked the killings to world-wide conspiracies (fronted by The Roman Catholic Church, The National Council of Churches, or Jews in general). Most tried to relate the killings to larger national and cultural frameworks. A representative selection is given here.

Letters from newspapers and magazines are reproduced next, with the emphasis on newspapers of the Kent-Akron-Cleveland area. We have tried for a selection representing the variety of opinion, not the statistical proportions of different opinions. That task awaits sociologists with computers. We think, after reading thousands of letters, that it may be fair to judge that the *Akron Beacon Journal's* statement that responses ran heavily in favor of the Guard's actions would hold true for almost all general circulation newspapers.

Telegram from a Whittier, Calif., couple to Pres. White, May 6, 1970.

We are parents of college student. We are not horror stricken. Students participating in destruction and rioting should be shot if that's what it takes to stop them.

From a Jesuit priest in Dublin, Ireland, to Pres. White, May 6, 1970.

I have offered Mass this morning for the deceased, their families and friends and for the whole university community—that God may guide you in this time of crisis and confusion. The sad news really grieved me.

I know that the causes of the event are extrinsic to K.S.U., and it could just as well have been on another campus. The sacrifice of the students in K.S.U. will, I hope, be a reminder to Government and society of the urgent need for a new social order and for a viable alternative to violence in the pursuit for social good and in our methods of redressing established social wrong. The happening at K.S.U. has become headlines all over the world.

May God bless and support you and the White family in this period of challenge. I know He will. I also pray for the student body that they may be enabled to bear the grief of loss, without becoming embittered.

From a Toledo, Ohio, woman to Pres. White, May 6, 1970.

Early this year I had the "underprivilege" to hear a speech given by General Sylvester Del Corso, a guest speaker and head of the Ohio Army National Guard.

The Guard is necessary for the protection of the citizen and the keeping of the peace and it is made up of many men with different political ideas, liberal and conservative, but this man with his "captive" audiences around the state, interjected his own arch-conservative views, smacking of "Wallacism" and one was made to feel that anyone who did not share the general's political views was a traitor. . . .

Just as I strongly deplore subversive groups such as the SDS and militant students who destroy public property to emphasize their dissent, I deplore this position of power being filled by a military man who does not have a calm, deliberate objectivity, and whose speaking engagements are instruments for whipping up "saber rattling" enthusiasm among his listeners, all this under the guise of "super patriotism". . . .

I feel General Del Corso's many inflammatory remarks may have made it easier for many guardsmen to feel freer with their "trigger finger" and may have contributed to what could be a blot on the fine record of the Ohio Guard.

From an Evergreen, Ill., mother to Pres. White, May 7, 1970.

My heart is heavy with sorrow for you, your faculty and the student body, but most of all for the parents of the four murdered kids. My daughter is a senior [in college] in Chicago, so I can really feel what all the parents of your students are feeling. Must we be afraid to send our children to college? If it happened at Kent can it happen anywhere?

Mr. White, may I humbly suggest that you demand a complete investigation of these trigger happy, panic stricken boys who did the shooting. The National Guard of Ohio has really proven to the world that they lack leadership and training. I hope and pray this investigation will not turn out to be a white wash.

From a Pacific Palisades, Calif., boy to the University, May 8, 1970.

I want all in Kent to hear this. Dear Kent State Universitey [sic] I have heard about the fight you all had. I think that we would live better without the National guards [sic] All they do is KILL. It's stupid to be paid to kill. I am very sorry about the people that died. I am only 9 but I understand. Call me [phone number].

From a Parma, Ohio, K.S.U. student to Pres. White, May 9, 1970.

As a student of Kent State University, I feel I must urgently appeal to you to re-open our university. . . .

I want an education. We, the students of K.S.U., want an education. Do *not* close the doors of learning to us.

What happened last week certainly is tragic, and the loss of four lives is regrettable and disheartening, but do not let these four lives stand in the way of the other 20,000 who want to learn.

Please, sir, re-open our university. Do it now. Have faith in us.

From a North Olmsted, Ohio, man to Pres. White, May 12, 1970.

As a taxpayer I am fed up with your lack of control of minority or radicals on your campus. We pay your salary to see that all students are taught the good old American traditions. We do not expect you to employ "Free Thinking" socialists to corrupt all the years of training we have given our children, before sending them to your (OUR) university.

We expect you to back our President and American principals before the students regardless of your personel feelings or opinions.

If you and your staff are not capable of controlling the students or if your teachings have caused them to riot—don't complain about the National Guard killing them! . . .

From a Topeka, Kan., man to the University, May 14, 1970.

. . . In Kent, Ohio, we witnessed the awesome spectacle of a second Golgotha. Only this time there were four victims instead of one. Like the first Golgotha the crowd was there and confusion prevailed; the soldiery was there, but they were not the well disciplined Roman soldiers of the first Golgotha; they were young frightened boys of the Ohio National Guard. The mighty rulers were not there—just people, mostly young people, dreaming of constructing a new world, a world that nobody had ever known; a warless world where all nations will live together and none will be masters. . . .

Jesus of Nazareth was crucified. Allison Krause, Sandy Scheurer, Jeffrey Miller and William K. Schroeder were cut down with bullets.

Like Jesus of Nazareth they gave their lives but they won a glorious victory—they settled the issue for all time—the New Age is here. . . .

From a Mansfield, Ohio, man to Pres. White, May 18, 1970.

Today our daughter received your letter to "future KSU students."

Both my wife and I would like to thank you for this act of thoughtfullness. We appreciate the fact that you and your staff, in the midst of these hectic days, took the time and had the foresight to give a thought to these sure to be frightened young people getting ready to enter college. It's unfortunate that their nervousness isn't a result of the awe and mystery of leaving home and going after and seeking out an education; but rather an understandable fear of an arena of nightmares of violent actions and reactions.

We, like you, hope that the university scene this fall finds an emphasis directed towards learning how to develop and better what we already have, than to concentrate on creating a charred void of nothingness.

From a Richmond, Va., woman to Pres. White, May 20, 1970.

I should think that now you and the students who attend Kent State would take a good long look at yourselves. All of you are responsible for the lives of the four kids who died on your campus. They were there of their own free will and they took part in what is a criminal offense. Anyone who got caught in the cross fire—injured or otherwise asked for it. We have seen on TV the arsenal of weapons taken from the rooms of Kent students—certainly, the nation cannot believe anything a student says and certainly we cannot respect you for allowing such actions on a college campus. . . . If you are afraid of a bunch of radical, selfish, spoiled kids, and cannot stay in control of the situation—resign and let someone who can do the job. . . .

From a Pittsburgh, Pa., man to Pres. White, May 21, 1970.

I am sure the repercussions from the recent tragedies have been many and loud, and no doubt of great concern to you, the president.

As the father of a future student, I want you to know that the proud feeling of having my daughter educated at your fine school has not changed. [My wife and I] look forward to four fruitful and happy years at Kent State University for our daughter.

From a Hannibal, Ohio, man to "Fuehrer White" of "Kent State Penitentiary," May 22, 1970.

Congratulations, when the Fascist State that you so ardently espouse is a reality, they may possibly delegate you to operate one of the local Dachaus. Together with Pig Rhoades [sic] and your beloved Gestapo and Stormtroopers, you should then find ample use for your meagre talents, or perversions, depending on one's point of view. I make the charge without the slightest fear of contradiction that your arrogant, Hitlerian attitude in the recent tragedy (or joyful event, again according to one's point of view) was the prime contributing factor in the murder of four (4) human beings by the hired butchers and draft dodging pigs of Rhoades's hired assassins. I hope you can live with what you call your conscience, if you even have one, which I seriously doubt.

From an educator to Pres. White, May, 1970.

At last, a chance to send you a note to let you know our sorrow for you, your good wife and the university you built. No one else can really feel your sadness but we know it exists, deep and full of personal anguish. No other college or university president, of the hundreds we have known, has as compassionate a spirit as yours. Always you put students first, talking with them all the time and trying to build an open institution in which they could be heard, could be individual persons, and could learn from dedicated teachers in a warm, friendly environment. . . . It is a tragedy that it could happen in quiet, peaceful Kent, in a place where the president, his staff, and many faculty *really* put students first. No one in America has done more, out of personal conviction and desire, than you have!

From a Pomeroy, Ohio, man; the *Gallipolis* (Ohio) *Daily Tribune,* May 6, 1970.

. . . Those of us who yet believe in law and order realize that within minutes after the orders to clear the area were given, there were no "innocent bystanders" left on the campus scene. Those students who stayed on despite the warnings did so with wilful and deliberate intent to violate the law.

In their unjustified attacks upon the Guardsmen and Highway Patrol units, they compounded their criminal activities, causing severe bodily harm to legally constituted authorities. In recognition of the physical suffering endured by those men who were there to protect the properties and rights of all citizens of the state of Ohio, I again urge that we, as church members, raise prayers of supplication to God that His healing hand will be upon them. Painful indeed were their injuries. Some may carry to their graves the scars inflicted by ferocious mobs turned loose by spineless campus authorities. Until such time as those campus authorities and faculty members exhibit the courage to stand erect as men, and cease permitting the mobs to burn and plunder at will, may we continue to ask God's blessing upon the Ohio National Guard and the State Highway Patrol.

These men now appear to be our only hope that communism on the campus will be held in check. Make Sunday, May 10, a day of prayer in your church; a day of prayer for the men who are fighting communism here at home.

From a Cleveland Heights, Ohio, woman; the *Cleveland* (Ohio) *Plain Dealer*, May 6, 1970.

I am a recent graduate of Kent State University, and, in the light of the tragic events which have occurred at that university, I feel that I must speak. Please do not be quick to condemn the actions of protesting students. Try, instead, to understand that they are desperate people— people without hope. This hopelessness and desperation is due to the continuation of a war which demands under penalty their participation and consent.

. . . [L]et us remember that young people are taught that to take a life is a crime, an uncivilized and immoral act. Yet if a young man chooses not to commit such an act he must leave the country which is his birthright or face imprisonment simply because he chose to live up to an ideal instilled in him by the same people who now tell him to disregard it.

On the other hand, I fail to understand how one can say he despises the violence of this war and then turns around and commits similar acts of violence such as bombing, burning buildings, and deliberate attempts to excite violent response from police officers. It is this contradiction which defeats the validity of peace protests. It greatly resembles the contradiction of being taught "thou shalt not kill" and being handed a rifle which defeats the validity of the war. . . .

It is easier to talk than to listen. It is easier to condemn than it is to try to understand. If there is to be any future for America, we all must choose the harder way and choose it now, before all America becomes a battleground and the tragedy at Kent a single scrimmage.

From a Napoleon, Ohio, man; the *Northwest Signal* (Napoleon, Ohio), May 7, 1970.

. . . More and more in today's every day scene, we see protesters and dissenters turn to violence. Here in America, we are historically patient and sympathetic to dissenters. As they daily grow more violent in nature, we are quick to find other causes to blame for their violence. We put the blame everywhere but where it belongs; that being an overly permissive society.

It would be well to ponder the words of Hilaire Belloc; "We sit by and watch the barbarian, we tolerate him; in the long stretches of peace we are not afraid. We are tickled by his irreverences; his cosmic inversion of our old certitudes and our fixed creeds refreshes us; we laugh. But as we laugh we are watched by large and awful faces from beyond; and on those faces, there is no smile."

From a Wadsworth, Ohio, KSU graduate student; the *Akron* (Ohio) *Beacon Journal,* May 6, 1970.

I was with two of the students who were shot and killed by National Guardsmen at Kent Monday and for their sake I want to tell it like it was.

The Guardsmen had marched up the hill after leaving the football practice field. Kids were following them up, some shouting and probably some throwing small stones—there were no "baseball size" rocks available. Without warning the Guards stopped at the top of the hill and fired a long volley of rifle shots into the crowd below.

Many of the kids dropped to the ground and others ran behind the building. There was discussion as to whether the shots were blanks but in seconds we knew they were not. There were kids gathering around the wounded.

The boy who died first was shot in the back of the neck. He lay in a vast puddle of his young blood. His friends tried to stop the flow, but he had no pulse nor breath and we all realized he was dead.

There was a cry from a group trying to help a big, beautiful young girl who was lying in the parking lot, shot in the armpit. We tried to put enough scarves and handkerchiefs into the hole to stop the bleeding. She was breathing a little but as we waited for the ambulance I saw her lips go white and her eyes glaze over, and I realized she wouldn't make it, either.

Five or six victims were picked up on stretchers and those of us who had been fired on stood in small groups trying to figure out why the soldiers had turned and fired without warning. Most of us in that area had been walking away when the shooting started.

Those who died weren't wild, SDS bearded hippies. They were kids like my sons and daughters. They came to Commons for a peace rally. They wanted to know how to get the word to our government that the Vietnam war is immoral and its extension into Cambodia intolerable.

After the shooting one young man said, "You think this bloody mess is awful, just imagine what these kids have to do every day in Vietnam —kill, kill, kill. Plenty of blood in the streets there."

Listen to them. You know in your hearts, they're right.

I'm no kid. I'm over 40 and the mother of seven children.

From "For the Law"; the *Akron Beacon Journal,* May 7, 1970.

When a soldier of the United States, under orders and in uniform, is attacked in any way, this constitutes an act of treason. Every country in the world specifies death the penalty for treason.

Let the Kent radicals realize they were, in fact, in violation of the law of the land, like it or not. It is too bad that death must be the price of preservation of the law. The price of freedom from anarchy is high.

From an Akron man; the *Akron Beacon Journal,* May 8, 1970.

. . . David supposedly killed Goliath with a small stone. Many Americans have been killed with stones, bottles, etc. If a rock the size of a baseball isn't as deadly as a rifle at 20 feet, then brother, you flunked physics.

It's about time that "these" people realize laws and Constitutional rights are meant for all Americans, not just a few.

Hell, yes, students were shocked when they realized they were being shot at. They've broken the law so long and not even had their hands slapped that to find a few National Guardsmen who felt the law applied to all was sure to come as a surprise.

It's just too bad this couldn't have happened four or five years ago. Then these people would have realized that there is a right and a wrong way to go about things.

Rise up, good, decent, and honest people of America. Stand and be counted in support of our American ideals. If you don't, you won't have them much longer.

From a Washington, D.C., man; the (Washington, D.C.) *Post,*
May 8, 1970.

The killing of four Kent State University students by Ohio National
Guardsmen was a tragic event for the United States and the blackest
hour in the long history of the National Guard.

The D.C. National Guard, of which I am a member, could never be
guilty of such an act. Although we carried ammunition while on the
street during such demonstrations as that of last Nov. 15, our weapons
remained unloaded, and we were instructed time and again to load
and fire only under the most extreme circumstances. Certainly it was
made clear that we should never fire indiscriminately into an unarmed
crowd. Also we knew that we would be held individually accountable
for any use of our weapons. Apparently the Guardsmen at Kent State
were under different orders.

Of equal importance is the seemingly unrepentant attitude of those
Guardsmen. A large group of D.C. Guardsmen are college students and
graduates. There are also many blacks within our unit. Perhaps these
facts explain our different orientation toward crowd control.

I believe this incident has greatly harmed the image and credibility
of the National Guard as a peacekeeping force.

From "Very Worried Mother"; the *Akron Beacon Journal,* May 8, 1970.

. . . I have two boys in the Guard and a boy on campus. That means
I have them on both sides of the street. Which side would I take?

All three boys have the same convictions about the world today.
Their thinking is no different. So if I had to make that choice I would
have to say the boy on campus has a choice where he wants to be and
the boys in the Guard are ordered there. So really I have no choice.

The TV and news have given me the feeling that the students are
children and the Guard grown men. Actually there is no difference
in age. In fact, some of the Guardsmen are much younger. Where are
the people to stick up for the Guard?

These boys have had more garbage thrown at them—not pebbles or
stones, but concrete, bricks and iron from a construction site on campus.
They were surrounded and out-numbered 50 to one that day the horrible tragedy happened. Consider the threats and name-calling that
went on before and after the tragedy.

I'm asking the public to answer one question with an open mind:
How much can one take, frightened, fearing for your life (which is a
very precious thing), with a mass of people surrounding you, out-num-
bering you, while they carry boys off the field hit with these objects.
Can you honestly call them murderers, pigs, etc., and put the blame
on the National Guard?

From a Cuyahoga Falls, Ohio, woman; the *Akron Beacon Journal,*
May 9, 1970.

It was a sad day indeed, when a minority mob of radical students
could threaten the existence of our government and then be made
heroes of the day by men and women of the news media, presidents
and professors of universities, and even elected officials of this government. Protesting buildings were pelted with rocks resulting in broken
windows. Businessmen were threatened and ordered to display peace
signs, the alternative being destruction to their property. A few militant
reactionaries burned the ROTC building to the ground and prevented
firemen from extinguishing this blaze by slashing their water hoses.

Some attempted arson on the Music and Speech buildings but were
unsuccessful. Last but not least, National Guardsmen were assaulted
with rocks or anything else available, including obscenities. . . .

Let us not blame the majority of students, law enforcers, nor an
overseas war for this crisis on our home front. Instead, we should seek
out and uproot a corrupt element bent on destroying our government
from within through the use of mob psychology on the impressionable
minds of youth.

From "273 Concerned Citizens"; the *Kent-Ravenna* (Ohio)
Record-Courier, May 9, 1970.

To Dorothy Fuldheim:

Concerning your special thirty-minute panel discussion on WEWS
of May 4, 1970. Subject: Kent State University unrest.

Were you informed of the situation which caused the calling up of
the National Guard? We feel you were not. The City of Kent would be
a shambles now, not to say anything of the campus at the university
which we as taxpayers helped build. The undesirable students (or non-
students) tore through Kent Friday breaking 50 windows of innocent
business owners. The estimated crowd of young people doing the harm
was anywhere from 500 to 1000. This, mind, you, was before the National Guard was called up. The city was a mess! The signs on some of
the windows and brick buildings were a disgrace. No, SHOCKING is
a better word. Was this to be forgotten?

We thank God our country has such able bodied men as our law enforcers and or our National Guard. For you to call these men murderers
is outrageous. I recall your program on the Hough riots and you stated
then that the National Guard should go in with ammunition. That was
a riot, and this also Miss Fuldheim, was a riot. Don't underestimate
the damage which was caused and the damage which was halted. We
live here and are very much aware of this.

These men are every bit as upset over this as the innocent students,
the rioters, and we the citizens of Kent. They were doing their job.

They were to disperse crowds. They were, above all, to be on the campus at their posts at this time. On the other hand, the students were not to assemble in crowds—which they did. They were to dis-assemble —which they did not.

We do feel bereavement for the families who suffered a loss because of this tragedy, but we do not blame this on any law enforcement agency for trying to defend our city and its citizens.

Don't you feel you were a bit one-sided? If you are going to report on such a touchy situation why not give a report on what the citizens of Kent think. We do live here.

From a Los Angeles, Calif., man; the *Los Angeles Times,*
May 9, 1970.

And now, those who oppose the war must die on the campus battlegrounds. Four young students are dead in Ohio, murdered by America's "defenders." The students were advancing upon the troops, armed with rocks. Rocks. The troops were armed with bullets. When will our supposedly intelligent leaders learn that war is an obscenity, and that murder (no matter how they justify it) is the ultimate evil? I never thought I would hate the country, I was born in—but I do now.

From "Silent Majority"; the *Akron Beacon Journal,* May 9, 1970.

Well, it has finally happened. Death on our campus.

What did the rioters expect? It is tragic to think innocent people were killed and injured, but we sent the National Guard in to protect the campus and the City of Kent. That is what they did, and rightly so.

If anyone is in a riot they should be expelled immediately, never to be admitted again.

If parents would put their foot down and tell the kids, "any rioting and your money is cut off," how many would work for a college education?

It is high time the tax payers express their views and demand that pressure be put to college officials to clean out their faculty and get rid of the agitators.

From an Air Force man; the *Kent-Ravenna Record-Courier,*
May 12, 1970.

I just read about the hometown and the college I was once proud of in the Pacific Stars and Stripes. I think it's disgusting the way the students there are rioting, burning down buildings, etc. and then having the nerve to say that they are against violence . . .

As far as the Guardsmen being brought in, the majority of the people here look at it this way:

Would you stand for people throwing rocks and stones at you, and having no way to protect yourself.

I ask this, would the people of Kent and the U. S. rather have themselves under control of the Communists or the system of government we now have? I know what the majority of us want and I have a good feeling that the vast majority of us want the same thing and that is U. S. democracy.

It is my personal belief that the majority of the public is for the war, but won't speak up for fear they will be persecuted by the rest of the public.

From a KSU graduate; the *Kent-Ravenna Record-Courier*, May 12, 1970.

I was appalled and grieved by the news about Kent State.

I was one of some 200 to graduate from Kent the year it became a university—1936. How proud I was, and have always been of that lovely school "on the hill." All 200 of us had the same feeling.

Kent citizens were proud also of the college. We respected the town of Kent.

Why isn't respect and pride part of most students anymore? Why have they lost it? Where did it go? These are important values of life to disappear.

What about the word "expell?"

The campus rebels who are disrupting the education of hundreds, grieving the alumni, and instilling fear in the hearts of Kent citizens should again be familiar with the word.

In 1935 I was summoned to Dean [of Women] Verder's office. I had been smoking in my room in Lowry Hall. In a few words she told me the next time I would be expelled. There was no next time!

Thank God for the opportunity I had, to go to Kent State from 1934–1936. Can the 19,000 enrolled there now, say the same?

From a Ravenna, Ohio, man; the *Kent-Ravenna Record-Courier*, May 12, 1970.

On Monday, May 4, I witnessed the KSU killings. As horrible and frightening as the memories of those experiences are, they are not nearly so terrifying as the hostility that has been revealed in their aftermath.

I am disgusted to find [a letter writer suggest], "a very simple compound with barbed-wire and a minimum of conveniences" as a possible solution to today's student unrest. Frighteningly, [he] is not alone in his advocacy of the "get tough" policy. Many people even go so far as to suggest that the four deaths at Kent State should be only the beginning.

I am not a radical. I do not believe that arson and violence should go unpunished, but I know of no state in which arson carries a death sentence, and there are certainly none in which "illegal" assembly is punishable by execution.

I have recently heard a multitude of comments such as, "They should have mowed them all down," or "I'll bet they think twice next time," or "They got what they deserved." It is in the people who make these statements that the real violence is to be found. They seem to be permeated with an intense desire to see destroyed or shackled anything they do not understand. . . . [T]hey would destroy freedom! And is not freedom supposed to be what America is all about?

I work at night to pay for my education. I do not take it lightly, but, if as a result of the disturbances at Kent there is a "cleaning house" of the faculty and student body, as some are suggesting, then I will also leave. I will not leave because I am a radical or a "hooligan," but because I will not become an automaton when I might have been an individualist.

I will not be programmed when I might have been educated, I will not paraphrase when I might have written. Can "1984" really be so near?

From a Louisville, Ky., man; the *Courier-Journal* (Louisville, Ky.), May 12, 1970.

I protest lowering of the American flag in honor of the men who died last week in Vietnam and the students who died at Kent State University.

The mayor, aldermanic president and police judge until now have not found it proper to honor those brave men, over 40,000, who previously died for our country. What kind of emotional quirk possessed them to do so late what ought to have been done all along? It was political fence-straddling, to say the least, that caused them to use the honor of brave men to express their sympathy with a bunch of rioting, rabble-rousing students.

What twisted thinking could place the Sons of the Flag on the same honor roll with burning, cursing, looting students who defy the government, abhor its traditions and do despite to its honor? To associate the two is to blaspheme the names of countless Americans who have died to make us free and hold the flag high.

Such political degeneracy and moral blasphemy as these officials demonstrate make us unworthy of the men who guard our freedoms around the world, much less those who have died for them.

From "Concerned Resident"; the *Kent-Ravenna Record-Courier*,
May 12, 1970.

. . . I'd like to express my thanks and appreciation to all our law
enforcement officers, firemen and the National Guard who worked long
hours, under great stress to protect our homes and yes, even our lives
from rioting, rock throwing, destructive human beings. Seeing our city
policed by capable people let me go to sleep at night without wondering if our home might be firebombed or the windows broken next. After
being awakened on Saturday night by the noise of the crowds and the
shattering of glass as the windows were being broken downtown, I
certainly needed the feeling of that protection. . . .

From Martin Scheuer, Youngstown, Ohio; the *Cleveland Plain
Dealer,* May 13, 1970.

I am referring to the "One-Sided Story" column of television reporter
William Hickey. He was trying to degrade the emotions and human
feelings for others who were made to suffer. The reader is made to
believe, that the killing of the four innocent bystanders at Kent State
University was excusable, by connecting this incident with the rioting
that took place in downtown Kent three days before. These riots, which
incidentally were perpetrated by a motorcycle gang, not by innocent
"nice college kids." The picture of police being reduced to living vegetables by rock throwing students was horrible, and I know that the
Ohio National Guardsmen will have no moral or physical after-effects
when they mowed down my lovely daughter Sandy, the flower of my
life.

I also want to defend the able and dedicated reporters from Huntley-
Brinkley and Dorothy Fuldheim who by showing their compassion
might arouse the public to a state of awareness, so that this tragedy
may never be repeated.

I feel that The Plain Dealer reporter was distorting the news and
failed to distinguish the difference between rock wielding rioters and
innocent, sensitive college students. He tries to find excuses for senseless killings, and I am quite sure that this same reporter could find a
valid excuse for the brutal beating that students suffered at the hands
of the New York construction workers. I only hope, that now the country will wake up and stop killing its own college students.

From a Canal Fulton, Ohio, mother; the *Akron Beacon Journal,*
May 13, 1970.

. . . There are two sides to everything and I certainly don't have any
sympathy for the hippie Communist protesters who are only going to
college for the draft deferment and the agitation they can cause.

Just take a look at the queer sights they are. You took pictures of them and put them in your paper. They sure don't look like clean-cut students to me. Who would hire a freak like that that dresses like a slob and has shaggy unkept hair and beards? Even if he had a degree I sure wouldn't hire him or want to work with him.

The Beacon Journal has been very unkind to the National Guard and I personally think you and your reporters should take another look at the National Guard before you condemn them. . . .

Shame on you!

From a Kent man; the *Akron Beacon Journal,* May 13, 1970.

As a citizen and former Guardsman, I must insist—I must insist— even the rock throwers and burners would not have deserved an instant death sentence on Taylor Hill.

It is dangerous, foolhardy, dictatorial, and un-American to think that way. Therefore, it is absurd, ignorant, blind folly to congratulate my former company Guardsmen for opening fire on that crowd of students.

I know the frustration, terror, and panic that stirs in Guardsmen on duty and I know how inflammatory remarks from National Guard superiors can make it easier for a private to feel protected when he opens fire. This is an insidious danger!

I also know the frustrations students face when their peaceful protests over American foreign policy evils are ignored by our national leaders and by our comfortable, but ignorant and unaware silent majority. . . . I, for one, am through with shooting or silencing intelligent, sensitive, idealistic, and beautiful, really beautiful, young Americans.

From "A Concerned Mother"; the *Kent-Ravenna Record-Courier,*
May 13, 1970.

To the People of the United States:
Do you not see what is really happening to our country?

On May 1, 1970 the young people at Kent State University were protesting (they said) the war in Vietnam, the movement of our troops in Cambodia and other things.

These young people are being USED by the Communists. They like excitement and some of them think they are protesting for a good and worthwhile cause. I am sure they have not had enough experience in leading a nation to know.

All our labor strikes are Communist backed. I refer to the "Communist Manifesto" by Karl Marx and Friedrich Engels in which they call on workers of all countries to unite against 'capitalist oppression.' Class struggle with workers always opposing employers. Communists use this belief to stir up unrest in non-Communist countries. They spread disorder so they can start revolutions more easily. They support movement against social and political order of things.

Communists often use other groups such as student organizations, to create unrest and disunity in non-Communist countries. They have encouraged demonstrations against our presidents and other great men in many countries. They have ruined our good name.

From a Skokie, Ill., man; the *New York Daily News,* May 13, 1970.

I'd like to shake the hands of those construction workers who clobbered the "peace" hypocrites at City Hall. Decent Americans have had it up to here with these protesting bums, on campus and off.

From a Valley Stream, N.Y. woman; the *New York Daily News,*
May 13, 1970.

I strongly advise President Nixon to put Dr. Spock on an advisory board to handle the current temper tantrums of our militant Youth. Since he helped to form this generation, he should be able to provide the proper prescription for a cure.

From a Manhattan, N.Y., man; the *New York Daily News,*
May 13, 1970.

I am mystified. Why didn't the National Guard call for an air strike first at Kent State?

From a Springfield, Ohio, KSU student; the *Sun*
(Springfield, Ohio), May 13, 1970.

Last Wednesday I was interviewed by one of your reporters, and it seems that he interpreted my comments other than I intended. It was reported that I was happy to see the ROTC building gone. I did not say this.

The reporter asked me when I last saw Allison [one of the two girls among the four students who were killed at Kent State University] alive, and I told him, "Sunday morning, when the students were allowed to see that burnt-down building. There she said jokingly, 'Ain't it pretty?' and I answered her in a low tone of voice, 'Yeah, I guess so.' "

The reporter didn't print this. So it sounds as though I was really happy, and this made me seem like some kind of radical. I really didn't want the building to go down, but I will admit that it will relieve a lot of problems on campus.

The reporter also said that I used every obscenity I knew in regard to the Guard when I saw Allison get shot and die. This is not true.

For one thing I told the reporter that I did not see her get shot but I did see her die. When I saw her suffer, then finally die, I called the Guardsmen one obscenity, then "pig."

I apologize for this but I lost my head. After seeing one of your friends foam at the mouth, then die right in front of you, you are bound to act differently. I hope you can see my point, but I don't mean to sound like some kind of revolutionist.

I hope you can straighten this out. Thank you for your time.

From an Akron, Ohio, man; the *Akron Beacon Journal,* May 14, 1970.

Based upon total costs, college students are about one-fifth as expensive to kill as Viet Cong. Perhaps soon we will be able to murder as economically as Adolf Hitler.

From a Lorain, Ohio, man; the *Journal* (Lorain, Ohio), May 15, 1970.

. . . In the act of their dissidence, the Kent students were putting into effect what the residents of Lorain County had taught them since they were little children, namely that America is a democracy where each individual is free to question his government and what it is doing.

I wish to ask a question of those residents who are members of any one of the multitude of locals of unions in our community. How did you feel when you were founding these unions? Was it so long ago that you have forgotten the conflict you were engaged in, the names you were called, the outrageous shootings, the beatings and the mass dismissal of employes even suspected of unionism? You stood your ground against this as was your privilege in a democracy, dissented, picketed and eventually won your cause not always without violence. Were you so very different in your dissent than the college student of today's in his?

From a Kent couple; the *Kent-Ravenna Record-Courier,* May 16, 1970.

Everyone must obey the state authorities; for no authority exists without God's permission, and the existing authorities have been put there by God. Whoever opposes the existing authority opposes what God has ordered; and anyone who does so will bring judgment on himself. . . .

This bit of God's word pretty much expresses our feelings on the recent happenings in our town.

From a KSU student; the *Akron Beacon Journal,* May 16, 1970.

For the past month and a half, I have been the victim of the most blatant, back-stabbing social hypocrisy I have ever had the misfortune to witness.

I am trying to earn enough money to finish college this year, but I cannot get a job. Why? Because I am a student at Kent State University.

For this dubious but obviously serious "crime," I have been refused employment in Kent, Ravenna and surrounding areas. I am qualified for all the positions for which I apply. I appear before the interviewer clean and neatly dressed. I don't have long hair.

I am refused a job when the interviewer learns I am a student at Kent State. At this point one of two things happens: Either a polite but firm brush-off, or an evasive "Call you when we get an opening" answer.

I am fed up. . . .

From an Akron, Ohio, man; the *Akron Beacon Journal,* May 17, 1970.

The tragic days of May are the reaping of the sowing of the winds of an intemperate free society. These days were predictable, but not their hour, nor their place, nor their time. They were precipitated by those most intemperate, schooled and hardened to be so, and not anxious to change their ways. . . .

Edmund Burke said it best: "Men are qualified for civil liberties in exact proportion to their disposition to put moral chains upon their own appetites . . . Society cannot exist unless a controlling power upon will and appetite be placed somewhere, and the less of it there is within, the more there must be without. It is ordained in the eternal constitution of things that men of intemperate minds cannot be free. Their passions forge their fetters."

Now, death came to a university at Kent. Physical and institutional deaths, and abortion of better ideas and ideals will continue until there is a change back to a "controlling chain" from within. The alternative is fetters for all.

We may be closer to a dictatorship, a society of informers, and armed guards on every corner, than we like to think. This will be a reality unless we change back to a self-disciplined, law-abiding society.

No government can do this for us. This is an individual effort, private yet totally public.

Let the Kent State University bell toll for its student dead! Let it also ring for the resurrection of the idea of our basic and only way to freedom—a self-imposed controlling power over our wills and appetites, from within! The alternative is chaos, and an escalation toward the tyranny of the police state. Intemperate minds cannot be free!

From a Kent woman; the *Kent-Ravenna Record-Courier,*
May 20, 1970.

. . . Perhaps apathetic Americans will wake up to what ideals are really being taught to the college students by liberal professors. It also worries many of us in the teaching profession that a great number of the rioters are in the college of liberal arts and it is from this group that we get a high percentage of our teachers. These riotous students seem to have rationalized that it is all right to do anything necessary to have their own way regardless of other people's rights. These immature students think that they will be excused on the grounds that they are only releasing their emotions. Maybe they should have learned to control their emotions long ago as mature youth and adults do.

Because it is highly probable that schools will be getting more and more of these liberal-oriented teacher, all parents, school administrators, and boards of education should be on guard. Parents, discuss with your children school philosophies advocated by their teachers. Also, visit classrooms to see and hear first-hand what is going on. School boards, carefully interview your administrator and teacher applicants about their philosophy of education. . . .

From "Loyal Citizen"; the *Kent-Ravenna Record-Courier,*
May 21, 1970.

Well, Mr. Kane, you've certainly done it! You've searched the rooms of approximately 8,000 students at KSU and come up with a grand total of (and I quote the Record-Courier) "a variety of 60 knives, 50 guns and drugs of all types." Quite a haul! However, I suspect that if you were to search the homes of an equal number of residents in Kent, you might have even better results.

And not so incidentally, Mr. Kane, no citizen of Kent who knew his rights would allow you to enter his premises without a search warrant. But the students of KSU are not entitled to the same protection of their constitutional rights as are the citizens of Kent, are they, Mr. Kane.

From a letter by a KSU faculty wife quoted by a contributor to
the *Sunday Times* (London, England), May 24, 1970.

. . . Groups of four or more are subject to arrest in Kent still. The
townspeople, inflamed by the local government, are only sorry more
weren't killed—this is true, believe me.

On the basis of a few broken windows downtown and a frame shack
burned on campus, they have made the fantastic assumption that the
students would have destroyed the town and burned the larger part of
the campus. Vigilante groups have formed, armed. Many of the townspeople literally hate the "bums" and "punks," those dead and those
mercifully still alive.

Until Friday we heard the continual noise, day and night, of helicopter flights at tree top; we saw troops with loaded rifles and bayonets
everywhere; we endured what I call tanks lumbering about the streets.

[My daughter's] school was taken over before the children could
even get safely away, and in my frantic attempt to leave the campus to
reach her that Monday afternoon, I was sworn at by guardsmen; imagine how they felt about long-haired, bearded students. Whatever Nixon,
Hoover, *et al.* may come up with, there was no provocation for what
happened and no panic on the part of individual guardsmen. Someone
gave a direct order to at least a platoon to fire in unison from formal
positions.

I did not see the shootings—I was still on my way to the commons;
but I know *many* eye witnesses, professors as well as students. The students were retreating from tear gas, they were 25–50 yards away from
the troops when the order came.

Yes, they threw stones (small; there are no rocks or bricks on the
commons) and hurled insults; that is all. For this they were slaughtered, because they rightfully insisted on their right to assemble without soldiers and tanks present, because they hated our actions in South-
East Asia. I shall never forget the first student who reached me, crying
in disbelief, "They are shooting us; they are shooting us." I cannot go
on. . . .

From a Kent man; the *Kent-Ravenna Record-Courier*, May 20, 1970.

I have been appalled by many vicious and even cruel statements
made by some local residents in recent letters. For example, one letter
included the following comments: ". . . We feel sorry for and pity the
parents of the students killed and put in the hospital. But it is a shame

that the news media didn't show the four killed students the way they really were instead of old, probably high school pictures. If your readers want to form their own opinions, if they will, give them all the facts the way they are. . . ."

Let me ask directly, how do you know that the four students were not exactly as they appeared in their pictures? Did you ever try to find out what kinds of persons they were? How do you know that the pictures were "old, probably high school pictures?" Talking about readers getting all of the facts, why don't you get some facts on this yourself? And finally, did you send any letters of condolence to the grieving parents?

I have read about would-be citizen vigilante groups who would be "willing to help (police) physically" in future civil disturbances and heard rumors that local residents are storing armed weapons in their homes.

Only a relative few of the letters ask for more understanding between young and old, to try to avoid future bloodshed. Indeed, many of the letters indict all of the students, the good and bad together, in a threatening way that can only lead to further misunderstanding and possible violence in the future. It is indicative of an attitude of fear and distrust that so many local residents are unwilling to sign their actual names to these letters.

I certainly do not condone violent and destructive acts by students, or teamsters, or anybody else for that matter. We have a problem which, hopefully, can be resolved in a peaceful way. More dialogue, more understanding, more sympathy will be required if students and townspeople are to get along together.

From a Brandford, Conn., woman; *The National Observer,*
May 25, 1970.

In your editorial of May 11, you say, "In their [students'] outrage . . . they collect in the streets and scream the short words of contempt. They spit and throw rocks. They break and they burn. And finally, after years of such behavior . . . four students are killed at Kent State University."

I am 23 years old and am a year out of the university. I have been protesting our involvement in Vietnam since the election of 1964. I have written letters, talked to friends and fellow workers, marched and protested for six years. *Never* have I shouted more contemptible words than "Peace Now!" *Never* have I spat! *Never* have I thrown a rock! *Never* have I broken a window! *Never* have I burned a building! And I know scores of people, including my parents, who have been march-

ing, protesting, and pleading in letters for the end of this insane war
who have never committed a violent act.

And I do not regard myself as a member of "a privileged class, possessing the right to have their way because they believe so passionately
in their cause." I simply, along with thousands, maybe millions of
Americans and other people in the world (including the late Jesus
Christ), abhor violence and killing of anyone, be they an American soldier, a North Vietnamese soldier, or a college student. All I am asking
is the end to purposeful killing of human beings.

From two Kent women; the *Kent-Ravenna Record-Courier,*
May 26, 1970.

We should like to commend and thank Mayor Satrom and Prosecutor
Kane for their actions taken for our protection during our present dis-
aster, and endorse especially calling for the National Guard, closing
KSU, invoking the curfew, etc.

It's good to know that they, along with Chief Thompson and his
men, are looking out for the City of Kent, which seems to have been
forgotten by all the news media in their so-called factual reporting;
in the various "analyses of the situation"; in the resolutions, proposals
and declarations by the so-called "college community"; and in the letters and speeches by students who want KSU to reopen, like now.

We also wish to thank Governor Rhodes for sending the Ohio National Guard to our rescue and to let the men of the National Guard
know that we stand 100 per cent behind them, their actions and conduct while here.

We are both lifelong residents of Kent.

From a Kent woman; the *Kent-Ravenna Record-Courier,* May 26, 1970.

. . . After living in the Kent-Ravenna community for about 20 years,
I went to Kent State University and finished B.S. and M.A. degrees.
I taught in university extension classes for eight years. For all those
years, and especially all this month, I have been listening to the people
of the community and to university students and faculty members. All
of us need to listen to each other, to understand each other, to work
WITH each other. Maybe we should stop waiting for someone else to
bring us together, and bring ourselves together.

One method that I advocate is for the university to use its facilities to
develop free, noncredit, evening classes for adults in the community.
These facilities—now standing empty—have never been used to full
capacity in the evening. Looking at the problems we confront in this

country as the students do might help us understand both the students and the urgency of these problems.

Is it possible to make a better university, a better community, a better America out of all this tragedy? Then it will not have been entirely senseless and useless.

From "Mother of a National Guardsman"; the *Canton* (Ohio) *Repository*, May 27, 1970.

. . . [A student] said he was not so sure he'll support the National Guards anymore because he could have been shot leaving his class. Wasn't he and other students told not to go outside their classrooms or dorms while the trouble was going on? Why then did he not obey?

In the same article, a [writer] said he discounted the idea that the SDS leaders, who had just been released from jail, had anything to do with the demonstrations because he would have recognized them. How would this student have recognized them?

I do not agree with everyone but I do not intend to go out and destroy to prove my point. This is like burning down your neighbor's home because you don't agree with each other's beliefs. I did not believe in the college students getting out of going to service, but I did not invade their colleges to prove my point.

Maybe I will live long enough to see the troublemakers on campus (girls and boys alike, since they want to be equal) put into trucks by our national guards, taken to the nearest point of export and shipped over to Vietnam where they can do their laughing, stone throwing and building burning. This would leave the campus open to those who really want an education.

From a Barberton, Ohio, man; the *Akron Beacon Journal*, May 27, 1970.

If all the news media handled facts as carelessly as you handled the Kent State report [May 24] I pray that more men with the courage of Mr. Agnew will pin the correct label on you.

You should be intelligent enough to know that sensational untruths you used to picture the casualties as innocent bystanders only serve to inflame the mind of those who do not know the facts. . . .

Please imagine yourself in place of a National Guardsman who is being stoned, spit upon and the target of epithets of a foreign ideology. What would you do? Run like a coward, I suppose, and let the Communist hippies destroy the institutions the law-abiding element has worked to build and preserve. . . .

From a KSU student and Army Reservist; the *Akron Beacon Journal,*
May 28, 1970.

I would like to know who gave the police permission and the right
to enter Kent State University dormitory rooms. The rooms are the
private locked residences of the students.

Law provides that a search warrant be issued to the person who rents
the room before the room is searched. There were no search warrants
issued.

The police entered and searched over 3,000 rooms, uncovering various items. Rifles were found, neglecting the fact that Kent State has
a rifle club was neglected and the fact that many of the members own
their rifles was neglected, too. Pills and drugs were found neglecting
the fact that some students do take medicine.

Knives were uncovered but knives are an essential to camping students just as turpentine is an essential to art students and wood workers.

As a student who had his turpentine confiscated, I wonder why they
didn't confiscate my shellac which was next to it. What legal right did
they have to remove such items without my permission?

The dormitories are not owned by the state. They receive no tax aid.
They are completely supported by the students who reside there.

From a Youngstown, Ohio, man; *Life,* May 29, 1970.

My whole world has been snatched away from me by the bullet of
a confused national guardsman's rifle ("Kent State: Four Deaths at
Noon," May 15). Sandy Scheuer, one of the students killed at Kent
State, and I had been going together for five years and I loved her
dearly. Her parents are like second parents to me and I mourn for them
also. It is most difficult to write this letter at this time, but I feel I must
because there is something I want the people of this country to know
about Sandy. Sandy felt the same way about the world situation as most
of us do today, but she was not a radical. She was not involved in the
demonstrations. She was not the type. Sandy always spread joy, happiness and laughter wherever she went. She couldn't understand why
there couldn't be happiness and joy throughout the world.

At the time Sandy was shot she was on her way to class with one of
her speech and hearing therapy students. She was giving him lessons
to clear up his speech impediment.

The funeral is over. I can cry no more, but the pain and sorrow will
always be with me. Sandy's death was so senseless. Please, pray to God
that such senseless killing never happens again.

From a Canandaigua, N.Y., man; *Newsweek,* June 1, 1970.

In Cleveland, Ohio, when a convoy of trucks escorted by "armed National Guardsmen" was attacked by 200 rock-throwing Teamsters union strikers, the convoy and guardsmen retreated to a nearby terminal. When armed National Guardsmen at Kent State University were treated the same way, four students were killed in a blaze of gunfire.

Are rock-throwing protests tolerable if done in the name of higher salaries and more fringe benefits, but punishable by death if done to prevent further killing in Indochina?

From a KSU student; the *Akron Beacon Journal,* July 1, 1970.

It is a known fact that Jerry Rubin was on campus at Kent State University in early April. It is a known fact, because the Silent Majority wishes to connect his visit with the tragedy less than a month later.

It is not a widely known fact, however, that other men spoke on campus after Rubin—namely John Glenn and Ralph Nader.

My point is that since this country is still a democracy, all men have the right to speak and be heard; not just a sifted-out few chosen by campus administrators . . . IF this country is still a democracy. . . .

From a Waukegan, Ill., man; the *Akron Beacon Journal,* Aug. 10, 1970.

It's a shame that people and the news media will not let events die. It has been almost three months since the shooting at Kent State and everyone acts as if it happened yesterday. . . . Even though I support the National Guard's actions at the KSU fiasco, I'd like to see the whole affair buried, once and forever.

3

Official
Reports

The impact of the deaths at Kent State was both deep and widespread. The intensity of personal and public reactions to the events of the first weekend in May got quick responses from local, state, and national authorities. A number of investigatory bodies were appointed, and as their reports became known they provoked rather than stilled controversy.

A 3,000-page report by the Ohio State Highway Patrol was not made public but was reported in newspaper articles like the one excerpted in this section.

The United States Justice Department prepared a 35-page "general background summary" based on over 7,500 pages of findings by 100 Federal Bureau of Investigation agents for the use of Congressional, state, and local authorities. The Knight newspapers (including the *Akron Beacon Journal*) leaked major elements of this summary on July 23, 1970. Extended excerpts were printed in *The New York Times* on October 31, 1970, and are reprinted here.

President Nixon announced the creation of a President's Commission on Campus Unrest on June 13. The Commission's members (listed below) were generally charged to seek out the causes of the growing turmoil which had reached tragic climaxes at Kent State University and Jackson State College.

The general report, issued on September 26, emphasized that "campus unrest" was a complex phenomenon "manifested in many kinds of protest activity," most of them "entirely peaceful and orderly manifestations of dissent" protected by the First Amendment. It condemned violence and called for students, college faculty and administration members, and the public at large to work for reconciliation in the full knowledge of the difficulties and complexities of a problem which was really "the aggregate result of thousands of individual beliefs and discontents. . . ." The report strongly recommended that neither police nor the National Guard be armed with lethal weapons when controlling disturbances except "in the face of sniper fire or armed resistance"; that "under no circumstances should the police attempt to disperse a crowd by firing over it"; and that the Guard be reequipped with non-lethal weaponry so that deadly force would be used only "as the absolute last resort." University officials should handle non-criminal, non-violent disruptive conduct, calling on law enforcement agencies promptly when criminal violence occurs. The President was urged to "exercise his reconciling moral leadership as the first step to prevent violence and create understanding." "To this end, nothing is more important than an end to the war in IndoChina." The war, racism, and social dehumanization were identified as the main causes for despair in students.

The Commission's special report on the Kent State affair was released on October 4 and is reprinted in this section.

An interim report of the Select Committee to Investigate Campus Disturbances prepared for the 108th Ohio General Assembly, issued on October 5, put the major responsibility for campus unrest on faculty and administration members. In this it was prophetic of the report of the Special State Grand Jury, which is reproduced here.

These were the major documents resulting from investigations which were closely followed by the public, and which themselves set off newly intensified debate.

Ohio State Highway Patrol Report Completed

Excerpt from the *Akron Beacon Journal*, July 22, 1970.

Patrol's KSU Report:
3,000 Pages, Photos

By Ray Redmond

RAVENNA—The State Highway Patrol presented a 3,000-page, photo-studded report on the May 4 Kent State University riots and slaying of four students to Portage County Prosecutor Ronald Kane Tuesday.

It shows:

Between 2,500 and 3,000 students milling on the campus during the anti-war fracas.

"Remarkable" photos marking several hundred as "suspects" and "possible grand jury indictees."

National Guard troops in the act of firing their rifles "but no falling bodies . . . or felled bodies."

There was no mention of sniper fire, Kane said.

It took Capt. Chester Hayth six hours to present the blockbuster report behind closed doors in Kane's office.

The two-month investigation produced a 3-foot-tall stack of evidence, including hundreds of photos. Also turned over were 30 minutes of film clips.

The news media was barred.

Only sketchy details were available, since the information is labeled confidential for future grand jury use.

"The patrol did a tremendous, thorough job," Kane said.

"It will be a terrible waste if this report can't be placed before a grand jury," Kane said.

Justice Department Summary of FBI Report—Excerpts

From *The New York Times,* October 31, 1970.

Excerpts From Summary of
F.B.I. Report on Kent State U. Disorders
Last May

WASHINGTON, OCT. 30—*Following are excerpts from a summary by the Justice Department of a Federal Bureau of Investigation report on the Kent State University disorders of May 4.*

At about 11:30 A.M. [May 4] some members of Company C and Troop G, on patrol since 6 A.M., were told to move to the R.O.T.C. building. The troops were moved into position around the R.O.T.C. building facing the students about 175 yards away at about 11:45 A.M. Ninety-nine men from the National Guard were present, all led by General Canterbury, Lieut. Col. Fassinger and Maj. Jones. Apparently no plan for dispersing the students was formulated.

Most persons estimate that about 200–300 students were gathered around the Victory Bell on the Commons with another 1,000 or so students gathered on the hill directly behind them. A few high school students were present at this rally. A few non-students were also present—some dropouts from Kent State. The overwhelming majority were, however, students enrolled at Kent State.

Apparently, the crowd was without a definite leader, although at least three persons carried flags. An unidentified person made a short speech urging that the university be struck. We are not aware of any other speeches being made. The crowd apparently was initially peaceful and relatively quiet.

Order to Disperse

At approximately 11:50 A.M., the National Guard requested a bullhorn from the Kent State University police department. An announcement was made that the students disperse but apparently it was faint and not heard since it evoked no response from the students.

Three National Guardsmen and a Kent State University policeman got in a jeep and, using the bullhorn to order the students to disperse, drove past the crowd. Many students made obscene gestures. Victim Jeff Miller was one of this group. The jeep drove past the students a second time. At this time, the students in unison sang/chanted "Power to the People."

The announcement to disperse was made a third time at which time the students chanted "One, two, three, four, we don't want your war," and after which they continuously chanted "Strike, strike . . ."

The jeep then apparently came closer to the crowd saying clearly, "Attention. This is an order. Disperse immediately. This is an order. Leave this area immediately. This is an order. Disperse."

Chanted "Sieg Heil"

The above announcements were again repeated at which time the students responded "Pigs off campus." The Kent State University policeman then announced, "For your own safety, all you bystanders and innocent people, leave." The crowd replied with chants of "Sieg Heil."

At some point when the jeep drove by the crowd of students, a few rocks were thrown at it—one hitting the jeep and a second striking a guardsman but doing no damage.

About five grenadiers were ordered to fire tear gas from M-79 grenade launchers toward the crowd. The projectiles apparently fell short and caused the students to retreat only slightly up Blanket Hill in the direction of Taylor Hall. Some students . . . retrieved the tear gas canisters and threw them back in the direction of the Guard. This action brought loud cheers from the students.

They also chanted "Pigs off campus." Again an announcement was made over a loudspeaker ordering the students to disperse. The students responded by chanting "Sieg heil" and "One, two, three, four, we don't want your war."

Weapons Loaded

Between 12:05 P.M. and 12:15 P.M., the 96 men of Companies A and C, 145th Infantry, and of Troop G, 107th Armored Cavalry, were ordered to advance. Bayonets were fixed and their weapons were "locked and loaded," with one round in the chamber, pursuant to rules laid down by the Ohio National Guard. All wore gas masks. Some carried .45 pistols, most carried M-1 rifles, and a few carried shotguns loaded with 7½ birdshot and 00 buckshot. One major also carried a .22 Beretta pistol.

Prior to the advance, Company C was instructed that if any firing was to be done, it would be done by one man firing in the air. It is not known whether any instructions concerning the firing of weapons was given to either Company A or Troop G.

General Canterbury moved with the troops. As they approached the students, tear gas was fired at the crowd. The combination of the advancing troops and the tear gas forced the students to retreat. Some rocks were thrown by the students at this time but were for the most part ineffective. Some students probably came "equipped" with bags full of rocks in anticipation of a confrontation.

Pursued Main Group

Fifty-three members of Company A, 18 members of Troop G and two members of Company C, all commanded by General Canterbury and Lieut. Col. Fassinger, moved to the south and east of Taylor Hall, pursuing the main body of students.

[One] group retreated to the area of a football practice field southeast and approximately 150 yards from Taylor Hall. The guardsmen apparently momentarily halted to allow the students on the practice field time to pass through the two gates in the fence surrounding the field. The Guard then moved down the steep incline from Taylor Hall and onto the field where it took up a position in the northeastern portion of the field close to the fence. Seven guardsmen claim they were hit with rocks at this time. They were also cursed constantly.

Some of the students who had retreated beyond the fence obtained rocks and possibly other objects. They then began to pelt them [guardsmen] with objects. The number of rock throwers at this time is not known and the estimates range between 10 and 50. We believe that the rock throwing reached its peak at this time. Four guardsmen claim they were hit with rocks at this time. Fourteen others claim they were hit with rocks but do not state when they were hit.

Rocks Thrown by Guard

Some rocks were thrown back at the students by the Guard. The majority of students, who had merely stood aside and allowed the Guard to pass through their ranks, massed on the hill in front of Taylor Hall to observe . . . Thus, the Guard appeared to be flanked on three sides by students while on the practice field.

The Guard shot tear gas at the students in the parking lot and at those to the south of them . . .

It was, as far as we can tell, ineffective. A small amount of tear gas was also fired without result at the mass of onlookers gathered in front of Taylor Hall.

Just prior to the time the Guard left its position on the practice field, members of Troop G were ordered to kneel and aim their weapons at the students in the parking lot south of Prentice Hall. They did so, but did not fire. One person, however, probably an officer, at this point did fire a pistol in the air. No guardsman admits firing this shot.

The Guard was then ordered to regroup and move back up the hill past Taylor Hall.

Followed the Guard

The students at this time apparently took up the chant, "one, two, three, four, we don't want your war." Many students believed that the Guard had run out of tear gas, and they began to follow the Guard up the hill.

Some guardsmen, including General Canterbury and Major Jones, claim that the Guard did run out of tear gas at this time. However, in fact, it had not. Both Captain Srp and Lieutenant Stevenson of Troop G were aware that a limited supply of tear gas remained and Srp had ordered one canister loaded for use at the crest of Blanket Hill.

Some rocks were thrown as they moved up the hill and seven guardsmen claim that they were struck at this time. The crowd on top of the hill parted as the Guard advanced and allowed it to pass through. When the Guard reached the crest of Blanket Hill by the southeast corner of Taylor Hall at about 12:25 P.M., they faced the students following them and fired their weapons. Four students were killed and nine were wounded.

The few moments immediately prior to the firing by the National Guard are shrouded in confusion and highly conflicting statements. Many guardsmen claim that they felt their lives were in danger from the students for a variety of reasons—some because they were "surrounded;" some because a sniper fired at them; some because the following crowd was practically on top of them; some because the "sky was black with stones;" some because the students "charged" them or "advanced upon them in a threatening manner;" some because of a combination of the above. Some claim their lives were in danger, but do not state any reason why this was so.

Approximately 45 guardsmen did not fire their weapons or take any other action to defend themselves. Forty-seven guardsmen claim they did not fire their weapons. There are substantial indications that at least two and possibly more guardsmen are lying concerning this fact.

Heard Others Firing

Most of the guardsmen who did fire do not specifically claim that they fired because their lives were in danger. Rather, they generally simply state that they fired after they heard others fire or because after the shooting began, they assumed an order to fire in the air had been given. As a general rule, most guards add the claim that their lives were or were not in danger to the end of their statements almost as an afterthought.

Six guardsmen, including two sergeants and Captain Srp of Troop G, stated pointedly that the lives of the members of the Guard were not in danger and that it was not a shooting situation. The F.B.I. interviews of the guardsmen are in many instances quite remarkable for what is not said, rather than what is said. Many guardsmen do not mention the students or that the crowd or any part of it was "advancing" or "charging." Many do not mention where the crowd was or what it was doing.

We have some reason to believe that the claim by the Guard that their lives were endangered by the students was fabricated subsequent to the event. The apparent volunteering by some guardsmen of the fact that their lives were not in danger gives rise to some suspicions. One usually does not mention what did not occur . . .

A chaplain of Troop G spoke with many members of the Guard and stated that they were unable to explain to him why they fired their weapons.

The students tell a conflicting story of what happened just prior to the shootings. A few students claim that a mass of students who had been following the Guard on its retreat suddenly "charged" the Guardsmen hurling rocks.

A few other students claim that the students were gathered in the parking lot south of Prentice Hall—a distance of 80 yards or better from the Guard—when some of the Guardsmen suddenly turned and fired their weapons at the gathered crowd. They generally either do not mention rock throwing or say that it was light and ineffective.

Around the Parking Lot

A plurality of students give the general impression that the majority of students following the Guard were located in and around the parking lot south of Prentice Hall. They also state that a small group of students—perhaps 20 or 25—ran in the direction of the Guard and threw rocks at them from a moderate to short distance. The distance varies from as close as 10 feet to 50 feet or more. However, available photographs indicate that the nearest student was 60 feet away. At this time, they allege that the Guard began firing at the students.

There are certain facts that we can presently establish to a reasonable certainty. It is undisputed that the students who had been pursued by Troop G and Company A in turn followed the guardsmen as they moved from the practice football field to Taylor Hall. Some rocks were thrown and curses were shouted. No verbal warning was given to the students immediately prior to the time the guardsmen fired.

We do not know whether the bullhorn had been taken by the Guard from the R.O.T.C. building. There was no tear gas fired at the students, although, as noted, at least some guardsmen, including two officers in Company G, were aware that a limited number of canisters remained. There was no request by any guardsmen that tear gas be used.

There was no request from any guardsman for permission to fire. Some guardsmen, including some who claimed their lives were in danger and some who fired their weapons, had their backs to the students when the firing broke out. There was no initial order to fire.

Testimony on "Command"

One guardsman heard someone yell and believed he'd been given an order to fire. Another "thought" he heard a command to fire. He, however, claims he did not fire. Another heard a warning to "get down" just before the firing. Another "thought" he heard "someone" say "warning shots." Another "thought" he heard "someone" say "if they continue toward you, fire." Most guardsmen heard no order and no person acknowledges giving such an order. Colonel Fassinger states that all orders are given verbally and that there are no hand signals used to communicate with troops.

One guardsman, Sergeant McManus, stated that, after the firing began, he gave an order "fire over their heads."

The guardsmen were not surrounded. Photographs and television film show that only a very few students were located between the Guard and the commons. They could easily have continued in the direction in which they had been going. No guardsman claims he was hit with rocks immediately prior to the firing, although one guardsman stated that he had to move out of the way of a three-inch "log" just prior to the time that he heard shots. Two guardsmen allege that they were hit with rocks after the firing began.

Although many claim they were hit with rocks at some time during the confrontation, only one guardsman, Lawrence Shafer, was injured seriously enough to require any kind of medical treatment. He admits his injury was received some 10 to 15 minutes before the fatal volley was fired. His arm, which was badly bruised, was put in a sling and he was given medication for pain.

Testimony on "Sniper"

There was no sniper. Eleven of the 76 guardsmen at Taylor Hall claim that they believed they were under sniper fire or that the first shots came from a sniper. Two lieutenants of Company A, Kline and Fallon, claim they heard shots from a small-caliber weapon and saw the shots hitting the ground in front of them. Lieutenant Fallon specifically claims the shots came from a sniper. Sergeant Snure of Company A was facing away from the students when, he alleges, something grazed his right shoulder. He claims it was light and fast and traveled at a severe angle to the ground near his right foot. Captain Martin and Specialist 4 Repp of Company A claim they heard what they thought were small-caliber weapons from the Johnson-Lake Hall area. Others including General Canterbury merely state the first shot was fired by a small-caliber weapon.

A few guardsmen do not state that they thought the first shot was from a sniper but do state that the first shot, in their opinion, did not come from an M-1 rifle; it is alleged the sound was muffled or came from what they thought was an M-79 grenade launcher, converted for firing tear gas.

Some construction workers also reported hearing fire from a small-caliber weapon prior to the firing by the National Guard. The great majority of guardsmen do not state that they were under sniper fire and many state that the first shots came from the guardsmen.

The F.B.I. has conducted an extensive search and found nothing to indicate that any person other than a guardsman fired a weapon. As a part of their investigation, a metal detector was used in the general area where Lieutenants Kline and Fallon indicated they saw bullets hit the ground. A .45 bullet was recovered, but again nothing to indicate it had been fired by other than a guardsman.

The Guard clearly did not believe that they were being fired upon. No guardsman claims he fell to the ground or took any other evasive action and all available photographs show the Guard at the critical moments in a standing position and not seeking cover. In addition, no guardsman claims he fired at a sniper or even that he fired in the direction from which he believed the sniper shot. Finally, there is no evidence of the use of any weapons at any time in the weekend prior to the May 4 confrontation; no weapon was observed in the hands of any person other than a guardsman, with the sole exception of Terry Norman, during the confrontation. Norman, a free-lance photographer, was with the guardsmen most of the time during the confrontation.

Gun Checked Later

His gun was checked by a Kent State University policeman and another law-enforcement officer shortly after the shooting. They state that his weapon had not been recently fired.

Each person who admits firing into the crowd has some degree of experience in riot control.

Seven members of Troop G admit firing their weapons, but also claim they did not fire at the students. Five persons interviewed in Troop G, the group of guardsmen closest to Taylor Hall, admit firing a total of eight shots into the crowd or at a specific student.

Specialist 4 James McGee claimed that it looked to him like the demonstrators were overrunning the 107th. He then saw one soldier from Company A fire four or five rounds from a .45 and saw a sergeant from Troop G also fire a .45 into the crowd. He claims he then fired his M-1 twice over the heads of the crowd and later fired once at the knee of a demonstrator when he realized the shots were having no effect.

Specialist 4 Ralph Zoller claims he heard a muffled shot which he alleges came from a sniper. Thereafter, he heard the Guard shoot and he fired one shot in the air. He then kneeled, aimed and fired at the knee of a student who he claims looked as if he was throwing an object at Zoller.

Specialist 4 James Pierce, a Kent State student, claims that the crowd was within 10 feet of the guardsmen. He then heard a shot from the Guard. He then fired four shots—one into the air; one at a male 10 feet away with his arm drawn back and a rock in his hand (this male fell and appeared to get hit again); he then turned to his right and fired into the crowd; he turned back to his left and fired at a large Negro male about to throw a rock at him.

S. Sgt. Barry Morris claims the crowd advanced to within 30 feet and was throwing rocks. He heard a shot which he believes came from a sniper. He then saw a 2d lieutenant step forward and fire his weapon a number of times. Morris then fired two shots from his .45 "into the crowd."

Sgt. Lawrence Shafer heard three or four shots come from his "right" side. He then saw a man on his right fire one shot. He then dropped to one knee and fired once in the air. He then saw a male with bushy, sandy hair, in a blue shirt (Lewis) advancing on him and making an obscene gesture. This man had nothing in his hands. When this man was 25–35 feet away, Shafer shot him. He then fired three more shots in the air.

In addition to Herschler, at least one person who has not admitted firing his weapon, did so. The F.B.I. is currently in possession of four spent .45 cartridges which came from a weapon not belonging to any person who admitted he fired. The F.B.I. has recently obtained all .45's of persons who claimed they did not fire, and is checking them against spent cartridges.

The "Scranton Commission Report"

We reproduce here the complete text of the special report on the Kent State incidents prepared by The President's Commission on Campus Unrest and released on October 4, 1970. The report included 59 photographs, of which some are presented here. We have combined the report's two maps locating campus sites and fallen students.

The commission members were William W. Scranton (Chairman), former Governor of Pennsylvania; James F. Ahern, Chief of Police, New Haven, Connecticut; Erwin D. Canham, Editor-in-Chief, *The Christian Science Monitor;* James E. Cheek, President, Howard University; Lt. Gen. Benjamin O. Davis, USAF (Ret.), Director, Civil Aviation Security, U.S. Department of Transportation; Martha A. Derthick, Associate Professor, Boston College; Bayless Manning, Dean, School of Law, Stanford University; Revius O. Ortique, Jr., Attorney-at-Law, New Orleans, Louisiana; and Joseph Rhodes, Jr., Junior Fellow, Harvard University.

The Executive Staff members were William Matthew Byrne, Jr. (Executive Director); John J. Kirby, Jr. (Deputy Director); Paul H. Weaver (Editor); James D. Arthur (Administrative Officer); and

Christopher T. Cross, Director, and Abby L. Chapkis, Deputy (Office of Public Affairs).

Members of the Kent State Task Force were Kenneth I. McIntyre (Coordinator), James A. Strazzella (Chief Counsel), Richard Andrews, Terry W. Baker, Urbane Bass, Steven L. Friedman, Jaqueline M. Howard, Peter Nickles, Charles E. Stine, George V. Warren, M. Lee Winfrey, and Lloyd R. Ziff.

Special Report
The Kent State Tragedy

Blanket Hill is a grassy knoll in the center of the campus of Kent State University, named by students who use it as a place to sun themselves in the day and to romance at night. From here, shortly after noon on a sunny spring day, a detachment of Ohio National Guardsmen armed with World War II-vintage army rifles fired a volley of at least 61 shots killing four college students and wounding nine.

All of the young people who were shot that day were students in good standing at Kent State University.

The National Guardsmen were there under orders from both civilian and military authorities. Duty at Kent State had not been pleasant: they had been cursed and stoned, and some feared physical injury.

Stones were thrown, then bullets fired.

The events at Kent State over the long May weekend were tragic. They need not and should not have occurred. The Commission has drawn on the lessons learned from Kent State in making its report. This special report is made to give an explicit context to the recommendations made there.

The Commission staff spent several weeks studying reports of other investigations of the May 1970 events at Kent State, including 8,000 pages of reports by the Federal Bureau of Investigation. Three weeks were spent in Ohio interviewing hundreds of witnesses including students, faculty, university administrators, law enforcement personnel, National Guardsmen, townspeople, and others in possession of relevant information. Special efforts were made to gather contemporaneous photographic and audio evidence from all available sources. The Commission was able to study motion picture films and tape recordings of parts of the events, and hundreds of photographs taken by persons present at the scene. The Commission held hearings at Kent State University in Kent, Ohio on August 19, 20, and 21, 1970.

The Commission's task at Kent State was especially sensitive. At the outset of the investigation, the Kent incidents had not been placed before any grand jury, either county, state or federal. During our investigation, the Attorney General of Ohio announced the convening of a state grand jury. The grand jury began proceedings in September as this report was being written.

We deem it of paramount importance that the Commission do nothing to interfere with the criminal process. We therefore have not sought to establish and report the names of persons who might be guilty of city, state, or federal offenses—persons who fired weapons or who may have caused property destruction or personal injury by rock throwing, arson, or other means. The Commission has not attempted to assess guilt or innocence but has sought to learn what happened and why.

The Setting

Kent State University is a state-supported school with some 20,000 students, more than four-fifths of them graduates of Ohio high schools. Its main gate is only four blocks from the center of the business district of Kent, a city of some 30,000.

Compared with other American universities of its size, Kent State had enjoyed relative tranquility prior to May 1970. Two sizable disturbances had occurred, however, and were widely remembered.

On November 13, 1968, members of the Black United Students (BUS) and the Kent State chapter of the Students for a Democratic Society (SDS) participated in a five-hour sit-in to protest the appearance on campus of recruiters from the Oakland, California, police department. When the university announced it planned disciplinary action, 250 black students walked off the campus and demanded amnesty. Kent State President Robert I. White consulted university attorneys and, two days after the walk-out began, announced no charges would be brought, whereupon the black students returned.

The university established an Institute of African-American Affairs several months later. Blacks pressed for further changes, including enrollment of more black students and the addition of more Black-oriented courses. No further race-related disturbances occurred, and black students played virtually no part in the turmoil at Kent State last May. But Blacks at Kent State remained less than content, and after the sit-in, relations between them and the administration were uneasy.

In the spring of 1968, SDS launched a campaign centered around four demands which still remain as campus issues. In this campaign, the Kent State chapter followed tactics used elsewhere, finding issues that would attract mass support, demanding that action be taken, and then attempting to organize a confrontation to push for the demands. At Kent State these demands were: abolition of the campus ROTC training program; removal of Liquid Crystals Institute, a university agency which had a grant from the Department of Defense; removal of a state crime laboratory from campus; and abolition of the university's degree program in law enforcement.

On April 8, 1969, a group of about 50 white students, including SDS leaders, went to the administration building planning to post the abolition demands on an office door. Campus police met them outside, pushing and shoving ensued, and some officers were struck. Several students were charged with assault and battery and summarily suspended from school. In addition, the university revoked the SDS charter, a campus ban that is still in effect.

A disciplinary hearing for two of the students involved in the April 8 incident was set for the Music and Speech Building eight days later. The University said it scheduled a private hearing at the request of one of the students, but about 100 supporters of the suspended students demanded that the hearing be public. Fist fights broke out between the demonstrators and about 200 counter-demonstrators, including conservative fraternity men and campus athletes. The demonstrators entered the building and broke open a door on the third floor. Campus police sealed exits and called the Ohio State Highway Patrol, which arrested 58 persons. Some students complained that they were permitted to enter and then held inside for arrest.

In Autumn 1969, four SDS leaders were prosecuted for their part in the April incidents. Each was convicted after a jury trial of assault and battery and pleaded guilty without trial to a charge of inciting to riot. The "Kent State 4" served six months each in Portage County jail. They were released April 29, 1970—two days before Kent State's disruptions of May 1970 began.

After these incidents of April 8 and April 16, some students charged that the university had deviated from its own student conduct code in its handling of the disruptions. On the day after the second incident, an organization called the Concerned Citizens of the KSU Community (CCC) was formed to protest the university's suspension of some demonstrators without a hearing and before they were convicted of criminal charges. One week later, the CCC lost a campus-wide referendum on this issue and others, including reinstatement of the SDS charter.

There was high campus interest in the referendum, which drew the largest vote ever cast in a campus election. Some tactics employed by the university and student leaders left many CCC supporters resentful. These tactics included a rare extra edition of the campus newspaper, the Daily Kent Stater, featuring a front-page editorial headlined, "Evidence Links SDS, 3-C." Some CCC supporters who characterized themselves as liberal or moderate felt that this extra edition, plus an anonymous leaflet circulated about the same time, was an unfair effort to paint them as either dupes or agents of the SDS.

Five months after the April 1969 events, the Kent State chapter of the American Association of University Professors (AAUP) published the findings of a Special Committee of Inquiry. In general, the report was critical of the University administration's handling of the April incidents. It failed, however, to resolve several questions, including divergent views of the Music and Speech building incident. Administration supporters generally felt that the persons who had been arrested had tried to disrupt or to take over a building. Many radicals and activists felt that police tactics used at that time constituted entrapment.

After the April incidents, the administration maintained its position that national politics and foreign policy were not issues on which the university as an institution should take a formal stand.

The university did take several steps in the late 1960's to liberalize university regulations. Women's curfew hours were abolished, visits by the opposite sex to dormitory rooms were permitted, and the sale of beer on campus was allowed.

A year of quiet followed the April 1969 disturbances. Most students were either conservative or apolitical. On April 10, 1970, for example, Yippie leader Jerry Rubin spoke at Kent State but drew only a tepid response when he urged students to join "the revolution."

In retrospect, however, the absence of major disturbances between April 1969 and May 1970 appears to have been deceptive. Interviews with black students show clearly that they were discontented during this time. Many activists, militants, and radicals believe that the university was not only opposed to them but also ready to use any tactics necessary to suppress them.

Present on the Kent State campus during the period 1968–70 were six organizations considered by some to be radical. Almost all were comparatively small, ranging down to the Young Socialist Alliance with only eight to twelve members. The most prominent of these organizations was the Students for a Democratic Society.

The Kent State chapter of SDS was organized in the spring of 1968. In the beginning it drew poor support, with less than 10 persons attending most of its meetings. By autumn, however, attendance grew to about 50 or 60 per meeting.

In October 1968, Mark Rudd, a leader of SDS activity at Columbia University, addressed the Kent State chapter. The next month, a regional conference of SDS chapters in northeastern Ohio was held at Kent State, with a speech on that occasion from Rennie Davis, one of the founders of the SDS.

Davis asked for local cooperation on demonstrations in January 1969, against the inauguration of Richard M. Nixon as President. Subsequently 45 Kent State students participated in this demonstration in Washington, including all of the Kent State 4.

After the SDS was banned from Kent State in April 1969 the group held no open meetings and directed no demonstrations on campus.

Nationally, in June 1969, the SDS divided into three factions: Revolutionary Youth Movement I, generally called Weatherman; Revolutionary Youth Movement II, often called RYM II; and the Progressive Labor Party, commonly called the PLP. All espouse some variety of Marxist doctrines and view the United States as an imperialist nation. The Weatherman wing is considered the most prone toward violence.

RYM II petitioned for official recognition at Kent State in the autumn of 1969 and was active in limited ways. Neither Weatherman nor the PLP has ever been recognized as a campus organization at Kent State.

The FBI reports do not indicate that any of the disturbances at Kent State during May 1–4, 1970, were planned by members of the SDS.

The campus is patrolled by a 30-man security force. Downtown, the 22-man Kent Police Department is normally at its busiest on weekends patrolling North Water Street, where many bars draw a heavy student patronage. The two police agencies have had a loose agreement to help one another if severe trouble developed, but clearly even at combined strength they are too few to handle any assemblage of more than a few hundred.

Also available if trouble comes are the Portage County sheriff's department, with 29 full-time employees and 83 part-time deputies, and the highway patrol, with a statewide force of 1,075 men.

If civilian authorities were not enough, two regiments of the Ohio National Guard, the 107th Armored Cavalry and the 145th Infantry, called to active duty on April 29, 1970, as a result of a truckers' strike, were in nearby Akron.

This was the situation when on the night of Thursday, April 30, President Richard M. Nixon announced that United States troops were being ordered into Cambodia.

Kent State President White did not hear President Nixon's speech. When his wife told him about it later he had a "sinking feeling," he said. Downtown, in the North Water Street bar area, slogans denouncing the Cambodian action were being painted on walls. Many students viewed the move as a shocking reversal of President Nixon's announced policy of withdrawal from Vietnam and as an aggressive action which flouted widespread anti-war sentiment in the United States.

Friday, May 1

Friday, at noon, a small group of history graduate students, entitling themselves World Historians Opposed to Racism and Exploitation (WHORE), held an antiwar rally on the Commons, a grassy field in the center of the campus and a traditional site for student rallies and outdoor meetings. The New University Conference, an organization of younger faculty members and graduate students considered radical by some, also sponsored this rally.

Near the Victory Bell, an old railroad bell normally rung to celebrate Kent football victories, rally leaders buried a copy of the United States Constitution, declaring that it had been "murdered" when troops had been sent into Cambodia without a declaration of war or consultation with Congress. A sign asking, "Why is the ROTC building still standing?" was hanging on a tree nearby.

The ROTC building, a small wooden barracks officially named East Hall, stood at the northwestern corner of the Commons overlooking the rally site.

About 500 persons attended the rally and no disorder occurred. The meeting closed with a call for another rally at noon Monday to discuss the attitude of the university administration toward Cambodia and toward other student demands, including the abolition of the ROTC program.

Few if any Blacks were present at the Friday noon rally, having been urged by their leaders to avoid white rallies and to concentrate on Black concerns. Throughout the weekend virtually all black students remained apart from the student demonstrations. Many black students stated they preferred to concentrate attention on black-oriented issues, and that, after the Guard had arrived, they feared physical violence at the hands of the Guard. At 3:00 P.M. on Friday, the Black United Students held a rally to hear black students from Ohio State University discuss the campus disturbances which had recently occurred there. This rally, which drew about 400 persons, ended peacefully at 3:45 P.M.

Late Friday afternoon, after receiving reports on the two peaceful rallies, President White decided that the situation was sufficiently calm for him to depart for Iowa for a long planned visit with his sister-in-law and a Sunday meeting of the American College Testing Program. He did not return to Kent until Sunday noon, after the city and campus had experienced two nights of turmoil.

The first disturbance began on North Water Street, a downtown area where six bars, popular with young people, are located. Some of these bars feature rock bands. The sale of 3.2 beer to persons 18 or older, and of liquor to 21 year olds, is legal in Kent. Because several surrounding counties prohibit the sale of beer or liquor, the Kent bars draw young people from as far as 50 miles away, in addition to Kent State students.

May 1 was one of the first warm Friday nights of the spring. A sizable crowd of young people, some of whom were discussing Cambodia, gathered in and around the bars. About 11:00 P.M., they began to jeer passing police cars.

Kent's small police force had fewer than 10 men on duty when the disturbance began. Four of these men in two patrol cars were specifically assigned to North Water Street.

The crowd grew increasingly boisterous. They began to chant slogans, and a motorcycle gang called the "Chosen Few" performed some tricks with their bikes. Shortly before 11:30 P.M., someone threw a bottle at a passing police car. The Kent City police ceased efforts to patrol the street and waited for reinforcements from the day shift and from other law enforcement agencies.

Some of the crowd, which had grown to about 500, started a bonfire in the street. Soon the crowd blocked the street and began to stop motorists to ask their opinion about Cambodia.

One motorist accelerated when approached, narrowly missing people standing in the street. This incident, according to witnesses, angered bystanders. Shortly thereafter a false rumor that black students were "trashing" on campus circulated among the crowd.

Some demonstrators began to break store windows with rocks. A few items were stolen from the display windows of a shoe store and a jewelry store. A fertilizer spreader was taken from a hardware store and thrown through the window of a bank. In all, 47 windows in 15 establishments were broken, and two police officers were cut by thrown missiles.

At 12:30 A.M., after the trashing had begun, Kent Mayor LeRoy M. Satrom declared a state of emergency and ordered the bars closed. The assembled force of city police and sheriff's deputies then moved to clear the street, which became even more crowded as evicted patrons poured out of the bars.

Mayor Satrom initially estimated the damage to property at $50,000, a figure he subsequently reduced to $15,000. Still later a study by the Kent Chamber of Commerce placed maximum damage at $10,000.

At 12:47 A.M. Mayor Satrom telephoned the office of Governor James A. Rhodes in Columbus and spoke to John McElroy, the Governor's administrative assistant. Satrom reported that SDS students had taken over a portion of Kent. A few minutes later, McElroy phoned the Ohio Adjutant General, Major General Sylvester T. Del Corso, and Del Corso sent a National Guard liaison officer to Kent to assess the situation.

Between 1:00 and 2:00 A.M., a force composed of 15 Kent city police and 15 Portage County deputies used tear gas to force the student crowd out of the downtown area, several blocks up East Main Street, and back onto the campus at the main gate, at Lincoln and East Main Streets. The city police were annoyed when Kent State University police officers did not arrive at the gate to take over from there. City police did not know that students were simultaneously congregating on campus and that the University Police Chief Donald L. Schwartzmiller had decided to use his men to guard campus buildings. A small amount of property damage was done on campus, including a broken window at the ROTC building.

City police, who would not enter the campus, and students faced each other over the border of the campus, and a virtual stand-off developed. A freak automobile accident on Main Street is generally credited with dispersing the crowd.

An electrical repairman was standing on his truck repairing a traffic light in front of Prentice Gate. A car hit the truck, knocking the scaffold from beneath the repairman and leaving him hanging onto the traffic light above the pavement. His odd predicament completely captured the attention of the crowd. They drifted away quietly after he was rescued.

Fifteen persons, all with Ohio addresses, were arrested that night, most of them on charges of disorderly conduct.

The disturbance on North Water Street angered and frightened many merchants, and left the city administration fearful that it did not have enough manpower available to keep order. On the next day, these circumstances were to lead to the calling of the Ohio National Guard.

Some city and university officials suspected that the disturbances had been fomented by the Kent State 4, who had been released from jail two days earlier after serving sentences for their actions during the campus uproar in April 1969. The FBI uncovered no evidence that the Kent State 4 were involved in planning or directing any of the events of the May 1–4 weekend. The presence of at least one of the Kent State 4, who was seen on the street downtown early Friday evening, has been confirmed.

Many of the students who were in the crowd on North Water Street were there only because the bars were closed. Some were disgruntled because they had paid cover charges to hear rock bands and then had to leave before they felt they had had their money's worth.

The pattern established on Friday night was to recur throughout the weekend: There were disorderly incidents; authorities could not or did not respond in time to apprehend those responsible or to stop the incidents in their early stages; the disorder grew; the police action, when it came, involved bystanders as well as participants; and finally the students drew together in the conviction that they were being arbitrarily harassed.

Saturday, May 2

Against the background of Friday night's activities, rumors proliferated.

When 40 uniformed ROTC cadets gathered early Saturday morning at the ROTC building to be transported to a rifle range, students who saw them spread a report that the National Guard was on campus. At this time, only one guardsman—liaison officer Lt. Charles J. Barnette—was actually in Kent. In mid-afternoon, as cadets returned from the range, some students heckled them, and one student told an officer, "You'd better watch your building. It would make a pretty fire."

Some Kent State students helped downtown merchants clean up Friday night's rubble. In the minds of many merchants and the Mayor, however, their good deeds were outweighed by threats which a few merchants said they received from young people whom they presumed to be Kent State students. The owners of a shoe store and a music store were among those who said they were told to put an antiwar sign in their window with a message like, "Out of Cambodia" or "Get Out of Vietnam," or run the risk of having their shops burned or damaged.

Troubled by these reports and fearful that he did not have enough policemen to protect his city, Satrom began efforts to secure a force of 75 auxiliary deputies from Portage County Sheriff Joseph G. Hegedus. Satrom could not call on the Ohio State Highway Patrol because its jurisdiction is limited to state highways and state owned or leased property.

Early Saturday, Mayor Satrom formalized his proclamation of civil emergency. He banned the sale of liquor and beer, firearms, and gasoline unless pumped directly into the tank of a car. He established an 8:00 P.M. to 6:00 A.M. curfew in Kent which was to take effect Saturday night.

In the wake of Friday night's window-breaking in Kent, the university administration launched a strenuous effort to restore order among students. Chester A. Williams, Kent State's Director of Safety and Public Services, attended five separate meetings with university and civic officials.

In the first of these meetings, held at 8:30 A.M., university officials, including Robert E. Matson, Vice President for Student Affairs, and Williams, decided to seek an injunction barring further property damage on campus. The name of a male student arrested Friday night on charges of breaking a window in the ROTC building, together with 500 "John Does," was placed on the court order, which enjoined anyone from "breaking any windows, defacing any buildings with paint, starting any fires on campus, and damaging and destroying any property . . ." The injunction did not include a ban on rallies.

In a meeting at city hall at 11:00 A.M., Mayor Satrom agreed to exempt the university from his 8:00 P.M. curfew. He set the curfew on the campus to begin at 1:00 A.M.

At a 1:00 P.M. meeting, Lt. Barnette told university officials that if the National Guard were called, it would make no distinction between city and campus and would assume complete control of the entire area. University officials were still hoping that if trouble arose on campus they could secure help from the Highway Patrol whose handling of the Music and Speech building disturbance in 1969 had been widely praised.

At a 3:00 P.M. meeting, university officials reviewed the special steps they planned to take to entertain students who would be prevented by the curfew from visiting the downtown area. They had arranged for special late hours for the cafeterias and for bands to play at dormitory dances. The university had also activated its Rumor Control Center and its emergency Operations Center. Vice President

Matson and Student Body President Frank Frisina prepared and distributed a leaflet that informed students of the injunction and of the 8:00 P.M. curfew in Kent, but that failed to mention the 1:00 A.M. curfew on campus. The leaflet said specifically that peaceful campus assemblies were not banned.

The administration was aware of rumors that a rally was to be held on the Commons that evening, and during the day an informal corps of faculty marshals assembled. The original suggestion for faculty marshals had come the previous year from Vice President Matson in response to criticism by some faculty members of the handling of the Music and Speech building incident. Matson discussed the role of the marshals on this Saturday with Professor Glenn W. Frank, a faculty leader. That evening, Frank related the discussion to the marshals. Many of them nevertheless continued to be confused about their exact role. Ultimately, most of the marshals decided that they would not physically intervene in case of disturbances, but would confine their activities to discussion and persuasion, fact-finding, and reporting events to the administration's Emergency Operations Center. Frank purchased armbands and gave them to the marshals, who stationed themselves around the campus in groups of two or three where they circulated among students and distributed the informational leaflets.

The final meeting of the day was held at 5:00 P.M. in Mayor Satrom's office in city hall. Several times during the day, Lt. Barnette told the Mayor that 5:00 P.M. was the deadline for calling the National Guard, which would need some time to assemble and move. The Mayor continued to defer a decision, hoping he could secure the sheriff's deputies instead. Williams and the university were holding to their position that Kent State would prefer the presence of the Highway Patrol if severe trouble developed.

Satrom felt strongly that help was needed. Rumors, reports, and complaints had been pouring into city hall all day. Kent Police Chief Roy Thompson said a usually reliable campus informant had told him that plans were afoot to destroy the ROTC building, the local U.S. Army recruiting station, and the Kent Post Office that night. He had forwarded this information to the university police.

Satrom told the group at the meeting that he had learned that the sheriff's deputies would not be available. He asked Williams if Kent State officers could help downtown. Williams replied that his men were needed on campus, and Satrom left the room with Lt. Barnette to ask for National Guard assistance. Williams and University Vice President for Financial Affairs Richard E. Dunn, who supervises the campus police, then left the meeting; they were under the impression that the National Guard was being requested for duty only in Kent, not on the Kent State campus.

Mayor Satrom spoke to John McElroy in the Governor's office and requested that the Guard be sent to Kent.

McElroy believed that Governor Rhodes' proclamation of April 29, which called out the Guard to control disturbances resulting from a Teamsters' strike, was sufficient to cover the Kent case because it authorized the Guard to "take action necessary for the restoration of order throughout the state of Ohio. . . ." He telephoned General Del Corso and told him to inform Mayor Satrom that troops would be available. Then McElroy telephoned Governor Rhodes and told him about the situation. Governor Rhodes authorized the commitment of guardsmen to Kent.

At 5:35 P.M. General Del Corso, following McElroy's instructions, phoned Mayor Satrom and told him that troops would be available that evening. Del Corso then called Colonel John Simmons, the duty officer at National Guard headquarters near Columbus at Fort Hayes. He ordered guardsmen bivouacked in the Akron area, about 10 miles from Kent, to be placed on stand-by.

At 6:15 P.M., Del Corso notified Simmons that he and Assistant Adjutant General, Brigadier General Robert H. Canterbury, were leaving for Kent. Del Corso told Simmons that, if Simmons received an urgent request for help from Kent while he and Canterbury were enroute, Simmons should dispatch troops to Kent. But, Del Corso added, the commander in Akron should be told that no troops were to be committed to the Kent streets until Del Corso and Canterbury arrived. The troops were to assemble on the grounds of Wall Elementary School on the west side of Kent and wait until the generals arrived.

At the university, a crowd had assembled on the commons around the Victory Bell by 7:30 P.M. The group appeared to be an idle collection of students whom the curfew had prevented from going downtown. As a precaution, Kent State Police Chief Donald Schwartzmiller called the Highway Patrol for assistance; but the patrol said that unless arrests were necessary, they would not come to the campus. Schwartzmiller stated that there was no present basis for arrests.

On the Commons, a young man is reported to have jumped up on the brick structure from which the Victory Bell is suspended and to have said, "They're trying to keep the kids penned up in the dorms. Let's go."

The crowd soon moved off toward Tri-Towers, a complex of dormitories, where one of the specially arranged dances was being held. Faculty marshals observed them as they followed the usual student parade route around the dormitories, picking up new recruits as they went. By the time they headed back toward the Commons, the crowd had grown to around 2,000, and some were chanting, "Ho, Ho, Ho Chi Minh," and "One, two, three, four, we don't want your fucking war." As they crossed the Commons near the ROTC building, some shouted, "Get it," "Burn it," and "ROTC has to go."

The ROTC building was an obvious target. It was a two-story wooden structure—an old World War II-type Army barracks—and it looked easy to ignite. Many students saw it as evidence that the university supported the Vietnam war effort by maintaining a military training program on campus.

About 8:10 P.M., a few students began to throw rocks at the ROTC building. In a short while, flying rocks had broken some of the building's windows. A few in the crowd appeared to have brought bags of rocks to the scene. A group used an ash can as a battering ram to break in a window; some started throwing lighted railroad flares into and onto the building. A curtain caught fire. In the crowd, someone burned a miniature American flag. A student taking pictures was attacked and wrestled to the ground, and his film was taken and exposed. Professor Frank said that when he intervened in the student's behalf, he was grabbed from behind. Frank was saved from further attack only when recognized by one of his students. Finally, a young man dipped a cloth into the gasoline tank of a parked motorcycle. Another young man ignited it and set the building afire. The building began to burn about 8:45 P.M.

The mood of the part of the crowd nearest the ROTC building was one of anger. "I have never in my 17 years of teaching," said Frank, "seen a group of students as threatening or as arrogant or as bent on destruction as I saw and talked to that night." Faculty marshals did not intervene.

Many spectators behaved around the ROTC fire as though they were at a carnival. Only a dozen or so persons appeared to have made active efforts to set the building afire, and another two or three dozen threw stones, but many others cheered and shouted with glee as the building was destroyed, and sat on the hills surrounding the Commons to watch the conflagration.

One student protested the burning of the ROTC building, telling his fellows, "You can't do this." He was shouted down. A faculty marshal who feared that the student was in danger of physical injury led him from the area.

About 9:00 P.M., a truck from the Kent Fire Department arrived. No police protection was provided. Members of the mob grabbed the hose from the firemen. They slashed and stabbed the hose with pocket knives, an ice pick, and a machete. They threw rocks at the firemen, who then withdrew. At this point, the fire seemed to subside.

Yet the fire quickly began to grow again. When the building was burning furiously and live ammunition was exploding inside, the campus police appeared. Their headquarters were only 200 yards from the ROTC building.

Kent State Safety Director Williams explained later that he and Schwartzmiller had decided not to commit their men to the threatened building promptly because, given the size and mood of the crowd, they feared for the lives of some of their men. Security Officer Schwartzmiller had asked Kent police for help but had been told that almost the entire force had been mobilized and stationed to protect the downtown area. Schwartzmiller said later he received the impression that the Kent Police Department was "getting even" with him for his failure to dispatch his men to Prentice Gate to disperse the crowd there on Friday night.

As the campus police marched up in riot gear, someone shouted, "Here come the pigs." The police fired tear gas at the crowd. It left the ROTC building area and moved across the Commons to the tennis courts. Some students bent down the strong metal fence around the courts.

About 9:30 P.M., a small shed near the tennis courts, which was used to store archery equipment, was set afire. Flames shot up from the shed and threatened nearby trees. Students hurried into buildings, filled wastebaskets with water, and put out the fire.

Aware of the turmoil on campus, Mayor Satrom had called General Del Corso's office at 8:35 P.M. to renew his request for troops. He spoke to Colonel Simmons. Acting under the directions left him by General Del Corso, Simmons called the Akron bivouac and ordered the troops to Kent.

At 9:30 P.M., Generals Del Corso and Canterbury arrived in Kent. As their troops were pulling into town, the flames from the burning ROTC building lit up the horizon.

The generals went to city hall and were briefed by Mayor Satrom. Del Corso then dispatched one detachment of guardsmen to prevent students from entering downtown Kent, and sent another detachment to protect firemen who were returning to the burning building. As the first detachment approached the campus, it was stoned by persons hidden among trees on East Main Street. Specialist 4th Class Ronald West of Troop G of the 2nd Squadron, 107th Armored Cavalry Regiment, was cut in the mouth by glass when a rock broke the windshield of a jeep in which he was riding, and several other guardsmen in the unit reported they were hit by stones or pieces of brick.

Neither Del Corso nor Canterbury requested permission of any university official before sending troops onto campus. General Canterbury said later that because the building was located on state property, the Guard needed no specific invitation to enter the campus.

At the same time that Del Corso was ordering troops to the ROTC fire, an unidentified guardsman called Matson at the Emergency Operation Center in the administration building to inquire if the Guard was needed at the fire. Matson asked the advice of Vice President Dunn, who supervises campus police and who was at the Kent Police Station at this time. Dunn in turn asked Williams and Schwartzmiller if they needed the Guard at the ROTC fire. The Highway Patrol had been called a second time by Schwartzmiller, after the fire had been set. Now that there was a basis for arrests, they agreed to come. But, by now Williams and Schwartzmiller had abandoned hope that the Highway Patrol would arrive in time and agreed that they needed the Guard. They communicated this to Dunn, who in turn advised Matson. Unknown to them the Guard was already enroute.

Part of the crowd had already left the Commons and was heading for town. Matson was informed of this fact at the same time he heard from Dunn. Matson said later that he told the Guard that the matter was no longer in his hands because the crowd was now off campus and in the town. Guardsmen previously dispatched by Del Corso intercepted the students before they got downtown.

At about this time, campus police, sheriff's deputies, highway patrolmen, and National Guardsmen had assembled on campus. The patrolmen deployed to patrol the campus. The Guard and campus police gave protection to firemen, who now came on campus in a second attempt to put out the fire in the ROTC building. The building could not be saved and soon burned to rubble. The university set the loss of building and contents at $86,000.

Information developed by an FBI investigation of the ROTC building fire indicates that, of those who participated actively, a significant proportion were not Kent State students. There is also evidence to suggest that the burning was planned beforehand: railroad flares, a machete, and ice picks are not customarily carried to peaceful rallies.

Students continued to roam about. A faculty marshal dissuaded half a dozen persons from setting fire to a small information booth at the edge of the campus. Along East Main Street, just off campus, a group of about ten wrecked a telephone booth and tried to uproot a bus stop sign. Others dragged an air compressor into the street from a construction site, piled up sawhorses and debris, and built a bonfire. Other students followed along trying to prevent damage and put fires out.

At 9:50 P.M., Del Corso telephoned McElroy and reported that he had already sent troops onto the campus and into downtown Kent. McElroy relayed this information to Governor Rhodes.

The Guard set up a campus headquarters in the meeting room of the Board of Trustees in the administration building. The next day, Sunday, they moved their headquarters to Wills Gymnasium, near the administration building.

The National Guard cleared the campus with dispatch, using tear gas freely. Some students had to spend the night in dormitories other than their own because the clean-up was so quick and emphatic. At 11:55 P.M., General Canterbury phoned his staff at Fort Hayes and reported that the situation was under control.

Antagonism toward law enforcement personnel already was evident among many students. A faculty marshal reported seeing a young woman trying to dissuade a young man from throwing a rock toward officers and guardsmen near the ROTC building. She said, "Hey, don't throw that. You might hurt somebody." "That's all right," the young man replied, "they all have helmets on." He threw the rock and ran.

When a group of faculty marshals wearing blue armbands attempted to identify themselves as guardsmen approached, the guardsmen knelt in a skirmish line and pointed rifles at them. Abandoning explanations, the marshals fled.

The university had made no effort beforehand to prepare the students for the possibility that the Guard might come to the campus. Administration officials had met with student leaders several times during the day, but the discussions were confined to the subject of dances and other diversionary social events. There was no discussion of what might happen if another disorder occurred—a subject administrators discussed only among themselves or with city officials.

President White and his wife were at the home of his sister-in-law in Mason City, Iowa, all day Saturday. After repeated telephone conversations Saturday morning with his aides in Kent, he called for the Kent State airplane to be sent to bring him back to his troubled campus. He took off for Ohio early Sunday morning.

As the ROTC building burned, the pattern of the previous night reappeared—authorities arrived at the scene of an incident too late to apprehend the participants, then swept up the bystanders and the participants together in their response. Students who had nothing to do with burning the building—who were not even in the area at the time—resented being gassed and ordered about by armed men. Many students returning to the campus on Sunday after a weekend at home were first surprised at the Guard's presence, then irritated when its orders interfered with their activities. Student resentment of the Guard continued to grow during the next two days.

Sunday, May 3

At 10:00 A.M. Sunday, while Kent State President White was on his way home from Iowa by plane, Governor Rhodes arrived in Kent and held a news conference. Among those present to hear Rhodes were his chief aid, McElroy, General Del Corso, Mayor Satrom, KSU Vice President Matson, Ohio Highway Patrol Superintendent Robert N. Chiaramonte, Portage County Prosecutor Ronald J. Kane, U.S. Attorney Robert Krupansky, and Kent Fire Chief Fred Miller.

Governor Rhodes called the Kent disturbances "probably the most vicious form of campus-oriented violence yet perpetrated by dissident groups and their allies in the state of Ohio" and told his listeners that "we are going to employ every force of law that we have under our authority." Rhodes alluded to information that he seemed to suggest indicated that the Kent State 4 were involved in the Kent disorders.

After referring to recent disturbances at two other Ohio universities, Governor Rhodes said:

> We have the same groups going from one campus to the other and
> they use the universities state-supported by the state of Ohio as a

sanctuary. And in this, they make definite plans of burning, destroying, and throwing rocks at police and at the National Guard and at the Highway Patrol.

"We are going to eradicate the problem," Governor Rhodes said. "We are not going to treat the symptoms."

Rhodes described the troublemakers as

worse than the brown shirts and the communist element, and also the night riders and the vigilantes. They are the worst type of people that we harbor in America. And I want to say this—they are not going to take over the campus and the campus now is going to be part of the county and the state of Ohio. It is no sanctuary for these people to burn buildings down of private citizens of businesses, in the community, then run into a sanctuary. It is over with in the state of Ohio.

Other officials commented at this point. Highway Patrol Superintendent Chiaramonte said, "We have men that are well trained, but they are not trained to receive bricks; they won't take it. The next phase that we have encountered elsewhere is where they start sniping. They can expect us to return fire." Mayor Satrom said, "We will take all necessary and I repeat, all necessary action to maintain order."

After the news conference, Governor Rhodes met briefly in private with Prosecutor Kane. According to Kane, he suggested that the university be closed. Rhodes declined, saying that would be "playing into the hands of the Weathermen," the most militant faction of the SDS. A university official tried to attend this meeting, but he was excluded.

Many persons felt that the Governor had spoken firmly and forthrightly. Others felt that his remarks were inflammatory and worsened an already tense situation. Some, including many Kent students, believed the Governor was hoping that his words and actions at Kent would win him additional votes in the primary election, to be held two days later, for nomination to the United States Senate.

Governor Rhodes delayed his departure until noon so that he could meet and talk briefly at the university airport with President White as he arrived from Iowa. White later stated that the Governor told him, "Bob, you have 400 of the worst riffraff in the state from all of the campuses. They are trying to close you down. Don't give in. Keep open." White said he was told by Chiaramonte, who was with the governor, that the State Highway Patrol had supplied this information.

After the Governor departed, widespread uncertainty regarding rules, prohibitions, and proclamations remained. Many people were unsure about what was to be legal and what not, particularly with respect to rallies and demonstrations.

Governor Rhodes had told his news conference, "We are going to ask for an injunction . . . equivalent to a state of emergency," and added that "we're trying to work on it right now." There is no official record that such an injunction was ever sought or obtained. The rules Governor Rhodes intended to apply were never precisely defined. Mayor Satrom had placed Kent under a state of civil emergency but had not banned peaceful rallies.

After Rhodes' news conference, university officials spent several hours trying to define the precise meaning of the "state of emergency" to which the Governor had referred. Finally, John Huffman, Matson's executive assistant, talked with a Guard officer, and received the impression that the state of emergency permitted "no gatherings or rallies at all."

Based on this discussion, the university prepared and distributed 12,000 leaflets again signed by Matson and Frisina. The leaflet listed curfew hours; said the Governor through the National Guard had assumed legal control of the campus; stated that all outdoor demonstrations and rallies, peaceful or otherwise, were prohibited by the state of emergency; and said the Guard was empowered to make arrests. Canterbury later cited this leaflet, which was based on an interpretation given to a university administrator by one of his officers, as one source of his authority for banning rallies.

White broadcast a statement of his own, indicating the university had no control over when the Guard might depart, declaring, "Events have taken decisions out of the university hands."

Some students disregarded the informational leaflet distributed Sunday when they saw the names of Matson and Frisina on it. Many students disliked the roles these two had played in opposing the old CCC during April 1969.

Many students remained confused all day Sunday about the rules governing the campus and what they permitted.

About noon, the National Guard asked Schwartzmiller for a bullhorn to use in dispersing sightseers at the ROTC ruins. Schwartzmiller complied, although he believed the Guard was being overzealous. In the afternoon, a group of 23 faculty members issued a statement deploring the Guard's presence on campus and student rock-throwing and violence during the previous two days. But the statement also suggested that the building burning should be viewed in the context of the war in Vietnam and the American move into Cambodia. Another group of about 60 teachers asked White to call a full faculty meeting immediately. He declined—permission of the Guard would have been required for such an assembly, and in any case the request did not come from the proper body.

Generals Del Corso and Canterbury had left Kent that morning, leaving Colonel Harold Finley in charge of the Guard.

On Sunday afternoon, the campus was generally quiet, and many students felt the worst was over. Sightseers visited the ruins of the ROTC building, and some students conversed with guardsmen.

Students began gathering on the Commons about 8:00 P.M. The crowd was peaceful, and included a group of coeds kicking a soccer ball around. But by 8:45 P.M., it had grown large enough that campus police and the highway patrol suggested to Colonel Finley that the 1:00 A.M. campus curfew be cancelled and an immediate curfew imposed. As a result, shortly before 9:00 P.M., Major Jones read the Ohio Riot Act to the crowd on the Commons and gave them five minutes to disperse. When they did not, police proceeded to disperse them with tear gas. One group headed toward President White's house, another toward Prentice Gate.

The students were driven away from White's home by tear gas. At Prentice Gate, there was a more serious confrontation. A sizable crowd sat down in the intersection of Lincoln and Main next to the gate and asked to speak with Satrom and White about six demands: abolition of ROTC; removal of the Guard from Campus by Monday night; lifting of the curfew; full amnesty for all persons arrested Saturday night; lower student tuition; and granting of any demand made by BUS.

Matson and Ronald Roskens, Vice President for Administration, were at the administration building when a police officer told them the crowd wanted to talk to White. Matson and Roskens rejected the idea. They felt that the Guard was in charge of the campus and that there was no point in negotiating in the streets.

Matson said he contacted White, who agreed with his decision. White's recollection is that he was not personally contacted about the student's request. Matson himself was asked to go to the gathering, but declined.

Mayor Satrom was informed of the situation at Prentice Gate and left for the scene; before he arrived, the Guard dispersed the crowd.

A tape recording, made at the scene, assists in reconstructing the following account of the dialogue:

An unidentified young man who was permitted to use the police public address system, told the crowd that Mayor Satrom was coming to discuss their demands and that efforts were being made to contact President White. (John Huffman, Matson's executive assistant, later said he had just told the young man specifically that White was not coming.) The young man said that if the students would move out of the street, the guardsmen at the scene would reciprocate by moving off campus. Both the Guard and the students did in fact withdraw slightly.

At 11:00 P.M., police where told that the two officials would not talk to the demonstrators. The Riot Act was read to the crowd and Colonel Finley told them the curfew was in effect as of 11:00 P.M.

The students, previously nonviolent, became hostile. They felt that they had been double-crossed. They cursed the guardsmen and police and threw rocks at them. Tear gas was fired and the crowd ran back from the gate across the campus lawn.

During the confusion of the dispersal, two students were bayoneted and sustained minor cuts. Three guardsmen received cuts and bruises from thrown stones and a wrench.

Guardsmen drove one group of about 300 young persons across the campus with tear gas to the Tri-Towers dormitory area. A helicopter had been hovering over the Prentice Gate sit-in. Its spotlight illuminated the scene, following the students as they ran. Its wash increased the effectiveness of the gas along the ground. Among the fleeing Kent State students was Allison Krause.

Another group of students ran to the Rockwell Memorial Library, the building closest to the gate, and climbed through windows to get inside. A coed was reportedly bayoneted as she attempted to climb through a window. Some of the library windows were broken by rocks. The night guard locked the doors, sealing the students inside. They were later given a 45-minute grace period to leave the building and return to their dormitories.

Fifty-one persons were arrested Sunday night, mostly for curfew violations. This brought the total of arrests to more than 100 since the disturbances began. By the time General Canterbury returned to Kent at 11:40 P.M., the campus was quiet. He called a meeting of law enforcement and other officials for 10:00 A.M. Monday. He was concerned about the lack of coordination and wanted to resolve the confusion over the applicable curfew hours.

Despite a promising start, the situation in Kent had appreciably worsened during the day. Students were more resentful of the Guard as a result of what they considered to be broken promises at Prentice Gate. The university was anxious to restore normal conditions, and law enforcement officers and guardsmen seemed to be growing more impatient with student curses, stones, and refusals to obey.

Monday, May 4

As they lined up opposite students on the Commons shortly before noon, the three National Guard units involved in the Kent State shooting had had an average of three hours of sleep the night before.

Company C of the First Battalion, 145th Infantry Regiment, went off duty at 2:00 A.M. Monday morning. At 5:30 A.M., the company commander, Capt. James R. Snyder, received orders to return to patrol on city streets near Kent State.

At 6:00 A.M., Troop G of the Second Squadron, 107th Armored Cavalry Regiment, relieved Company A of the First Battalion, 145th Infantry, which had been on duty all night. Company A then had to move their bivouac area, however, and the company commander, Capt. John E. Martin, said none got to bed before 9:00 A.M. At about 11:30 A.M., they were roused to return to duty on the campus.

Troop G had gone off duty at 6:00 P.M. Sunday, according to the troop commander Capt. Raymond J. Srp. But they had just lined up for their first hot meal of the day, when they were sent back to duty on campus. They served until between midnight and 1:00 A.M. Monday and then were awakened between 4:00 and 4:30 A.M. to prepare to relieve Company A.

President Robert I. White met at 7:00 A.M. with his cabinet. At an 8:00 A.M. meeting with the executive committee of the faculty senate, he agreed to attend the senate's regular Monday meeting and to hold an afternoon meeting for the full faculty.

The Education building was closed at 7:45 A.M. before classes began because of a bomb threat. Several other Monday classes were cancelled by bomb threats. In many of the classes that did meet, the events of the weekend were the chief topic of discussion.

A call for a noon rally on the Commons was passed around the campus by word of mouth and by announcements chalked on classroom blackboards. The precise purpose was not made clear, but most students assumed it was to protest the presence of the National Guard, which by now was resented by many students, even by those who held no deep political beliefs.

Until this weekend in May, the student population of Kent State had generally been considered either conservative or apolitical. Under state law, the university must accept any graduate of an accredited Ohio high school, and five out of six Kent State students are from Ohio, mostly from Cleveland and Akron, from the steel towns of Lorain and Youngstown, and from small rural towns. They are predominately the children of middle class families, both white collar and blue collar, and in the main go on to careers as teachers and as middle-level management in industry.

General Canterbury called a meeting for 10:00 A.M. Monday to discuss plans for the day and to reduce confusion over the curfew hours. He attended the meeting in civilian clothes to avoid attracting attention. He never had time to change into his uniform. President White, Vice President Matson, Mayor Satrom, Paul Hershey, the Kent city safety director, Major Donald E. Manly of the Ohio State Highway Patrol, and Major William R. Shimp, legal officer of the Ohio National Guard, were also in attendance. They decided to apply the city's 8:00 P.M. to 6:00 A.M. curfew to the campus. The proclamation of civil emergency which Satrom had issued on Saturday was amended accordingly.

Thereafter the major topic of the meeting was what to do about the rally planned for the Commons at noon. A university official phoned Matson at the meeting and asked him about the status of the noon rally. Matson's reaction was that the rally was forbidden by the Guard's rules. He returned to the meeting and raised the issue of how the noon rally was to be handled. Participants in the meeting give differing accounts of this discussion.

Canterbury testified before the Commission that he first learned about the rally during this meeting. When he asked White if it should be permitted, White replied, "No, it would be highly dangerous."

White testified that during this meeting "it became apparent that any noon rallies or any rally would not be permitted. . . ." Asked what part he played in banning the noon rally, White testified, "None at all." In a statement after Canterbury testified, White denied making the statement attributed to him by the general and added, "From past history, all know that my response would have been affirmative to a rally."

Satrom, Hershey, and Major Manly do not recall that White asked that the rally be prevented, but each of them came away with the belief it was banned.

Matson said he thought it was "more or less assumed" by all present that Governor Rhodes' declaration of emergency on Sunday prohibited all rallies. Matson recalled that Canterbury told the group that the rally would not be allowed unless he heard strong objections to its prohibition.

After the meeting, Canterbury returned to Guard headquarters in the administration building at Kent State about 11:30 A.M. Two Guard officers present recall that, upon his return, he stated that the noon rally on the Commons would not be permitted. Major John Simons, chaplain of the 107th Armored Cavalry Regiment, expressed concern that the students might be unaware that the noon rally had been prohibited. He said a campus official told him that the university radio station would "spread the word."

Throughout the morning, guardsmen patroled the campus without notable incident.

About 11:00 A.M., students began gathering on the Commons, apparently for a variety of reasons. Some had heard vaguely that a rally would be held. Some came to protest the presence of the Guard. Some were simply curious, or had free time because their classes had been cancelled. Some students stopped by on their way to or from lunch or class. The Commons is a crossroads between several major university buildings.

Many students who described themselves as "straight," or conservative, later attributed their presence at the rally to a desire to protest against the National Guard. This attitude was reflected in the testimony of one Kent State coed before the Commission:

Q—What were your feelings at the time when you saw them [the Guard on May 3]?
A—I just really couldn't believe it. It was a very unreal feeling to walk up on your Front Campus and see these armed troops. You know, like you had been invaded, in a way.

Q—Did you go back on the campus on Monday, May 4?
A—Yes, I did. I have an 11 o'clock class in the Educational Building . . . After that time, I have a 12 o'clock class, which is around this side complex, so I had to cross the campus and I went the usual way and found I couldn't get across campus because the Guards were blocking the campus, across the Commons.

Q—Had you heard of the rally down on the Commons before you left your class at the Education Building?

A—Yes. One of the boys in the class had heard about it and mentioned that there was a rally. And that Governor Rhodes was taking hard lines about the rally.

Q—Did you plan to go to the rally?

A—No, I had my books with me and I had a report due in the next hour and I intended to go to class. It was when I found I couldn't go across campus, I decided to go to the rally.

Q—Had you been to any rallies before?

A—Just one, on October 15 [the war moratorium] was the first time I had gone to any kind of a rally.

Q—Why did you stay at this particular rally after you got there . . . ?

A—Well, I just couldn't believe the Guards were on campus. It was mostly, just outrage and disgust and fear, and all sorts of crazy things. I just couldn't believe that my campus had been taken over by Guards. You know, they said I couldn't cross the campus, they said we can't assemble on the campus. I stood on the Commons. I was watching the Guards and thinking, they are telling us to leave, but this is our campus, we belong here and they don't. That is why I stayed mostly.

This coed was gassed on the Commons, moved back over Blanket Hill to the Prentice Hall parking lot, and was within three feet of Allison Krause when Miss Krause was killed.

General Canterbury reached the Commons between 11:30 and 11:40 A.M. with Lt. Col. Charles R. Fassinger, commander of the Second Squadron of the 107th Armored Cavalry. Canterbury told a Commission investigator he did not feel that the crowd represented a significant threat at that time.

Fassinger estimated that by 11:45 the crowd had grown to more than 500. The principal group gathered around the Victory Bell about 170 yards across the Commons from the burned-out ROTC building, where the guardsmen were stationed. Canterbury ordered the crowd dispersed.

Fassinger then ordered troops to form up by the ruins of the ROTC building. Some 40 to 50 men from Company A, about 35 to 45 men from Company C, and 18 men from Troop G were hurriedly assembled. Those who had not already done so were ordered to "load and lock" their weapons. By this process an M-1 rifle is loaded with an eight-round clip of .30 caliber ball ammunition, and one bullet is moved up into the chamber ready to fire. The weapon will then fire immediately after the safety mechanism is disengaged and the trigger is pulled. Throughout the weekend, whenever guardsmen were on duty, their weapons were loaded and locked.

A Kent State policeman, Harold E. Rice, stood near the ROTC ruins and using a bullhorn ordered the students to disperse. It is doubtful that Rice was heard over the noise of the crowd. A jeep was brought up. Rice, a driver, and two Guard riflemen drove out across the Commons toward the crowd. Rice gave the dispersal order again.

The students responded with curses and stones. Some chanted "Pigs off campus" and "One, two, three, four, we don't want your fucking war." Rocks bounced off the jeep, and Rice said the occupants were hit several times.

Specialist Fifth Class Gordon R. Bedall, who was in the jeep, said Rice saw a student in the crowd who Rice believed was one of the instigators of the weekend disturbances. Rice asked the driver to direct the jeep into the crowd so that he could pick up this young man and take him back. According to the driver, a shower of rocks from several students forced the jeep back twice. Major Jones was dispatched from the Guard lines to order the jeep to return.

At 11:58 A.M., as the jeep returned, Canterbury ordered the 96 men and seven officers to form a skirmish line, shoulder to shoulder, and move out across the Commons toward the students. Each man's weapon was loaded and locked. Canterbury estimated the size of the crowd on the Commons at about 800; another 1,000 or more persons were sitting or milling about on the hills surrounding the Commons. His goal as he moved out was to disperse the crowd.

After the event, Canterbury was asked several times to indicate the authority under which he had issued his order to disperse the crowd.

On May 8, 1970, he told an FBI agent that his order was based on the proclamation of Governor Rhodes on April 29 which mobilized the Guard for a Teamster's strike. Canterbury contended that the proclamation incorporated the Ohio Riot Act even though it did not explicitly mention that Act.

On August 4, 1970, Canterbury told a Commission investigator that his authority was based on Governor Rhodes' April 29 proclamation, and also on the Ohio Riot Act which permits an officer to order dispersal of a crowd when it is engaged in "violent or tumultuous conduct which creates clear and present danger to the safety of persons or property."

On August 20, 1970, Canterbury testified before the Commission:

> The assemblies were not to be permitted because of the previous two days of rioting and to permit an assembly at this point would have been dangerous. This was my assessment, as well as the assessment of the President of the University, and the other authorities present.

Shortly before noon, students began to ring the Victory Bell. Two generalized emotions seem to have prevailed among the 2,000 or so young persons who were now on or near the Commons. One was a vague feeling that something worth watching or participating in would occur, that something was going to happen and that the Guard would respond. The other was antipathy to the Guard, bitter in some cases, accompanied by the feeling that the Guard, although fully backed by official pronouncements, was somehow "trespassing" on the students' own territory.

A majority of the crowd was watching the tableau from the patio of Taylor Hall, and from the slopes around the adjacent buildings of Prentice, Johnson, and Stopher Halls. The hills made a natural amphitheatre from which students could watch events on the Commons floor. Most of the onlooking students could not be described as neutral: in almost any quarrel between students and guardsmen, they would take the side of their fellow students.

The troops lined up with fixed bayonets across the northwestern corner of the Commons. On orders from Canterbury relayed by Fassinger, eight to ten grenadiers with M-79 grenade launchers fired two volleys of tear gas canisters at the crowd, which began to scatter.

Canterbury, in civilian clothes and unarmed, was in command. At the age of 55, he had 23 years of military experience behind him and had served during many previous civil disturbances in Ohio, including ones in Akron and in the Hough section of Cleveland. The Ohio National Guard units Canterbury commanded were also experienced in dealing with disorders. General Del Corso testified that Governor Rhodes, since appointing him adjutant general on April 1, 1968, had mobilized the Guard approximately 30 times for civil disturbances. "Twelve or thirteen" of these occasions, said Del Corso, had involved disturbances in the northeastern zone of the state, the location of Kent State University.

The day was bright and sunny, and a 14 mile-an-hour breeze was blowing. The tear gas did not at first scatter all the students: the wind blew some of the gas away; the aim of some of the grenadiers was poor, causing many who were only spectators to be gassed; and some of the students picked up the tear gas canisters and threw them back. Canterbury ordered the troops to move out.

The guardsmen were wearing gas masks. Company A was on the right flank, Company C was on the left flank, and Troop G was in the middle. Moving out with the men were Canterbury, Fassinger, and the third in command, Major Harry D. Jones, battalion staff officer of the 145th.

The guardsmen marched across the flat Commons, the students scattering before them up a steep hill beyond the Victory Bell. Canterbury's original plan was to march to the crest of Blanket Hill, a knoll beyond the bell between the northern end of Johnson Hall and southern end of Taylor Hall. When some of the students ran to the north end of Taylor Hall, he sent a contingent of men around there to disperse them. He had hoped, after clearing the Commons, to withdraw his troops to the ROTC building. When Canterbury reached the crest of Blanket Hill, however, he concluded that it would be necessary to push the students beyond a practice football field which lay about 80 yards below the crest of Blanket Hill.

By this time the crowd seemed more united in mood. The feeling had spread among students that they were being harassed as a group, that state and civic officials had united against them and that the university had either cooperated or acquiesced in their suppression. They reacted to the guardsmen's march with substantial solidarity. They shouted, "Pigs off campus," and called the guardsmen "green pigs" and "fascist bastards."

Rocks flew as the guardsmen marched across the Commons. Capt. Snyder, the C Company commander, said a young man near Taylor Hall struck him twice with stones. When the young man refused Snyder's order to put the rocks down, Snyder knocked him down with his baton. The youth scrambled to his feet and ran away.

The antagonism between guardsmen and students increased. The guardsmen generally felt that the students, who had disobeyed numerous orders to disperse, were clearly in the wrong. The razing of the ROTC building had shown them that these noisy youths were capable of considerable destruction.

Many students felt that the campus was their "turf." Unclear about the authority vested in the Guard by the governor, or indifferent to it, some also felt that their constitutional right to free assembly was being infringed upon. As they saw it, they had been ordered to disperse at a time when no rocks had been thrown and no other violence had been committed. Many told interviewers later, "We weren't doing anything."

The guardsmen marched down the east slope of Blanket Hill, across an access road, and onto a practice football field, which is fenced in on three sides. The crowd parted to let them down the hill to the field and then reformed in two loose groups—one on Blanket Hill, above the football field, and the other in the Prentice Hall parking lot at the north end of the field. The crowd on the parking lot was unruly and threw many missiles at guardsmen on the football field. It was at this point that the shower of stones apparently became heaviest. Nearby construction projects provided an ample supply of rocks.

Tear gas canisters were still flying back and forth; after the Guard would shoot a canister, students sometimes would pick it up and lob it back at the guardsmen. In some cases, guardsmen would pick up the same canister and throw it at the students. Some among the crowd came to regard the situation as a game—"a tennis match" one called it—and cheered each exchange of tear gas canisters. Only a few students participated in this game, however. One of them was Jeffrey Glenn Miller. A few minutes later, Miller was fatally shot.

As the confrontation worsened, some students left the scene. Among those who departed was a student who had gone to the rally with a classmate, William Schroeder. Subsequently, Schroeder was killed.

While on the practice field, about a dozen guardsmen knelt and pointed their weapons at the students in the Prentice Hall parking lot, apparently as a warning or a threatening gesture. Whether any shot was fired on the field is in dispute.

Richard A. Schreiber, an assistant professor of journalism at Kent State, said he was watching the action through binoculars from the balcony of Taylor Hall when he saw an officer fire one shot from a .45 calibre automatic pistol at a 45-degree angle over the heads of rock-throwers in a nearby parking lot. Sgt. James W. Farriss of Company A said an officer whom he did not know fired one shot from a .45 caliber pistol while on the field.

The next day, Tuesday, Specialist Fourth Class Gerald Lee Scalf found a spent .22 caliber shell casing near the edge of the football field. Major Jones was the only officer on the field with a .22 caliber pistol, a Beretta automatic. He said he did not fire this pistol on the football field or at any time on Monday.

After the guardsmen had been on the football field for about 10 minutes, Canterbury concluded that his dispersal mission had been sufficiently accomplished. He ordered his troops to retrace their steps back up Blanket Hill. He also thought—wrongly—that his men had exhuasted their supply of tear gas. Capt. Srp, commander of Troop G, ordered a tear gas launcher prepared for possible use as his unit marched back up Blanket Hill. One grenadier, Specialist Fourth Class Russell Repp, still had four unused tear gas grenades. Canterbury made no check to determine if tear gas was still available before the order to move out was given.

Later, in discussing his order to move off the field, Canterbury said, "My purpose was to make it clear beyond any doubt to the mob that our posture was now defensive and that we were clearly returning to the Commons, thus reducing the possibility of injury to either soldiers or students."

The Guard's march from Blanket Hill to the football field and back did not disperse the crowd and seems to have done little else than increase tension, subject guardsmen to needless abuse, and encourage the most violent and irresponsible elements in the crowd to harass the Guard further.

As the guardsmen withdrew from the field, many students thought they had run out of tear gas, or that there was nothing more they could do in their strategically weak position. Many felt a sense of relief, believing all danger was over. Most expected the Guard to march back over Blanket Hill to the ROTC building.

Some students grew more aggressive. A small group of two to four dozen followed the Guard closely. Some came as close as 20 yards, shouting and jeering and darting back and forth. One Guard officer said some students approached as close as six inches from the end of the guardsmen's bayonets. None of the many photographs examined by Commission investigators show any students to have been this close.

Many witnesses said that during the Guard's return march the intensity of rock-throwing appeared to diminish. The witnesses also said that most rock-throwers remained so far away from the guardsmen that most of their stones fell short, but that several guardsmen were hit and some rocks bounced off their helmets. Other student witnesses said the rock-throwing never slackened, and some say it grew heavier as the Guard mounted the hill.

The movements of the crowd in the last minute or two before the firing are the subject of considerable dispute. General Canterbury, in a statement to a Commission investigator on August 25, gave this description:

> As the troop formation reached the area of the Pagoda near Taylor Hall, the mob located on the right flank in front of Taylor Hall and in the Prentice Hall parking lot charged our right flank, throwing rocks, yelling obscenities and threats, "Kill the pigs," "Stick the pigs." The attitude of the crowd at this point was menacing and vicious.

> The troops were being hit by rocks. I saw Major Jones hit in the stomach by a large brick, a Guardsman to the right and rear of my position was hit by a large rock and fell to the ground. During this movement, practically all of the Guardsmen were hit by missiles of various kinds.

> Guardsmen on the right flank were in serious danger of bodily harm and death as the mob continued to charge. I felt that, in view of the extreme danger to the troops at this point, that they were justified in firing.

General Canterbury also testified that the closest students were within four to five yards of the Guard. In the direction the Guard fired, however, photographs show an open space in front of the guardsmen of at least 20 yards. To their side, the nearest student, one of several on the terrace of Taylor Hall, was at least 15 yards away. The nearest person wounded, Joseph Lewis, Jr., who was 20 yards away, said there was no one between him and the Guard. The closest person killed, Jeffrey Glenn Miller, was at least 85 yards away.

An 8-millimeter motion picture film, taken by an amateur cameraman from a point approximately 500 yards northeast of the firing line, indicates that the main body of aggressive students was about 60 to 75 yards away, at the foot of the hill near the corner of the Prentice Hall parking lot.

The crowd's movements can be reconstructed from testimony, photographs, and investigation.

As the guardsmen left the practice field on their way back up Blanket Hill, they encountered a crowd of several hundred students fanned around in a broad parabola from Memorial Gymnasium and Lake Hall on their left to Taylor and Prentice Halls on their right. The crowd divided to let the Guard through.

A small gathering of 25 to 50 persons stood on the crest of Blanket Hill. As the Guard approached them, they retreated down the west slope of the hill and away from the scene of action.

About 100 persons stood on the east terrace of Taylor Hall, watching the guardsmen approach the adjacent hill. They are not known to have thrown any rocks and seem to have been spectators throughout. Perhaps another 100 persons withdrew from the edge of the practice field to a slope just below the east side of the hall. They threw some rocks.

A crowd of about 200 persons near Johnson Hall had generally watched the guardsmen pass by and not followed them to the football field and back.

As the Guard crossed the road that lies between the football field and the foot of Blanket Hill, perhaps 200 persons moved off to the left of the troops through the trees toward Lake Hall. Among them was student James D. Russell, subsequently wounded as he stood more than 100 yards from the firing line on Blanket Hill.

In the Prentice Hall parking lot, to one side of the withdrawing Guard, were some 100 to 200 students, some throwing rocks, some carrying books. At the time of the firing, some thought the action was over and had started away toward classes, including student Douglas Wrentmore, whose back was toward the guardsmen when the firing began. He was wounded as he walked away.

About 20 to 50 persons were the most conspicuous part of the crowd, moving along the guardsmen's right flank, and later behind them. In this group were the students most active in throwing rocks. It is not known precisely how many of this group threw rocks, but perhaps half of them threw rocks at one time or another. Included in this group of 20 to 50 were two young men, one carrying a red flag and the other a black flag. This group was particularly aggressive, cursing and jeering the guardsmen, following and pursuing them at a range varying from about 20 to 80 yards. At the time of the firing, most of this group were just south of the Prentice Hall parking lot, just below the eastern side of Taylor Hall.

Movie film and testimony indicate that as guardsmen reached the top of the hill, some students surged from the east face of Taylor Hall and the southern end of the parking lot up toward the guardsmen on Blanket Hill. The film is too indistinct to tell how many of the students involved in this movement were throwing rocks. The leading edge of this crowd appears to have advanced to a point no closer than 20 yards from the guardsmen, with the main body 60 to 75 yards away, before the gunfire began and they reversed their direction. It is possible that some of them had no aggressive intent but instead began running up the hill in the direction of the Guard to get a good vantage point on Blanket Hill after, as they expected, the guardsmen retreated down the far side of the slope.

Near the crest of Blanket Hill stands the Pagoda, a square bench made of 4-by-4 wooden beams and shaded by a concrete umbrella. The events which occurred as the Guard reached the Pagoda, turned and fired on the students, are in bitter dispute.

Many guardsmen said they had hard going as they withdrew up the hill. Fassinger said he was hit six times by stones, once on the shoulder so hard that he stumbled.

Fassinger had removed his gas mask to see more clearly. He said the guardsmen had reached a point between the Pagoda and Taylor Hall, and he was attempting to maintain them in a reasonably orderly formation, when he heard a sound like a shot, which was immediately followed by a volley of shots. He saw the troops on the Taylor Hall end of the line shooting. He yelled, "Cease fire!" and ran along the line repeating the command.

Major Jones said he first heard an explosion which he thought was a firecracker. As he turned to his left, he heard another explosion which he knew to be an M-1 rifle shot. As he turned to his right, toward Taylor Hall, he said he saw guardsmen kneeling (photographs show some crouching) and bringing their rifles to their shoulders. He heard another M-1 shot, and then a volley of them. He yelled, "Cease fire!" several times, and rushed down the line shoving rifle barrels up and away from the crowd. He hit several guardsmen on their helmets with his swagger stick to stop them from firing.

General Canterbury stated that he first heard a single shot, which he thought was fired from some distance away on his left and which in his opinion did not come from a military weapon. Immediately afterward, he heard a volley of M-1 fire from his right, the Taylor Hall end of the line. The Guard's fire was directed away from the direction from which Canterbury thought the initial, non-military shot came. His first reaction, like that of Fassinger and Jones, was to stop the firing.

Canterbury, Fassinger, and Jones, the three ranking officers on the hill, all said no order to fire was given.

Twenty-eight guardsmen have acknowledged firing from Blanket Hill. Of these, 25 fired 55 shots from rifles, two fired five shots from .45 caliber pistols, and one fired a single blast from a shotgun. Sound tracks indicate that the firing of these 61 shots lasted approximately 13 seconds. The time of the shooting was approximately 12:45 P.M.

Four persons were killed and nine were wounded. As determined by the FBI, their distances from the firing lines and the types of wounds they received were as follows:

1. Joseph Lewis, Jr., 20 yards, wounded in the right abdomen and the left lower leg.
2. Thomas V. Grace, 20 yards, wounded in the left ankle.
3. John R. Cleary, 37 yards, wounded in the left upper chest.
4. Allen Michael Canfora, 75 yards, wounded in the right wrist.
5. Jeffrey Glenn Miller, 85 to 90 yards, killed by a shot in the mouth.
6. Dean R. Kahler, 95 to 100 yards, wounded in the left side of the small of his back. A bullet fragment lodged in his spine and he is paralyzed from the waist down.
7. Douglas Alan Wrentmore, 110 yards, wounded in the right knee.

8. Allison B. Krause, 110 yards, killed by a bullet that passed through her left upper arm and into her left side.

9. James Dennis Russell, 125 to 130 yards, wounded in the right thigh and right forehead.

10. William K. Schroeder, 130 yards, killed by a shot in the left back at the seventh rib.

11. Sandra Lee Scheuer, 130 yards, killed by a shot through the left front side of the neck.

12. Robert Follis Stamps, 165 yards, wounded in the right buttock.

13. Donald Scott Mackenzie, 245 to 250 yards, wounded in the left rear of the neck.

Of the casualties, two were shot in the front, seven from the side, and four from the rear. All 13 were students at Kent State University.

Schroeder and Kahler were hit while lying prone. MacKenzie and Canfora were wounded while running away from the line of fire. Russell and Stamps were apparently hit by ricochets. Two of the casualties, Lewis and Russell, were wounded twice.

Of the 25 riflemen who admitted firing, 21 said they fired their 41 shots either into the air or into the ground. Four riflemen acknowledged firing nine of their total of 14 shots into the crowd.

Two men fired pistols: one said he fired two shots into the crowd and the other said he fired three shots into the air.

The guardsman who fired a shotgun said he fired a single blast into the air. Russell was wounded by shotgun pellets believed to have ricocheted off nearby trees.

The guardsmen admit firing a total of only 11 rounds into the crowd. Besides the 15 wounds sustained by the casualties, however, a number of parked cars in the Prentice Hall parking lot afterward showed bullet holes.

Guardsmen have claimed that they were under an increasingly heavy barrage of rocks and other objects as they advanced back up Blanket Hill, and that students rushed toward them threateningly. Many indicated that they began firing when they heard one or some of their fellow guardsmen open fire.

Although General Canterbury said his men were "not panic-stricken," it is clear that many of them were frightened. Many suffered bruises and abrasions from stones, although only one guardsman, Sgt. Dennis L. Breckenridge, required overnight hospitalization. He passed out from hyperventilation and was removed from the field in an ambulance.

A few students and a few guardsmen claim to have heard something like an order to fire. One student testified to the Commission that he saw an officer raise and lower his pistol just before the firing, possibly as a signal to shoot. The weight of the evidence indicates, however, that no command to fire was given, either verbally or by gesture.

As the shooting began, students scattered and ran. In the parking lot behind Prentice Hall, where two were killed and two were wounded, students dove behind parked cars and attempted to flatten themselves on the pavement. On the slope east of Taylor Hall, where four were wounded, students scrambled behind a metal sculpture, rolled down the incline, or sought cover behind trees. The scene was one of pell-mell disorder and fright.

Many thought the guardsmen were firing blanks. When the shooting stopped and they rose and saw students bleeding, the first reaction of most was shock. Jeffrey Miller lay on the pavement of an access road, blood streaming from his mouth.

Then the crowd grew angry. They screamed and some called the guardsmen "murderers." Some tried to give first aid. One vainly attempted mouth-to-mouth resuscitation on Sandra Lee Scheuer, one of the fatalities. Knots of students gathered around those who had fallen.

Sandra Lee Scheuer, 20, a junior, is believed to have been on her way to a 1:10 P.M. class in the Music and Speech Building when she was struck. She has not been identified in any available photographs as having attended the prohibited noon rally on the Commons.

Allison B. Krause, 19, a freshman, was among the group of students gathered on the Commons by the Victory Bell shortly before noon. After her death, small fragments of concrete and cinder block were found in the pockets of her jacket.

Jeffrey Glenn Miller, 20, a junior, was present in the crowd on the Commons when the dispersal order was given and made obscene gestures with his middle fingers at guardsmen. He also threw back a tear gas canister at the Guard while it was on the football practice field.

William K. Schroeder, 19, a sophomore, was an ROTC cadet. A photograph shows him retreating up Blanket Hill from the rally on the Commons, but he is not shown taking part in any of the harassment of the Guard.

No evidence was found to establish that any of the casualties were under the influence of drugs at the time of the confrontation. A marijuana cigarette was found in a pocket of the jacket used to cover one of the wounded students, Cleary, after he was injured. Cleary's father said, however, that the jacket did not belong to Cleary.

At the moment of the firing, most of the nine wounded students were far beyond a range at which they could have presented any immediate physical threat to the Guard.

The closest casualties—Lewis, Grace, and Cleary—were all within 20 to 40 yards. At the moment shooting began, Lewis was standing between Taylor Hall and the metal sculpture, gesturing at guardsmen with the middle finger of his right hand. Cleary was standing on the other side of the sculpture, which was perforated by a bullet. Grace was near them, but a little farther away from Taylor Hall. His actions are not known.

Canfora, who said he had been chanting anti-war slogans earlier, had started to run for cover behind cars in Prentice Hall parking lot when he was hit.

Kahler was standing at the northwest corner of the football field, beyond stone-throwing range, when the firing began. He dropped to the ground and was hit while prone.

Wrentmore was in the Prentice Hall parking lot and said he was walking away to a class when he heard the firing begin, turned, and was wounded.

Russell, apparently hit by a ricochet, was standing far away from all the other casualties, near Lake Hall and Memorial Gymnasium.

Stamps, tear gassed on the Commons, had just left Prentice Hall after washing tear gas off his face. He was wounded in Prentice Hall parking lot as he tried to run away from the firing.

Mackenzie, the casualty most distant from the Guard, said he heard the firing begin and had turned to run when he was hit. The entire length of Prentice Hall parking lot and the east slope of Blanket Hill lay between him and the Guard.

After the shooting, students ran to Taylor, Prentice, and Dunbar Halls to telephone for ambulances. Others ran down to the Commons screaming for ambulances. Several minutes passed before the ambulances came. Students linked their arms and formed rings around the bodies to keep them from further injury. Some students wept. Others wandered around dazed.

The shooting on Blanket Hill was done principally by members of Troop G and Company A. Company C, except for two members who went down to the football field and returned to Blanket Hill with the main body of troops, remained at the northern end of Taylor Hall where they had been dispatched by General Canterbury. The C Company members at that position, which is at the opposite end of Taylor Hall from Blanket Hill, did not fire their weapons.

After the firing, the C Company commander, Capt. Snyder, took seven men down to the Prentice Hall parking lot to render first aid. He looked at two young men who had fallen, probably Miller and Schroeder, but concluded both were dead. While the detachment was in the vicinity of the body of Jeffrey Miller, enraged students began to scream at them. The guardsmen responded by throwing a tear gas pellet at the student group. Capt. Snyder withdrew his unit to its original position and then back across the Commons, leaving the casualties where they had fallen. Many students subsequently believed that no guardsmen made any effort to render first aid after the shootings, and added this to their catalogue of charges against the troops.

The scene after the shooting was tense, and there was a possibility of further trouble. After an ambulance removed Miller's body, a demonstrator who had carried a black flag during the confrontation dipped the flag into the pool of Miller's blood and waved it at nearby students in an apparent effort to inflame them further.

Canterbury withdrew his troops to the Commons almost immediately. He ordered a weapons check to determine how many guardsmen fired how many rounds. He commanded that no more rounds be fired except at a specified target and upon an officer's order.

After the casualties were removed, students began to gather again on the hills overlooking the Commons. The largest concentration, varying from 200 to 300, congregated on the slope below Johnson Hall at one corner of the Commons. Many of them would later have trouble describing their emotions.

Professor Glenn W. Frank obtained permission from General Canterbury to allow faculty marshals to attempt to persuade this crowd to leave without further military action. Frank and Dr. Seymour H. Baron, who had a bullhorn, persuaded the students to sit down instead of milling around. Baron warned the students they might be shot if they approached the guardsmen again. "They're scared to death," he said of the guardsmen, "a bunch of summertime soldiers. They're not professionals. They're scared kids."

"I'm a faculty member," said Baron, who is chairman of the Kent State psychology department. "I want you to understand the faculty is with you with regard to this Vietnam thing. . . . We're with you all the way."

Major Jones of the National Guard approached. Aware of the crowd's volatile mood, Frank told him, "For God's sake, don't come any closer." Jones said, "My orders are to move ahead." Frank replied, "Over my dead body."

Jones withdrew, but soon a detachment of guardsmen appeared along the hill behind the students. Frank pleaded with the students to leave. "I am begging you right now," he said, "if you don't disperse right now, they're going to move in, and there can only be a slaughter. Jesus Christ, I don't want to be a part of this."

When the guardsmen appeared behind the students, some of the students felt surrounded, some panicked and ran. Others adamantly refused to leave and had to be physically carried away by faculty marshals and graduate students. The entreaties of Baron and Frank induced others to walk away. Slightly more than an hour after the shooting, the Commons and the hills around it were clear.

Major Simons, chaplain of the 107th, was one of the officers who checked weapons among the guardsmen. He said when he asked the first guardsman how many rounds he fired and in what direction, the guardsman told him he had fired twice "right down the gully." Simons said the guardsman was tired, angry, and disgusted.

Lt. Stevenson said he felt like he was "swallowing dry lumps" as he checked weapons. He said he saw tears in a number of the guardsmen's eyes and described their mood as "having a lump in your throat and, although your lips are wet, you swallow dry." Stevenson said he felt it was psychologically a bad time for a weapons check so he decided to just make mental notes of who fired and write down the information later. Fifteen guardsmen told him that they had fired into the air, but he never established how many rounds each man fired and made no physical check of weapons or ammunition.

An investigation officer was appointed one hour after the shooting. Guardsmen who fired were instructed to fill out an incident report.

After the shooting, some Guard officers, including Generals Del Corso and Canterbury, said that the guardsmen were responding to a sniper shot. The FBI conducted an extensive investigation for evidence of a sniper, including a search of the Blanket Hill area with a metal detector in an attempt to find non-military bullets. Nothing was found to indicate that anyone other than a guardsman discharged a firearm during the incident. The Ohio State Highway Patrol investigation found no evidence to conclusively support the presence of sniper fire or shooting from the crowd. General Del Corso testified on behalf of the Guard: "We never identified a sniper as such, as defined in the military."

The activities of two persons at the scene may have given rise to the belief that a sniper was present.

Terry Norman, a free-lance photographer, was taking pictures of the demonstration and was seen with a pistol after the Guard fired. Several civilians chased him from Taylor Hall into the Guard line, where he surrendered a .38 caliber revolver. The gun was immediately examined by a campus policeman who found that it had not been fired.

Jerome P. Stoklas, a photographer for the campus newspaper, the Daily Kent Stater, was taking pictures of the demonstration from the roof of Taylor Hall with a camera equipped with a telephoto lens. Most of the camera, lens, and tripod were painted black and might have given the impression from a distance that Stoklas had a rifle. Stoklas had no firearm.

Dr. Joseph W. Ewing, an Akron plastic surgeon who has both military and civilian experience treating gunshot wounds, was called to St. Thomas Hospital in Akron at about 3:00 P.M. to examine the wound of Donald S. Mackenzie. Dr. Ewing was surprised to see that the bullet had gone completely through Mackenzie's neck and cheek without doing extensive damage. The bullet had entered approximately one inch left of the spinal column, making a small entrance wound, then had shattered part of the jawbone and exited through the left cheek, leaving a wound the approximate size of a five-cent piece.

Dr. Ewing told FBI agents he believed the wound could not have been made by an M-1 rifle or a .45 caliber pistol because either of these would have caused more extensive damage to Mackenzie's neck and face.

A Commission investigator showed photographs of Mackenzie's wound to Lt. Col. Norman Rich, an Army doctor at Walter Reed Army Medical Center in Washington, and to two physicians on his staff. All three physicians agreed with Dr. Ewing's conclusions.

The Walter Reed physicians also indicated their belief that the bullet which struck Mackenzie was not a ricochet or a deflected round, since it still had enough velocity to pierce his neck and cheek. They stated, however, that the velocity of a .30 caliber M-1 bullet could have been considerably reduced if the ammunition were defective. They concluded that the wound was more likely caused by a smaller caliber weapon, possibly a carbine.

General Canterbury said he did not believe that any of the guardsmen on Blanket Hill were carrying any long-barreled weapons other than M-1 rifles, M-79 grenade launchers, and the single shotgun.

A Commission investigator showed photographs of Mackenzie's wound and hospital records on his case to Dr. Milton Helpern, chief medical examiner of the city of New York. Dr. Helpern was told that MacKenzie had been located 245 to 250 yards from the position of men known to have fired .30 caliber M-1 rifles and .45 caliber pistols. Dr. Helpern said the wound definitely could have been caused by .30 caliber ammunition, and that he could not rule out that it had been caused by .45 caliber ammunition.

Helpern said that, in his opinion, the entry wound in Mackenzie's neck and the exit wound in his check indicated that the bullet struck him on a direct line of fire without deflection or ricochet. He said the bullet had travelled a great distance and that it definitely was not a close-range shot.

Dr. Helpern said that in view of the many variables of gunshot wounds he would like to see photographs of the other casualties in order to verify his opinion. He was shown the photographs of other victims, which he felt confirmed his initial judgment.

Mackenzie himself told a Commission investigator he believes he was shot by the Guard. He said he heard several shots and ran several steps before he was hit, and then heard shots after he was wounded.

The bullet that wounded Mackenzie was not recovered. No fragments from it were found in his jaw. He was wounded at the same time that the guardsmen fired, and the trajectory of the bullet which wounded him is in the line of fire from Blanket Hill. Since Mackenzie had time to turn and run after the first shot, he plainly was not hit by that initial shot. Listeners who said they distinctly heard a first shot said the Guards volley immediately followed it. To conclude that Mackenzie was struck by a sniper's bullet, unless a sniper stood between him and the Guard, would indicate that a sniper fired while the Guard fired and from behind and above them, missed them, and struck Mackenzie. There is no convincing evidence that this happened. And no guardsman who fired indicates he fired in the direction of a sniper.

Generals Del Corso and Canterbury stated that the guardsmen were well-trained in riot procedures and were seasoned veterans of previous civil disorders. Ohio guardsmen receive the same basic training as regular Army recruits, and 16 hours of riot training each year they remain in the Guard. Of the 28 men who admit firing, 22 had seen action in previous Ohio disorders.

Ohio Guard procedures require that a portion of the riot training manual be read verbatim to each guardsman at the outset of civil disorder duty. Included in this reading is the following:

ANNEX F (PRE-EMPLOYMENT BRIEFING) TO OPLAN 2 (AID TO CIVIL AUTHORITIES)

RULES OF ENGAGEMENT: In any action that you are required to take, use only the minimum force necessary. When the Riot Act has been read within hearing, it is unlawful for any group of three or more people to remain unlawfully or riotously assembled and you may use necessary and proper means to disperse or apprehend them. Keeping groups from assembling prevents crowds which may become unruly and take mob action. Your use of force should be in the sequence listed below:

a. Issue a military request to disperse.
  (1) Insure that an avenue of dispersal is available.
  (2) Allow ample time for them to obey the order.
  (3) Remain in area for sufficient time to prevent re-assembly.
b. Riot formations—show of force. Instructions in a. (1) (2) (3) above apply.
c. Simple physical force, if feasible.
d. Rifle butt and bayonet: If people do not respond to request, direction and order, and if simple physical force is not feasible, you have the rifle butt and bayonet which may be used in that order, using only such force as is necessary.
e. Chemicals. If people fail to respond to requests or orders, and riot formation and rifle butts or bayonets prove ineffective, chemicals (baseball grenades or jumping grenades) will be used on order when available. When large demands for chemicals are required, a chemical squad will be dispatched to assist you upon request.
f. Weapons. When all other means have failed or chemicals are not readily available, you are armed with the rifle and have been issued live ammunition. The following rules apply in the use of firearms:
  (1) Rifles will be carried with a round in the chamber in the safe position. Exercise care and be safety-minded at all times.
  (2) Indiscriminate firing of weapons is forbidden. Only single aimed shots at confirmed targets will be employed. Potential targets are:
    (a) Sniper—(Determined by his firing upon, or in the direction of friendly forces or civilians) will be fired upon when clearly observed and it is determined that an attempt to apprehend would be hazardous or other means of neutralization are impractical. . . .
    (c) Other. In any instance where human life is endangered by the forcible, violent actions of a rioter, or when rioters to whom the Riot Act has been read cannot be dispersed by any other reasonable means, then shooting is justified.

SUMMARY:

. . .

b. If there is absolute or apparent necessity and all other means of preventing the crimes of murder (such as sniper fire), robbery, burglary, rape or arson (fire bombing of inhabited building or structure) have been exhausted, then life may be taken to prevent these forcible and atrocious crimes.

c. When the Riot Act has been read within hearing and you are engaged in dispersing or apprehending rioters, using necessary and proper means, then you are declared by Ohio Statute (RC 3761.15) to be guiltless if any of the persons unlawfully or violently assembled is killed, maimed or otherwise injured in consequence of resisting. . . .

With specific reference to the discharge of weapons another Ohio Guard training manual states:

I will fire when required to save my life or when returning fire.

A sniper being an individual who fires a small caliber weapon from a concealed location represents a dangerous adversary to civilians and Guardsmen alike.

The following is a recommended method of eliminating or capturing a sniper: On coming under fire, the patrol take cover immediately. No fire is returned unless the sniper's location is definitely pinpointed, in which case, single aimed shots are fired as necessary.

Precisely how much of this training material was read to or discussed with the 28 men who acknowledge firing on May 4 is not known. Although General Canterbury speculated that the first shot may have touched off a chain reaction, he told a Commission investigator that the men who fired did not do so in panic.

During its investigation, the FBI collected rocks from the Blanket Hill area and the football practice field. Rocks collected by the National Guard and the Kent State Police Department were also turned over to the FBI. The FBI laboratory reported the gross weight of all of the rocks to be approximately 175 pounds and the number of rocks to be about 340. The rocks ranged in weight up to seven and one-half pounds. FBI agents collected ten pounds of rocks from the Blanket Hill area. The National Guard and the Kent State police also collected rocks, but it is not known how many of them came from the hill. Also collected from the areas where the Guard marched were a whole brick, two pieces of brick, five broken pieces of tile, a Vaseline jar containing rocks, a 2-by-2 stick 22 inches long, and a tree limb two and one-half inches in diameter and 20 inches long.

It is not known how many of these rocks and other objects were thrown and how many hit guardsmen.

At the time of the shooting Kent State President White was at a luncheon meeting at a restaurant one mile from the campus. His assistant, Ronald S. Beer, was called to the telephone and told about it.

The group returned immediately to the campus and White ordered the university closed for the rest of the week.

The Portage County Prosecutor Ronald J. Kane superseded White's directive. Kane heard about the shooting over the radio in his office and immediately attempted to telephone Governor Rhodes to tell him he intended to seek an injunction to close the university indefinitely.

Unable to reach Rhodes immediately, Kane told an assistant to begin preparing the appropriate papers. When Kane reached Rhodes about 3:00 P.M., Rhodes told him to confer with John McElroy, the governor's chief assistant. When McElroy questioned Kane's authority to close the school, Kane said he would worry about the legalities later. Rhodes asked Kane to delay for one hour. When Kane did not hear further from Rhodes, he obtained an injunction in late afternoon from Common Pleas Court Judge Albert S. Caris.

Under this injunction, the university was closed the day of the shooting and remained shut down for more than five weeks. It did not reopen until the beginning of summer school on June 13, 1970. During this period, the university improvised with correspondence courses and classes held in the homes of faculty and in churches.

On the day after the shooting, May 5, McElroy drafted a proclamation keyed to Governor Rhodes' April 29 proclamation which called out the National Guard for the Teamsters' strike. The new proclamation provided written authorization for the commitment of National Guard troops to the city of Kent.

Conclusion

Kent State was a national tragedy. It was not, however, a unique tragedy. Only the magnitude of the student disorder and the extent of student deaths and injuries set it apart from the occurrences on numerous other American campuses during the past few years. We must learn from the particular horror of Kent State and insure that it is never repeated.

The conduct of many students and nonstudent protestors at Kent State on the first four days of May 1970 was plainly intolerable. We have said in our report, and we repeat: Violence by students on or off the campus can never be justified by any grievance, philosophy, or political idea. There can be no sanctuary or immunity from prosecution on the campus. Criminal acts by students must be treated as such wherever they occur and whatever their purpose. Those who wreaked havoc on the town of Kent, those who burned the ROTC building, those who attacked and stoned National Guardsmen, and all those who urged them on and applauded their deeds share the responsibility for the deaths and injuries of May 4.

The widespread student opposition to the Cambodian action and their general resentment of the National Guardsmen's presence on the campus cannot justify the violent and irresponsible actions of many students during the long weekend.

The Cambodian invasion defined a watershed in the attitude of Kent students toward American policy in the Indochina war.

Kent State had experienced no major turmoil during the preceding year, and no disturbances comparable in scope to the events of May had ever occurred on the campus. Some students thought the Cambodian action was an unacceptable contradiction of the announced policy of gradual withdrawal from Vietnam, or that the action constituted invasion of a neutral country, or that it would prolong rather than shorten the war. Opposition to the war appears to have been the principal issue around which students rallied during the first two days of May.

Thereafter, the presence of the National Guard on campus was the focus of discontent. The Guard's presence appears to have been the main attraction and the main issue for most students who came to the May 4 rally. For students deeply opposed to the war, the Guard was a living symbol of the military system they distrusted. For other students the Guard was an outsider on their campus prohibiting all their rallies, even peaceful ones, ordering them about, and tear gassing them when they refused to obey.

The May 4 rally began as a peaceful assembly on the Commons— the traditional site of student assemblies. Even if the Guard had authority to prohibit a peaceful gathering—a question which is at least debatable—the decision to disperse the noon rally was a serious error. The timing and manner of the dispersal were disastrous. Many students were legitimately in the area as they went to and from class. The rally was held during the crowded noon-time luncheon period. The rally was peaceful, and there was no apparent impending violence. Only when the Guard attempted to disperse the rally did some students react violently.

Under these circumstances the Guard's decision to march through the crowd for hundreds of yards up and down a hill was highly questionable. In fact, the Guard never did disperse the crowd. The crowd simply swirled around them and reformed again after they had passed. The Guard found itself on a practice football field far removed from its supply base and running out of tear gas. Guardsmen had been subjected to harassment and assault, were hot and tired, and felt dangerously vulnerable by the time they returned to the top of Blanket Hill.

When they confronted the students, it was only too easy for a single shot to trigger a general fusillade.

Many students considered the Guard's march from the ROTC ruins across the Commons up Blanket Hill, down to the practice football field, and back to Blanket Hill as a kind of charade. Tear gas canisters were tossed back and forth to the cheers of the crowd, many of whom acted as if they were watching a game.

Lt. Alexander D. Stevenson, a platoon leader of Troop G, described the crowd in these words:

> At the time of the firing, the crowd was acting like this whole thing was a circus. The crowd must have thought that the National Guard was harmless. They were having fun with the Guard. The circus was in town.

The actions of some students were violent and criminal and those of some others were dangerous, reckless, and irresponsible. The indiscriminate firing of rifles into a crowd of students and the deaths that followed were unnecessary, unwarranted, and inexcusable.

The National Guardsmen on the Kent State campus were armed with loaded M-1 rifles, high velocity weapons with a horizontal range of almost two miles. As they confronted the students, all that stood between a guardsman and firing was the flick of a thumb on the safety mechanism, and the pull of an index finger on the trigger. When firing began, the toll taken by these lethal weapons was disastrous.

The Guard fired amidst great turmoil and confusion, engendered in part by their own activities. But the guardsmen should not have been able to kill so easily in the first place. The general issuance of loaded weapons to law enforcement officers engaged in controlling disorders is never justified except in the case of armed resistance that trained sniper teams are unable to handle. This was not the case at Kent State, yet each guardsman carried a loaded M-1 rifle.

This lesson is not new. The National Advisory Commission on Civil Disorders and the guidelines of the Department of the Army set it out explicitly.

No one would have died at Kent State if this lesson had been learned by the Ohio National Guard.

Even if the guardsmen faced danger, it was not a danger which called for lethal force. The 61 shots by 28 guardsmen certainly cannot be justified. Apparently no order to fire was given, and there was inadequate fire control discipline on Blanket Hill. The Kent State tragedy must surely mark the last time that loaded rifles are issued as a matter of course to guardsmen confronting student demonstrators.

Our entire report attempts to define the lessons of Kent State, lessons that the Guard, police, students, faculty, university administrators, government at all levels, and the American people must learn—and begin, at once, to act upon. We commend it to their attention.

Photos have been altered throughout to protect the identities of persons.

Above: Trash fire burning in middle of North Water Street in Kent before police arrived, Friday night, May 1.   Below: Students sitting in the inter-section of East Main and Lincoln Streets were subsequently dispersed with tear gas. Prentice Gate, the main entrance to the KSU campus, is visible at right.
(*Both photos:* Akron Beacon Journal)

Left: Aerial view of KSU campus. Large white building at upper right is Taylor Hall. In right center is the Prentice Hall parking lot. To the left of the parking lot is the football practice field. (**Douglas Moore**)

Below: Map of campus showing movement of the National Guard and locations of students killed or wounded. (Akron Beacon Journal)

Note the discrepancy in locations of students between this map and the one on the following page.

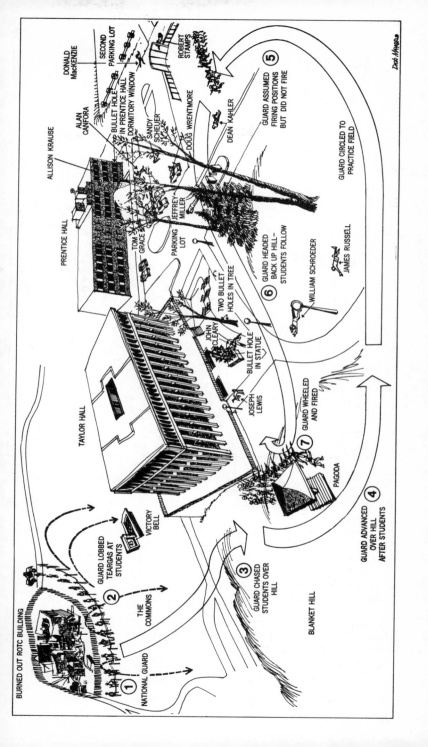

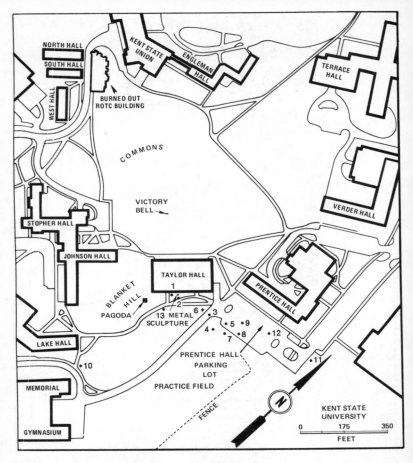

1. *Joseph Lewis, Jr.*
   wounded
2. *John R. Cleary*
   wounded
3. *Jeffrey Glenn Miller*
   deceased
4. *Dean R. Kahler*
   wounded
5. *Douglas A. Wrentmore*
   wounded
6. *Allen Michael Canfora*
   wounded
7. *Allison B. Krause*
   deceased
8. *William K. Schroeder*
   deceased
9. *Sandra Lee Scheuer*
   deceased
10. *James Dennis Russell*
    wounded
11. *Donald Scott MacKenzie*
    wounded
12. *Robert F. Stamps*
    wounded
13. *Thomas M. Grace*
    wounded

Map adapted with permission from the "Scranton Commission Report"
showing the locations of students killed or wounded.
(President's Commission on Campus Unrest)

Above: Students on the Commons taunt guardsmen. (Jack Davis)
Below: Students hurl tear gas canisters back at guardsmen. (Cleveland Plain Dealer)

Above: Guardsmen begin chasing students up Blanket Hill. (Howard E. Ruffner © 1970)

Opposite, above: After reaching the top of Blanket Hill, the guardsmen march down the other side toward the football practice field. Taylor Hall is the building at right. Also at right, partially obscured here by a tree, is the Pagoda. (Tim Olecki)

Opposite, below: The person in the center is throwing a missile of some type at the guardsmen, who are off to the right. The building in the background is Taylor Hall. (Akron Beacon Journal)

174

Opposite, above: Guardsmen on the football field kneel and point their weapons at the students in the parking lot, which is off to the left of this picture. This was apparently an admonitory gesture by the Guard, and these men did not fire at this point. (Harold C. Walker)

Opposite, below: Guardsmen leaving the football practice field with some students in the parking lot moving to follow them while the crowd on the hillside retreats. (Richard Harris, Jr. © *1970. All rights reserved.)*

Above: The Guard climbs the hill, at left in the background. Students stand and watch, while some follow the guardsmen. (Richard Harris, Jr. © *1970. All rights reserved.)*

The Guard arrives at the Pagoda. The second guardsman from the left, striding along, is Major Jones. The metal sculpture at right and the tree directly behind the Taylor Hall sign were pierced by bullets only a few seconds after this picture was taken.
(*John Paul Filo,* © Valley Daily News, *Tarentum, Pa.*)

Here the guardsmen are shooting. General Canterbury moves forward from extreme right of picture.
(*John A. Darnell,* Life Magazine © *Time, Inc.*)

On the patio of Taylor Hall, students scatter for cover as the shooting begins.
(Akron Beacon Journal)

Students in and around the Prentice Hall parking lot take cover during the shooting.
(*Douglas Moore*)

Above: Major Jones, wearing a soft cap and carrying a baton, has moved in front of the guardsmen as he orders them to cease firing. In the middle of the group of guardsmen is General Canterbury, distinguishable here by his white collar and dark tie. (John A. Darnell, Life Magazine, © Time, Inc.)

Opposite, above: Another view of the Guard immediately after the shooting, taken in front of Taylor Hall behind the metal sculpture. (John Paul Filo, © Valley Daily News, *Tarentum, Pa.*)

Opposite, below: The position of three of the students who were killed are pictured in this photograph of the Prentice Hall parking lot taken seconds after the shooting. At the extreme left are the bodies of William Schroeder and Sandra Lee Scheuer; at right center is Jeffrey Glenn Miller. The Pagoda and guardsmen beside it are visible at upper right. (Beverly K. Knowles)

A student being taken from the Prentice Hall parking lot to an ambulance after the shooting.
(*Howard E. Ruffner © 1970*)

Students looking at the Victory Bell, shortly after the shooting and before the campus was closed.
(Howard E. Ruffner © 1970)

Guardsmen patrolling the empty KSU campus which was closed indefinitely after the shooting.
(Wide World Photos)

Report of the Special State Grand Jury

On October 16, 1970, the Special State Grand Jury, its jurors drawn from Portage County, issued a "supplemental order" in addition to 25 secret indictments resulting from their one-month investigation. This supplemental report is presented below, except for the omission of procedural paragraphs at the beginning.

Heading the Grand Jury probe was Allen County Prosecutor Robert L. Balyeat, appointed by State Attorney General Paul W. Brown. Assisting Balyeat were Attorneys Seabury Ford and Perry Dickinson, both from Ravenna.

As reported in the *Akron Beacon Journal,* October 17, 1970, members of the Grand Jury were Robert R. Hastings (Foreman), insurance executive, Ravenna; Robert W. Brown, business machine service manager, Ravenna; Norman B. Hill, insurance agency owner, Ravenna; Elizabeth H. Heisa, school board secretary, Kent; Dallis Pigott, plant foreman, Kent; Lowell T. Davis, automobile parts employee, Kent; Anna R. Kaminsky, housewife, Kent; Carol Ann Balogh, hospital laboratory technician, Ravenna; Lewis B. Miller, factory worker, Garrettsville; James D. Deffenbaugh, automobile plant worker, Deerfield; Edward M. Gannon, farmer, Aurora; Thomas W. Yeager, factory worker, Windham; Malcolm P. Avery, plant employee, Mantua; Otha O. Drake, rubber worker, Rootstown; and Lewis G. Bacon, lumber company employee, Mogadore.

Report of the Special Grand Jury

TO THE HONORABLE Edwin W. Jones, Judge of the Court of Common Pleas, Portage County, Ohio.

The Special Grand Jury of the Court of Common Pleas of said County of the September term, A.D. 1970, hereby report to the Court that they have been in session 25 days, and herewith by their foreman present to the Court the Indictments found by said Jury.

We have carefully examined all such matters as have legitimately come to our notice and within our charge, having examined over 300 witnesses, and presented 30 true bills covering 25 defendants and 43 offenses considered by us. The business of this Special Grand Jury has been transacted in as expeditious a manner as possible.

As has already been reported here, this Special Grand Jury received testimony from more than 300 witnesses who have fairly represented every aspect, attitude, and point of view concerning the events which occurred in the city of Kent, Ohio and on the campus of Kent State University during the period from May 1, 1970, to May 4, 1970, inclusive. The persons called as witnesses, the order of their appearance, and the questions presented, clearly indicated an effort at complete impartiality with a full and complete disclosure of all available evidence. We are satisfied that each of these objectives was accomplished.

Many persons, some of whom claimed publicly to be in possession of pertinent information, and who were not subject to subpoena, were invited to testify. Some of those invited did appear, while others declined. All persons who requested to testify were permitted to do so.

In addition to the many witnesses summoned to testify, this Grand Jury viewed and otherwise received all physical evidence believed to have any probative value, including numerous audio tapes, photographs, motion picture films, and physical evidence recovered at the scene.

All requests for further information made by this Grand Jury have been complied with by the Special Counsel for the Attorney General as to the law applicable and the facts.

The Grand Jury has had available the independent investigative reports of the Federal Bureau of Investigation, Ohio Highway Patrol, Ohio Bureau of Criminal Identification and Investigation, and all other police agencies involved. Their reports and all pertinent information and evidence have been examined in detail. The Grand Jury expresses its appreciation to all investigative agencies for their cooperation.

In addition, the Grand Jury has received a substantial amount of additional information and evidence that was not available to the police agencies at the time of their investigations. Some facts were discovered subsequent to the investigation of other agencies.

This Grand Jury expresses its appreciation to Judge Edwin W. Jones for his leadership and guidance during our deliberations. We further commend the Court for its foresight in providing an atmosphere of judicial dignity within which our work could be accomplished. It is our sincere belief that the Court's order restricting publicity in no small measure provided this atmosphere. The Grand Jury wishes further to express its appreciation to the radio, T.V., and press media for following not only the letter, but the intent of the Court's order.

The Grand Jurors have determined numerous questions of fact relative to the issues presented. The Grand Jurors wish to stress the fact that our findings are entirely our own and no outside influences were exerted. In view of the many conflicting and contradictory accounts previously published concerning these events, we feel it appropriate to report those findings at this time. They are as follows:

I

The incidents originating on North Water Street in Kent, Ohio on Friday, May 1, 1970, and which spread to other parts of the downtown area and the University, constituted a riot.

We find that no provocation existed for the acts committed there and that many persons participating in this riot were not students, but were of a type who always welcome the opportunity to participate in the unjustified destruction of property.

The investigative techniques utilized by law enforcement agencies in connection with the suppression of the riotous conduct of May 1, 1970, were not adequate to permit the successful prosecution of many of the persons who participated. It is apparent that new methods and techniques designed to preserve the identity of future participants (rioters, etc.) must be made available to our law enforcement agencies. That those responsible for riots, etc. be held accountable, without exception, and to the maximum extent provided by law, is obvious.

II

We find that the rally on the Commons on Saturday, May 2, 1970, which resulted in the burning of the R.O.T.C. building, constituted a riot. There can never exist any justification or valid excuse for such an act. The burning of this building and destruction of its contents was a deliberate criminal act committed by students and non-students. Nor did the rioters stop with the burning of the R.O.T.C. building. They also set fire to the archery shed and moved from there to East Main Street on the front campus where they engaged in further acts of destruction and stoned the members of the National Guard as they entered Kent.

Arson is arson, whether committed on a college campus or elsewhere. The fact that some of the participants were college students changes nothing, except perhaps to further aggravate the seriousness of the offense.

It should also be said that the many hundreds of students who described themselves as merely "observers" or "cheerleaders" are not totally free of responsibility for what occurred there. It seems to us that many students are quick to say that "this is our campus," but slow to realize that this carries with it a responsibility to care for and protect that campus and the buildings situated there.

III

The Grand Jury finds from the evidence that the Kent State University Police Department, as presently constituted, is totally inadequate to perform the functions of a law enforcement agency. A clear example of this inadequacy was the shocking inability to protect the Kent City firemen who responded to the fire at the R.O.T.C. building on May 2nd. The fire was reported to the Kent Fire Department by a University Police dispatcher. One squad of Kent State University Police officers had mobilized in an area approximately three blocks from the R.O.T.C. building. They were readily available to lend the protection to which the firemen were entitled. That it was decided by those in command not to expose their officers to risk represents more than a question of judgment; it indicates a complete inability to respond in a manner expected of any police department. The persons who attacked the firemen numbered no more than 4 or 5. The total number of those persons who actually attempted to fire the building did not exceed ten or twelve. It is obvious that the burning of the R.O.T.C. building could have been prevented with the manpower then available. If the burning had been prevented it is reasonable to believe that the events which followed on May 3rd and 4th would not have occurred.

The inadequacy of the Kent State University Police Department was further demonstrated with its failure to respond to the events which occurred on Friday night, May 1, 1970, the early morning of Saturday, May 2nd and Sunday night, May 3rd. This is not intended to criticize any individual officer of that department. If the responsibility for providing adequate law enforcement on campus is to remain with an agency physically situated on that campus, the ultimate command, supervision, and control of that agency must be divested from the University administration and placed in the hands of professionally trained personnel.

IV

The Grand Jury finds that the events of Sunday, May 3, 1970, on campus and at the corner of Lincoln Street and East Main Street in Kent, Ohio, constituted a riot.

The avowed purpose of the leaders of this group was to march into the city of Kent in protest of, and in direct violation of the 8:00 P.M. curfew established by the mayor of Kent. As the students attempted to leave the campus, they were stopped at the intersection of Main and Lincoln Streets by the Ohio National Guard, Kent City Police Department, Ohio Highway Patrol and the Portage County Sheriff's Department. The protestors then sat down in the street and engaged in their usual obscenities, rock throwing, and other disorderly conduct. Had it not been for the combined efforts of the law enforcement agencies present, further extensive damage to persons and property would have resulted in the city of Kent that night. After their removal from the intersection of East Main and Lincoln Streets, the rioters were dispersed by tear gas and retreated to the dormitory complex known as Tri-Towers where some members of the mob continued to advocate further acts of violence and destruction.

V

The gathering on the Commons on May 4, 1970, was in violation of the directive of May 3rd issued by the University Vice President in charge of Student Affairs. We find that all the persons assembled were ordered to disperse on numerous occasions, but failed to do so. Those orders, given by a Kent State University policeman, caused a violent reaction and the gathering quickly degenerated into a riotous mob. It is obvious that if the order to disperse had been heeded, there would not have been the consequences of that fateful day. Those who acted as participants and agitators are guilty of deliberate, criminal conduct. Those who were present as cheerleaders and onlookers, while not liable for criminal acts, must morally assume a part of the responsibility for what occurred.

VI

We find that as of 5:28 P.M. on Saturday, May 2nd, the circumstances then present in the city of Kent, Ohio, necessitated the request for assistance of the National Guard.

The events which led to this request began with a telephone call at 12:47 A.M., May 2nd by Mayor LeRoy Satrom to the Governor's office to advise him of the riot and destruction which had taken place in Kent. This phone call resulted in the dispatching of an officer of the National Guard to assess the situation. As of Noon on Saturday, May 2nd, it had been determined by the Adjutant General that the situation did not require the presence of the Guard.

At 5:28 P.M. on Saturday, May 2nd, Mayor Satrom again called the office of the Governor and at this time formally requested the assistance of the National Guard. The factors which prompted Mayor Satrom to make this decision were:

1. Threats by students to downtown merchants of further damage if they did not post signs on the premises which protested the war in Vietnam and Cambodia.
2. Reports that two carloads of members of the Weathermen faction of the Students for a Democratic Society were in Kent and/or the University campus area.
3. Information that various weapons had been seen on the Kent State University campus.
4. Reports that the R.O.T.C. building, the Kent Post Office, and the Army Recruiting Office in Kent would be burned or otherwise destroyed.

In addition to receiving this information, Mayor Satrom had, by this time, been advised that substantial assistance would not be available from any local law enforcement agencies to assist in protecting the city and its residents.

We feel that it should be made clear that the Ohio National Guard was called solely for the purpose of assisting the civil authority. At no time during the period of May 1st through May 4th was martial law declared.

VII

It should be made clear that we do not condone all of the activities of the National Guard on the Kent State University campus on May 4, 1970. We find, however, that those members of the National Guard who were present on the hill adjacent to Taylor Hall on May 4, 1970, fired their weapons in the honest and sincere belief and under circumstances which would have logically caused them to believe that they would suffer serious bodily injury had they not done so. They are not, therefore, subject to criminal prosecution under the laws of this state for any death or injury resulting therefrom.

Fifty-eight Guardsmen were injured by rocks and other objects hurled at them as they moved across the "Commons" to Taylor Hall Hill and down to the practice football field, and were then forced to retreat. Whatever may have been in the minds of those who harassed and otherwise taunted the National Guard, it is clear that from the time the Guard reached the practice football field, they were on the defensive and had every reason to be concerned for their own welfare. Tear gas was admittedly ineffective because of wind direction and velocity and it was the belief of most of those Guardsmen present on the football practice field that their supply of tear gas had been exhausted. That it was later determined that one of ten grenadiers still had a small supply of tear gas remaining in no way changes this fact. The circumstances present at that time indicate that 74 men surrounded by several hundred hostile rioters were forced to retreat back up the hill toward Taylor Hall under a constant barrage of rocks and other flying objects, accompanied by a constant flow of obscenities and chants such as "KILL, KILL, KILL". Photographic evidence has established, beyond any doubt, that as the National Guardsmen approached the top of the hill adjacent to Taylor Hall, a large segment of the crowd surged up the hill, led by smaller groups of agitators approaching to within short distances of the rear ranks of the Guardsmen.

The testimony of the students and Guardsmen is clear that several members of the Guard were knocked to the ground or to their knees by the force of the objects thrown at them. Although some rioters claim that only a few rocks were thrown, the testimony of construction workers in the area has established that 200 bricks were taken from a nearby construction site. Various students were observed carrying rocks in sacks to the "rally"; others brought gas masks and other equipment from off campus in obvious anticipation of what was to happen. Rocks had been stockpiled in the immediate vicinity and cries of "GET THE ROCKS" were heard as the Guardsmen went onto the practice field. There was additional evidence that advance planning had occurred in connection with the "rally" held at Noon on May 4th.

It should be added, that although we fully understand and agree with the principle of law that words alone are never sufficient to justify the use of lethal force, the verbal abuse directed at the Guardsmen by the students during the period in question represented a level of obscenity and vulgarity which we have never before witnessed! The epithets directed at the Guardsmen and members of their families by male and female rioters alike would have been unbelieveable had they not been confirmed by the testimony from every quarter and by audio tapes made available to the Grand Jury. It is hard to accept the fact that the language of the gutter has become the common vernacular of many persons posing as students in search of a higher education.

The fact that we have found those Guardsmen who fired their weapons acted in self-defense is not an endorsement by us of the manner in which those in command of the National Guard reacted. To the contrary, we have concluded that the group of Guardsmen who were ordered to disperse the crowd on the Commons were placed in an untenable and dangerous position.

The Grand Jury also concludes that the weapons issued to the National Guardsmen are not appropriate in quelling campus disorders. Testimony presented to this Grand Jury reveals that the commanding officers of the National Guard are in agreement that the M-1 Rifle and other high powered weapons are not the type of weapons suited to such missions—except in those instances where required to return sniper fire. Unfortunately, however, under current procedures, no other weapons have been made available to the Guard by the Department of the Army. Non-lethal weapons more appropriate in connection with campus disorders should be made available to the National Guard in the future.

The Grand Jury takes note of some who have advocated that the Guard be committed to action without live ammunition. With this we cannot agree. Guardsmen should be furnished with weapons that will afford them the necessary protection under the existing conditions.

VIII

Among other persons sharing responsibility for the tragic consequences of May 4, 1970, there must be included the "23 concerned faculty of Kent State University" who composed and made available for distribution on May 3, 1970, the following document:

"The appearance of armed troops on the campus of Kent State University is an appalling sight. Occupation of the town and campus by National Guardsmen is testimony to the domination of irrationality in the policies of our government.

The President of the United States commits an illegal act of war and refers to his opposition as "bums." That students and faculty and, indeed, all thinking people reject his position is not only rational but patriotic. True, burning a building at Kent State University is no joke; we reject such tactics. Yet the burning of an *ROTC* building is no accident. We deplore this violence but we feel it must be viewed in the larger context of the daily burning of buildings and people by our government in Vietnam, Laos, and now Cambodia.

Leadership must set the example if it is to persuade. There is only one course to follow if the people of this country—young and old—are to be convinced of the good faith of their leaders: The war must stop. The vendetta against the Black Panthers must stop. The Constitutional rights of all must be defended against any challenge, even from the Department of Justice itself. If Mr. Nixon instead continues his bankrupt, illegal course, the Congress must be called upon to impeach him.

Here and now we repudiate the inflammatory inaccuracies expressed by Governor Rhodes in his press conference today. We urge him to remove the troops from our campus. No problem can be solved so long as the campus is under martial law.

We call upon our public authorities to use their high offices to bring about greater understanding of the issues involved in and contributing to the burning of the ROTC building at Kent State University on Saturday, rather than to exploit this incident in a manner that can only inflame the public and increase the confusion among the members of the University community."

Signed by 23 concerned faculty,
Kent State University, Sunday Afternoon,
May 3, 1970

Several hundred copies of this unusual document were distributed in the various dormitories situated on the Kent State University campus during the late afternoon and early evening of May 3, 1970. The offices and facilities of the Dean for the Faculty Council, known as the Ombudsman, were made available to those persons who participated in its preparation. If the purpose of the authors was simply to express their resentment to the presence of the National Guard on campus, their timing could not have been worse. If their purpose was to further inflame an already tense situation, then it surely must have enjoyed some measure of success. In either case, their action exhibited an irresponsible act clearly not in the best interests of Kent State University. Although the 23 persons referred to at the close of the statement did not actually affix their signatures to the document, they, together with one additional party, did leave their signatures with the Dean for the Faculty Council as evidence of their authorship and approval.

It should be pointed out that at least 60 faculty members were invited to the meeting, but a majority apparently elected not to be associated with the product that resulted.

The conduct of these faculty members is in sharp contrast to those of the faculty who, through their efforts on May 4th., restored order and prevented further rioting after the shooting.

IX

We find that the major responsibility for the incidents occurring on the Kent State University campus on May 2nd, 3rd, and 4th rests clearly with those persons who are charged with the administration of the University. To attempt to fix the sole blame for what happened during this period on the National Guard, the students or other participants would be inconceivable. The evidence presented to us has established that Kent State University was in such a state of disrepair, that it was totally incapable of reacting to the situation in any effective manner. We believe that it resulted from policies formulated and carried out by the University over a period of several years, the more obvious of which will be commented on here.

The administration at Kent State University has fostered an attitude of laxity, over-indulgence, and permissiveness with its students and faculty to the extent that it can no longer regulate the activities of either and is particularly vulnerable to any pressure applied from radical elements within the student body or faculty. One example of this can be clearly seen in the delegation of disciplinary authority under a student conduct code which has proven totally ineffective. There has been no evidence presented to us that would indicate that college students are able to properly dispose of criminal offenders within their own ranks any more than they are capable of devising their own curriculum, participating in the selection of faculty, or setting the standards for their admission to or dismissal from the University. Neither have we been convinced that the faculty is necessarily equipped to assume and successfully carry out responsibilities of a purely administrative character which for many years were considered to be totally outside the area of responsibility normally associated with the teaching faculty of our colleges and universities. In short, a segment of the student population and the faculty have demanded more and more control of the administrative functions of Kent State University. The administrative staff has constantly yielded to these demands to the extent that it no longer runs the University.

The student conduct code, as already indicated, has been a total failure. As a matter of policy, all criminal offenses uncovered by the University Police Department, except those which constitute felonies, were referred to judicial boards composed solely of students residing in the dormitory where the alleged offender resided. These students determined the guilt or innocence of the accused and prescribed the punishment. The end result has been, of course, that where any final disposition has been made at all it has consisted of recommended counseling or some other meaningless sanction.

Offenses for which suspension or dismissal from the University could be imposed were heard by the Student Faculty Judiciary Council. Membership consists of two faculty members, two students, and a fifth member who shall be a Dean of the defendant's college or a faculty member designated by him. A total of only 5 students were dismissed for non-academic reasons during the academic year 1969–70 out of a total enrollment of more than 21,000.

A second example of where the University has obviously contributed to the crisis it now faces is the over-emphasis which it has placed and allowed to be placed on the right to dissent. Although we fully recognize that the right of dissent is a basic freedom to be cherished and protected, we cannot agree that the role of the University should be to continually foster a climate in which dissent becomes the order of the day to the exclusion of all normal behavior and expression.

We receive the impression that there are some persons connected with the University who believe and openly advocate that one has a duty rather than a right to dissent from traditionally accepted behavior and institutions of government. This is evident [*sic*] by the administrative staff in providing a forum and available facilities for every "radical group" that comes along and the "speakers" that they bring to the campus. It has been the policy of Kent State University to routinely grant official recognition to every group that makes application. The few conditions that have been imposed are meaningless and we have been unable to find a single instance where recognition has been refused. This is the procedure by which the Students for a Democratic Society, Young Socialist Alliance, Red Guard, Student Religious Liberals, and other groups who advocate violence and disruption were granted recognition. Provisional recognition is automatic upon filing. During the period that is required to process the application, the organization is permitted the same use of the University facilities that it has when fully recognized. No distinction is made between ordinary student organizations whose objectives are related to legitimate activities on campus and the politically active organizations whose membership openly advocates revolution and anarchy. Once temporary or permanent recognition is granted the organization may sponsor speakers from off campus and have the use of University facilities and equipment for that purpose. It was in this manner that Jerry Rubin was brought to the campus in April, 1970, by the Student Religious Liberals. The inflammatory speech given by Mr. Rubin was so interspersed with vulgarity and obscenity that it could not be reported by the local news media.

A further example of what we consider an over-emphasis on dissent can be found in the classrooms of some members of the University faculty. The faculty members to whom we refer teach nothing but the negative side of our institutions of government and refuse to acknowledge that any positive good has resulted during the growth of our nation. They devote their entire class periods to urging their students to openly oppose our institutions of government even to the point where one student who dared to defend the American flag was ridiculed by his professor before his classmates.

We do not mean to suggest that these faculty members represent a majority of the faculty at Kent State University. To the contrary, we suspect that they form a small minority of the total faculty, but this does not mean that their presence should be ignored.

The most discouraging aspect of the University's role in the incidents which have been the subject of our investigation is that the administrative leadership has totally failed to benefit from past events. The same condescending attitude toward the small minority bent on disrupting the University that existed last May is still present. On Wednesday, October 7, 1970, the Youth International Party, more commonly known as the "YIPPIES," applied for and were granted permission from the University to use its auditorium. The request for use of the University facilities was granted in the customary routine manner with no apparent interest in the purpose of the gathering. The meeting was later billed as a "Yippie Open Smoker" and was attended by some 250 persons. The agenda consisted of several speakers who exhorted in the usual obscene rhetoric with the customary demands to free Bobby Seale, remove R.O.T.C. from campus, and to put an end to the Liquid Crystals Institute. In retrospect, no possible purpose could be attributed to the meeting except to disrupt the normal operation of the University.

On Sunday night, October 11, 1970, two appearances were scheduled at the Memorial Gymnasium for a rock music group known as the "Jefferson Airplane." During the second performance and while the "Airplane" were doing their musical numbers, color slides were projected onto a screen behind the group consisting of psychedelic colors, scenes of the Ohio National Guard on Kent State campus, and scenes of the shooting on May 4th complete with views of the bodies of the victims.

On October 12th the "YIPPIES" scheduled a second meeting at the Auditorium which was supposed in some manner to relate to the activities of this Grand Jury. Again, on October 14, 1970, the same "YIPPIE" group scheduled a Noon rally on the Commons. Neither of these events attracted more than a handful of spectators and this is to the credit of the student body. What disturbs us is that any such group of intellectual and social misfits should be afforded the opportunity to disrupt the affairs of a major university to the detriment of the vast majority of the students enrolled there.

Conclusion

The members of this Special Grand Jury find that all the conditions that led to the May tragedy still exist. It is apparent that an apathetic university community has allowed a vocal minority to seize control of the university campus. This will continue until such time as the citizens, university administration, faculty and students take a strong stand against the radical element bent on violence.

The time has come to detach from university society those who persist in violent behavior. Expel the trouble makers without fear or favor. Evict from the campus those persons bent on disorder.

This Grand Jury has in this report been critical of Kent State University, but let no one assume that we do not consider the University a valued part of our community. It is our hope that out of this chaos will emerge order and purpose. It is our belief that Kent State University has the capacity to become a greater university in the future.

Respectfully submitted,

October 16, 1970   (signed)   Robert R. Hastings
Foreman

There being no further business for said Special Grand Jury, they are recessed subject to the further order of the Court.

(signed)   Edwin W. Jones
Judge—Common Pleas Court

4

Aftermath

NEWS

After the memorial service of September 29, 1970, Kent State University settled into a fall quarter of tension, commitment, and suspense. As the campus nervously awaited the Grand Jury's decision, the local chapter of the Youth International Party tried to unite students in opposition to the war, ROTC, and the Grand Jury's anticipated activities. (A survey of KSU students taken in the spring reported 78% favored retaining ROTC; 55% favored giving academic credit for ROTC; 63% opposed Nixon's Cambodian decision; 47% favored immediate, complete withdrawal from Viet Nam; and 54% supported increased Vietnamization and gradual withdrawal.) The "Yippies" drew generally small attendance, even at the rally held at noon, October 16, about the same time as first reports of the Grand Jury's conclusions were being released.

The Grand Jury indicted 25 persons, including a sociology professor and the president of the Student Body, Craig Morgan. By the year's end, 22 of those indicted were arrested and charged. Portage County residents generally seemed to approve the action of the Grand Jury. (A survey reported in the *Akron Beacon Journal,* October 18, showed that 58% of Ohio high school students blamed dissidents rather than the National Guard for the tragedy at Kent.) A significant exception to the pattern was the response of the Kent Ministerial Association, which questioned the validity of the Jury's special report.

As for the University community, if it had not united around the extreme appeal of the "Yippies," it reacted quickly and almost in unison to the charges and assumptions contained in the special report. Within a few days, the Faculty Senate, the Student Body, the Graduate Student Council, and the KSU chapter of the American Association of University Professors all spoke out against some of the Grand Jury's conclusions. Professor Martin K. Nurmi, new chairman of the Faculty Senate, speaking on October 19 in support of a free university and of President White's leadership, said, "Our campus was thrown into a symbolic prominence by a fateful convergence of circumstances that cannot be explained away as simply as the Grand Jury in Ravenna would explain it."

When Craig Morgan, whose indictment was seen as symbolic harassment by some, called for a peaceful moratorium and rally on October 23, some 4,000 students and faculty gathered to hear speakers, among them liberal editor I. F. Stone, attack the Grand Jury, appeal for the empaneling of a federal grand jury, and call for the unified defense of the "Kent 25." Although the crowd was enthusiastic at this noon-hour rally, students generally attended classes, as did students around the country who had been invited to participate in the moratorium.

The witnesses and legal officers associated with the Grand Jury's investigation had been placed under legal constraint not to comment on the case. Despite this, Special Prosecutor Seabury H. Ford, on Saturday, October 24, was reported as having privately told a reporter that National Guardsmen "should have shot" all troublemakers at Kent in May. His infraction of the so-called "gag rule" was followed quickly by that of KSU Professor Glenn Frank, who within 24 hours deliberately took public issue not only with Ford but with the Grand Jury as well. While Republican party leaders in Portage County were disclaiming any connection between the party and the comments of Ford, a member of their Executive Committee, petitions were being circulated for Ford's resignation from the party position (*Kent-Ravenna Record-Courier,* October 26). Ford himself first attempted to retract, then ultimately acknowledged his remarks. On Monday, October 26, both Attorney Ford and Professor Frank pleaded guilty to contempt of court and were released on $500 recognizance bonds. On October 29, the *Record-Courier* reported a statement of Ohio Attorney General Paul W. Brown regarding the association of Special Prosecutor Ford with the Ohio National Guard in the 1920's: "I didn't know he had been a guardsman. I don't see that that makes any difference, but if I had known it, I would have avoided appointing him."

The legal aspects of the case assumed complex proportions during the fall, when among other developments, Attorney William Kunstler, defender of the "Chicago Seven," offered his aid to the indicted persons. On October 19, Kunstler told an audience of nearly 1,000 gathered in a one-time theater in downtown Kent that "I think the indictments are not defeats. They offer us an opportunity just as in Chicago. They indicted 25 people to clean the skirts of the National Guard. If a fight is going to be made, it might as well be made on the campus of Kent State." A few days later former United States Attorney General Ramsey Clark came to the assistance of Craig Morgan: "The moral and political issues involved in this case are so important that I am gratified that I am able to participate in Craig's defense." By this time the parents of Sandra Scheuer, Jeffrey Miller, and Allison Krause had all filed wrongful death suits. On October 29, in Cleveland, a judge of the Cuyahoga County Common Pleas Court dismissed a suit filed on behalf of Arthur Krause (Allison's father) on the grounds that the state could not be sued without the state's permission.

In late October and early November three suits were filed in a federal district court in Cleveland regarding the case. Two of them (one filed by 32 professors; the other by a combination of indicted students, an alumnus, and five clergymen) overlapped in asking the court to declare unconstitutional the Grand Jury's report, indictments, and certain parts of Ohio's campus riot law. Another, filed by the American Civil Liberties Union on behalf of two KSU students, requested the court to remove the "stay-silent" constraint on Grand Jury participants. (This suit was augmented 40 miles away in Ravenna by President White who filed a separate action in the Portage County Court to have the restraint removed.) Although the more sweeping suits were still pending at year's end, Federal District Court Judge Ben C. Green lifted the "stay-silent" order on November 3.

One of the more interesting legal questions arose in November about the question of whether the Grand Jury had used in its deliberations the Justice Department summary of the FBI findings and/or those findings themselves. On November 9, Chief Special Prosecutor Robert Balyeat said that the jurors never saw the Justice Department's summary; on November 10, Senator Stephen Young charged that the Jury was never shown the FBI report; and on November 11, Prosecutor Balyeat claimed, "We relied every day on the FBI report." Another index of the sensitivity regarding the FBI findings was the sharp exchange of letters in August (see below) between FBI Director J. Edgar Hoover and Editor John S. Knight, whose *Akron Beacon Journal* was to be honored in November by the Associated Press Managing Editors Association for "outstanding coverage" of the May events and their aftermath.

After the Grand Jury's report, two members of the Scranton Commission questioned the results. Police Chief James F. Ahern of New Haven said on October 17 that the Jury's complete exoneration of the National Guardsmen was "inconsistent with the facts" presented the Commission. Harvard Junior Fellow Joseph Rhodes, who had been criticized by Vice-President Agnew in June for prematurely deciding against the Guard, called the Jury a "kangaroo court" on November 1; and on November 29, he told a group in Boston that "there were a few Guardsmen who committed second degree murder. They went there with premeditation—meaning intending to kill students." The latter charge was rebutted by Ohio State Attorney General Brown the next day. On December 1, Rhodes said he regretted his remarks as "a severe mistake."

On November 9, speaking before a large audience at KSU's auditorium, Dr. Benjamin Spock, a leader in the anti-war movement, asked his audience to oppose the indictments. On November 17, well-known newscaster David Brinkley attacked the Jury's report as "absurd." And on December 12, speaking at Kent's commencement exercises, writer

James A. Michener called for understanding between youth and age. He mixed praise for the restraint shown in the Jury's low number of indictments with criticism for the Jury's report, and then went on record against the calling of a federal grand jury. He said that the only purpose of such a jury would be to place a greater share of blame on the Guard, which could not be prosecuted in Ohio courts and would receive only trivial penalties from a federal court. The resulting social disruption from this and from the additional indictments a federal grand jury would feel obligated to bring in on additional students and faculty, Michener felt, would be "a disaster."

The student unrest of the previous spring was bound to enter the national political elections in the fall of 1970. President Nixon and Vice-President Agnew, stumping for Republican congressional and gubernatorial candidates, set the tone by denouncing violence and, especially in the case of Agnew, implied that liberals (or "radic-libs") somehow approved of violence. Although Nixon claimed an ideological victory, many commentators agreed after the election that the administration's strategy was only minimally successful—despite the October 29th stoning of President Nixon's limousine by California protestors which had threatened to swing votes sympathetically to Republicans.

In Ohio, where the electorate presumably was highly sensitive to student activism, the two campaigns which perhaps most reflected the tension over student radicalism were the gubernatorial race between Republican Roger Cloud and Democrat John Gilligan, and the 14th Congressional District (Akron) contest between incumbent Republican William Ayres and Democrat John Seiberling. In both campaigns, the Republican candidates called for law and order and sought to link their liberal opponents to student radicalism. Both Gilligan and Seiberling won, however.

On November 9, Kent State University President Robert I. White, freed of the "stay-silent" order by Judge Green's decree, delivered his first public criticism of the Grand Jury report in a Washington speech (given in part below) and press conference. Later in the month, head football coach David Puddington resigned, giving as one of his reasons the school's atmosphere of negativism that had affected his team.

Until December, 1970, President Nixon had not publicly acknowledged the Scranton Commission's general report on the causes of campus unrest, which had emphasized the role of the President as a moral leader. Vice-President Agnew, on September 29, had stated that the Scranton report was "imprecise, contradictory, and equivocal" and would be taken as more "pablum" for the permissive. Although President Nixon was reportedly disturbed in October at the Commission's recommendations, he said at a press conference on December 10 that the report was "certainly not pablum." On December 12, Nixon sent a letter to Governor Scranton acknowledging his own role as a moral leader but placing the responsibility for campus disruption within academic communities themselves. KSU President White objected to the latter conclusion, but Governor Scranton expressed general satisfaction with Nixon's long-awaited analysis.

The National Guard also stayed in the news during the last months of 1970. A Guard chaplain in early November questioned the necessity of the Guard's shooting at Kent in May. At a more general level, Secretary of Defense Melvin Laird led the way in reassessing the training, weaponry, and tactics of National Guardsmen called out for riot control; and plans were afoot in Ohio to acquire non-lethal weapons for the Ohio Guard. On December 10, the *Akron Beacon Journal* reported that Guard Commander Del Corso had filed his annual report to the Governor in which the Kent affair was covered in one paragraph.

On Tuesday, December 8, Governor-Elect John Gilligan visited Kent and Kent State University to confer with townspeople, faculty, administrators, and students. Before a capacity crowd in the University Auditorium, Gilligan announced the establishment of a Volunteer Corps for Young Ohioans, and made a pledge: "What happened in Kent last May will never happen again if I, as Governor of Ohio, can help it. No university demonstration need ever be allowed to escalate into a general riot and there will be no more students shot by Ohio soldiers attempting to reestablish civil order."

From the *Akron Beacon Journal,* July 31, 1970.

Jury Wouldn't Indite Guard

By Lacy McCrary
Beacon Journal Columbus Bureau

COLUMBUS—[State] Attorney General Paul W. Brown said Thursday he did not believe a grand jury would indict any Ohio National Guardsmen in connection with the shooting deaths of four Kent State University students May 4.

"On evidence we have available—and we have as much as anyone —I don't see any evidence upon which a grand jury would indict any Guardsmen," Brown said. . . .

An exchange of letters between J. Edgar Hoover, Director of the Federal Bureau of Investigation, and John S. Knight, President and Editor of the *Akron Beacon Journal;* from the *Akron Beacon Journal,* August 7, 1970.

Dear Mr. Knight:

On July 23, 1970, your newspaper published an article which falsely stated that the FBI had drawn certain conclusions concerning the propriety of the activities of the Ohio National Guard in connection with the slayings of four Kent State University students.

I thought you would want to know that this inaccurate article— which has been quoted by news media across the Nation—has caused scores of knowledgeable and concerned citizens to write me inquiring whether the FBI has departed from its time-honored role of serving strictly as an investigative agency, and not as a prosecutor, jury or judge of the facts gathered by our Agents, such as you have strongly implied. These letters are being answered as follows:

"I can assure you any comments you may have seen in the news media to the effect that the FBI drew conclusions indicating guilt on the part of National Guardsmen in the shootings at Kent State University are absolutely and unequivocally false. The FBI is strictly an investigative agency and did not make any conclusions in this case and has not done so in any other case."

The results of our inquiries into the Kent State matter were furnished to the United States Department of Justice without recommendation or conclusion. Contrary to the misinformation contained in your newspaper, we have made no accusations nor expressed any opinions concerning prosecutive action to officials of the Federal Government or the State of Ohio.

In view of the wide attention which your distorted article has received, I must request that this factual refutation and clear statement of truth be accorded an equally prominent position in the pages of your newspaper.

Sincerely yours,

[Signature]
J. EDGAR HOOVER

Dear Mr. Hoover:

This will acknowledge your letter of July 31, 1970, in which you take exception to an article concerning an FBI report to the Department of Justice which appeared in the Beacon Journal on July 23, 1970.

We were in error in saying "The FBI has concluded . . ." rather than "the FBI has reported" the campus shooting by the Ohio National Guard which led to the deaths of four Kent State University students "was not necessary and not in order."

Our story accurately portrayed the facts of the FBI investigation as delivered to the Department of Justice. As our July 23 article pointed out, "a Justice Department spokesman told the Beacon Journal's Washington bureau that the document was a memorandum for Ohio officials prepared for the Justice Department's office of civil rights and signed by Jerris Leonard, chief of its civil rights division."

We are, of course, aware that the FBI does not draw conclusions nor make recommendations. We should have used "reported" rather than "concluded." I regret this mistake.

But an exercise in semantics must not be permitted to obscure the fact that our article was essentially correct and not "distorted," as you allege.

It is interesting that you have not contested the pertinent information contained in our story, but only the notation that the FBI made a "conclusion" about the tragedy at Kent State.

Furthermore, I am surprised at the hostile tone of your letter which is evidently intended to mollify public opinion.

There is no occasion to lecture the editor for, as you know, we are quite as dedicated to the quest for truth as the FBI.

Sincerely,

> [Signature]
> JOHN S. KNIGHT
> President and Editor

From the *Akron Beacon Journal,* October 7, 1970.

Ohio National Guard Getting Non-Lethal Weapons

COLUMBUS (OPS)—The Ohio National Guard hopes to have about $454,000 worth of non-lethal weapons to quell civil disturbances and equipment to protect troops within a month, Guard Commander Adj. Gen. Sylvester T. Del Corso said today.

"Some elements of the public are obviously unwilling to accept the use of troops armed with lethal weapons for riot control," Del Corso said. "And we are not going to send our men into these situations without some kind of weapons."

He referred to the recent report of the President's Commission on Campus Unrest which criticized the Guard's shooting at students at Kent State University May 4. Nine other students were wounded in the incident.

Del Corso said he plans to visit the National Guard bureau in Washington, D.C., within a week to request the Army to supply some of the equipment he considers necessary.

He plans to ask the State Emergency Controlling Board for funds needed to buy weapons and equipment which the Army does not regularly stock.

Riot shotguns—to fire light-weight birdshot—bayonets, M-79 grenade launchers to fire tear gas, flak vests and photographic equipment to record and identify rioters probably will be available from the Army, he said.

Face shields to protect men on riot duty and 37mm launchers to fire wooden blocks are among items to be purchased.

From the *Akron Beacon Journal,* October 16, 1970.

President Upset at Scranton

By Robert S. Boyd
Beacon Journal Washington Bureau

WASHINGTON—President Nixon is so irritated by the handling of recent commission reports on campus unrest and civil rights that he is likely to reject their key recommendations.

White House insiders say the President may refuse even to meet again with former Pennsylvania Gov. William Scranton to discuss his report on campus unrest.

The Scranton report was critical of Nixon's treatment of student problems, and Scranton personally accused the President of failing to provide "proper leadership."

The President's men feel Scranton's behavior was ungracious. It has given rise to considerable bad feeling in the White House, it was learned. . . .

The day the Scranton report was released, the President met in the morning with Scranton and the rest of his commission. He was photographed smiling and shaking hands with Scranton and the most militant member of the commission, Harvard graduate student Joseph Rhodes.

That afternoon the President took off for Europe in Air Force One, thinking all was well. As he roared over the Atlantic, the radio carried a report that Scranton, at a press conference, had said Nixon had not provided "the kind of leadership needed to bring about the kind of reconciliation that we're talking about."

Those aboard the President's plane said the reaction was instant and bitter.

The White House is inclined these days to sneer at the Scranton report as a routine, banal document. Even so, the report turned out better than earlier drafts which the President's men feel would have been disastrous.

An earlier version blamed campus unrest almost entirely on problems in society and not on the students themselves. It also gave what the White House feels was a dangerously rosy picture of the "youth culture."

Only the intervention of some hard-nosed social scientists, like philosopher Sidney Hook and sociologist Nathan Glazer, saved the document from what one White House source described as "hideous idiocy." . . .

From the *Kent-Ravenna Record-Courier,* October 20, 1970.

Craig's Father Says Son, Students Are Persecuted

COLUMBUS (UPI)—The father of indicted Kent State University student president Craig Morgan, charged by a special grand jury with second degree riot, believes the arrest is symbolic.

"If they (residents of Kent) think they can get back at the students by persecuting a student leader, then they are unlocking a lot of trouble for themselves," said Jack Morgan, a personnel technician with the state Department of Personnel. The Morgans live in Upper Arlington, suburb here.

"Look who comprised the grand jury—the people of Kent, and they just want to get the symbolic leaders of the students," Morgan said.

Craig Morgan, a senior Air Force ROTC student, was one of four persons arrested Monday in the first sweep toward rounding up the 25 persons the grand jury indicted on charges stemming from disorders at Kent State last May. The disorders culminated with the shooting of four students by National Guard troops May 4.

"I was shocked when I heard Craig was indicted," Morgan said. "He ran for student body president on a platform of non-violence and has stood for this.

"He spent his summer at Kent trying to calm things down and I feel that he deserves some of the credit for the calmness now on the campus," he added.

From the *Akron Beacon Journal,* October 24, 1970

Special KSU Prosecutor: "Should've Shot All Troublemakers"

By William Schmidt
Knight Newspapers Writer

KENT—One of the three special prosecutors of the Kent State Grand Jury said Friday that National Guardsmen on campus last May "should have shot all" trouble makers.

"There is no question that those boys (the Guardsmen) would have been killed up there—if they hadn't turned around and fired," said Seabury H. Ford, 68, a Ravenna lawyer and chairman of the Portage County Republican Party.

Ford said the incidents that led to the shooting deaths of four students on the Kent State campus last May 4 were "Communist inspired."

Ford is one of three appointed by Ohio Attorney General Paul W. Brown to act as prosecutors for the special 15-man Grand Jury impaneled Sept. 14 in Ravenna.

The Grand Jury report issued Oct. 16 exonerated Ohio National Guardsmen for the shooting deaths and indicted 25 persons, most of them students, for actions during four days of disruption on the Kent campus.

In addition to his role as prosecutor, Ford recently was appointed by the Ohio Board of Regents, the state's highest educational body, to preside at academic hearings for Kent State students arrested as a result of the Grand Jury.

Ford has the power to suspend students pending the outcome of criminal cases. He will not be involved in the prosecution of indicted students.

"I think the whole damn country is not going to quiet down until the police are ordered to shoot to kill," Ford said in an interview.

He said he agreed with what he called the "average" opinion of most people in the Kent-Ravenna area: "Why didn't the Guard shoot more of them?"

Ford said there have been numerous threats on his life. He keeps a .45 caliber pistol concealed under a manila folder on a table next to his desk.

Ford earlier warned two persons leaving his office—across the street from the Portage County Court House—to "be careful and hurry up" with their business at the Courthouse because of recent bomb threats.

"These kids have declared war on society. People had better wake up," said Ford.

He labels campus officials—including Kent State President Robert I. White—as "softies." Campuses across the country have "wilted" under pressure from subversive groups, he said.

But he praised Vice President Agnew for "speaking up."

Ford said he has strong personal feelings about the disorders at Kent, blaming it on a chain of subversive activities that began on the campus two years ago.

Evidence before the secret Grand Jury indicates that "Communists" were behind the activity, he said.

He labeled a number of groups on campus "subversive" and said they all "mouth the same Communist-inspired propaganda."

Ford speculated that money for such subversive groups comes to this country from "Russia through Cuba and the United Nations."

Pointing specifically to disorders on campus last May, Ford produced a copy of a message allegedly distributed on campus shortly before the shooting.

The message alleges that guns can be obtained from the Weatherman and says that a "tactical squad" of the SDS (Students For a Democratic Society) will lead an armed assault on the university's Commons.

The message also says that the group's slogan will be "Do or Die," and concludes by saying: "Some of these people will be wearing Army fatigues, will attempt to infiltrate N.G." (National Guard).

Referring specifically to the volley of National Guard bullets that killed four students and wounded nine others, Ford said:

"The point is, it stopped the riot—you can't argue with that. It just stopped it flat."

The Grand Jury's report clashed sharply with the President's Commission on Campus Unrest.

Whereas the commission divided blame between the students and Guardsmen and in fact recommended that Guardsmen not be sent into such situations with loaded rifles, the Grand Jury placed virtually all the blame on the students.

Ford said that "99 pct." of the people he had talked to supported the Grand Jury.

Of his experience as a prosecutor in the Grand Jury investigation, Ford said: "I wouldn't want to do it again. But I wouldn't have missed it for the world."

Ford is a long-time Ohio Republican. He was prosecutor of Portage County from 1945 to 1953.

From the *Akron Beacon Journal,* October 25, 1970.

Professor Breaks "Gag," Blasts Prosecutor Ford

By James Herzog

KENT—Purposely breaking a court order that he remain silent, a Kent State University professor Saturday said he is "ashamed of our system as it is working in Portage County right now."

Glenn W. Frank, emotionally taut after reading the remarks of a special state prosecutor, declared: "Someone must sacrifice himself."

Frank, 42, a geology professor, spoke out after Seabury H. Ford, one of three special prosecutors of the Kent State Grand Jury, said National Guardsmen on campus last May "should have shot all" troublemakers.

"I have spent 17 years teaching college students geology, a lust for life, and a respect for our laws and our system," Frank said.

"I speak now in contempt of court, in contempt of the naive and stupid conclusions of the special Grand Jury specifically as to their reasons for the May 4 disturbances, in contempt of Judge (Edwin) Jones for the gag rules placed on President White and in personal contempt for lawyer Ford for his lack of understanding after 68 years of what I believe is a wasted life."

Voicing this charge was a professor whose role has been one of hope during the Kent State investigations.

During the Scranton Commission hearings in August he said: "Nothing has gone beyond the possibility of return to order." He called himself "optimistic."

That is over.

"There is no middle any more," Frank said.

Since appearing before the special state Grand Jury that indicted 25 persons while exonerating the National Guard for the Kent State killings, Frank has respected a Portage County Common Pleas Court order by Judge Jones to remain silent. . . .

Frank said:

"Ford is a troublemaker. It is my feeling that the Republican Party must smash this student uprising in order to stay in power.

"Ford has made his statements in order to convince people who do not know the facts that he is a law-and-order man and will crack down on anyone who disagrees with the sytem he represents."

Frank continued: "I am a law-and-order man. I think anyone guilty of riot charges should be prosecuted.

"I was between the ROTC building and the rioting individuals (on May 2), and I know that some people deserve to be prosecuted.

"However, that should not allow a judge, a jury or a prosecutor to make what I consider to be a farce out of justice for their own gain or to gain favor with the voters.

"Freedom of speech is bigger than Judge Jones. . . . I defy Judge Jones to arrest me for contempt of court because I cannot see a system I believe in and respect subverted by man."

The professor said: "I was told by a young black student that we did have a great system but that man corrupts it. I agree with this student, and I understand better now what he meant.

"I cannot live with a conscience that permits people to say they 'should have shot all' troublemakers."

Frank said he was not afraid of the consequences of breaking the gag imposed by Judge Jones: "I'm hoping something will happen. I love KSU and love the students in it and I can't see this happening."

From the *Daily Kent Stater,* October 27, 1970.

Religious Group Desires Federal Investigation

Ed. note—Meeting in joint session the Kent Ministerial Association and the Kent State Campus Ministries formulated and adopted the following public statement on the recent Grand Jury report on Oct. 23, 1970.

We of the Kent State Campus Ministries Office and the Kent Ministerial Association have read with concern the report of the Special State of Ohio Grand Jury.

We are not unaware of the deep apprehension which campus unrest and, in particular, the events of May 1–4 have created in the minds of many in the community of Kent and society at large.

However, as we see it, the main role of religion is twofold: to reconcile man to God; and man to man. We, as religious leaders of the Kent community, would be seriously negligent if we did not fulfill our duty of leadership in reconciliation, by speaking out at this time.

We consider the Grand Jury report to be an inadequate treatment of the events and eventual tragedy of May 1–4, 1970. There are three areas of inadequacy which especially concern us:

First, the report fails to take with sufficient seriousness the findings of the Scranton Commission which points to the wider responsibility for the events than simply the students, faculty and administration of Kent State University.

Our traditions endow us with a particular perspective which maintains that responsibility for human events is a corporately shared responsibility among all men and institutions in a given society.

Therefore it is our conviction that long prior to May 1 the social fabric of our nation was rent by violent forces to which all of us have contributed; which forces were expressed anew in the events of May.

Second, the report misunderstands university life by assuming a greater degree of administrative control over faculty and student life than is possible in a university dedicated to the spirit of free inquiry.

Indeed, we wish to express our confidence in Kent State University and the ability of its faculty, students and administration to continue their pursuit of education and service with distinction and skill.

Third, the Grand Jury's statement that "the administrative leadership has totally failed to benefit from past events" is both unfair and false.

The university administration has made significant changes in internal structuring, and in external communications.

In addition, there has been a marked increase in awareness and responsibility both on the part of the students and faculty as well as the residents of the community of Kent.

Further, we are deeply troubled at the infringement of freedom in the injunction imposed upon President White and student and faculty leaders to respond publicly to the publicly aired report.

Finally, in light of these inadequacies, we must add our voice to those who have requested a fuller explanation of these events through a Federal Grand Jury investigation.

From the *Kent-Ravenna Record-Courier,* November 3, 1970.

Jones' Gag Rule Lifted: Grand Jury Report Hit By Federal Judge

A federal judge today lifted a ban on critical comment of a special grand jury report which investigated the spring disturbances at Kent State University and said "public officials may not wield an axe when a scalpel is required."

U.S. District Court Judge Ben C. Green issued the order in Cleveland on a suit filed by the American Civil Liberties Union of Ohio.

The special grand jury indicted 25 persons and said Ohio National Guardsmen fired in "self defense" when four students were shot to death May 4. The Portage County Common Pleas Court then imposed a ban prohibiting critical comment of the report.

"It is in this court's opinion that when the rules on grand jury secrecy are taken into conjunction with the basic law on the right of free speech," Green said, "the injunction restraining all grand jury witnesses from speaking out with reference to the comments of the special grand jury must fall as being overly broad."

Green indicated the special grand jury may have overstepped its boundaries by certain criticisms contained in the report.

The grand jury report "goes far beyond consideration of the offense on which the indictments are based," he said.

"It considers the conduct of not only those charged with violations of the law, but also makes a critical report of the actions and conduct of officials of Kent State, the Ohio National Guard and others caught up in the events which transpired at the university," he said.

"It condemns the conduct of the university officials and certain professors and students thereof, and seriously draws into question the very delicate matter of academic freedom," Green said.

The Portage County Common Pleas Court said only the approximately 300 grand jury witnesses are affected by the order.

"The difficulty with this argument is that the order prevents not only the 300 from speaking, but the rest of the world from hearing," said Green.

"The events which occurred at Kent State in the spring are a matter of national, social, political and moral concern and debate," he said.

The first reaction came from Ronald Beer, assistant to Kent State University President Robert I. White.

"Certainly the grand jury could not have had all the information and drawn the conclusion they did on the administration of this university," said Beer. "It would appear that they did not even make an honest effort to find out all the facts." . . .

From the *Akron Beacon Journal,* November 4, 1970.

Chaplain Says Guard Wrong

CLEVELAND (AP)—The chaplain of the National Guard unit involved in the Kent State University shootings in May says he disagrees with state guard policies and believes guardsmen should not have fired their weapons at students.

"I disagree with the guard policy of having troops load and lock weapons when going into these things, rather than loading and locking on the command of an officer," Maj. John W. Simons, chaplain of the 107th Armored Cavalry Regiment, Ohio National Guard, said Tuesday.

In an earlier interview with CBS News correspondent Robert Schakne, Mr. Simons said he did not believe the men should have fired at the students May 4. . . .

"I disagree with some of the tactical actions of Brig. Gen. Canterbury who was on the scene," he said. "We didn't have enough men and the shotguns didn't arrive until after the event." . . .

The minister is the son of a retired Army colonel and was a former military policeman. He said he has been in the guard for eight years. Two of his brothers and a brother-in-law also are in the ministry, he said. Mr. Simons is minister of Grace Episcopal Church in suburban Willoughby.

"I think," the minister said in the CBS interview, "the initial mistake was made at the state level with the general and the governor, who apparently feel that every campus disorder is another Normandy invasion.

"And, secondly, I think that we did not have men in enough numbers or the equipment to control that situation at noon on that day. Had we waited until, for instance, the shotguns arrived and reserves arrived from Ravenna, I think we could have done a better job. I think we could have done the job without bloodshed."

The minister added that he did not believe the guard unit to be a controlled, disciplined military unit.

"Some men were feeling threatened; others angry—up-tight—about what was going on, and confused," he said.

"They went too far away from the main troops," the minister said of the isolated guard unit. "They were caught in a box in which they felt trapped." . . .

Excerpt from President Robert I. White's Washington Speech,
November 9, 1970.

. . . Every one of the charges brought against us by the local Grand Jury has been made generally over the nation. However, every large-scale study—from the President's Commission on Campus Unrest to that by a segment of the republican congressional delegation—has pointed to factors far beyond any control of the university.

We know full well that the Grand Jury report was well received among the general public. On many occasions I have commented on the distressing polarization of views with regard to our, or any university, and the almost hopeless task of anyone who attempts to hold a balance against the rash extremists on either side.

In the Grand Jury's analysis, I see a prime example of a brewing national disaster.

In my opinion the Grand Jury report is inaccurate, disregarded clear evidence and, if pursued in all its nuances, would eventually destroy not only Kent State but all major universities in America.

In their essay report, Grand Jurors charged that the major responsibility for the May tragedy rested on the administration. More particularly, they noted what they called "general permissiveness" reflected in the nature of speakers, inability to control "radical elements," too much shared responsibility with the faculty, ineffectiveness of the student conduct code, tolerance of rallies, and overemphasis on dissent.

Throughout the pages of the Grand Jury report my colleagues and I are severally criticized. But directions of the findings transcend the Kent State administration. The charges are applicable to all higher education. In fact, the constitutional safeguards of American democracy are themselves under fire. Our judgments must not be parochial. We must view the policies of Kent State as they are intended to reflect the purpose and mission of all education and as a reflection of the democratic structure of our society.

Dissent and demonstration over the social and political problems which plague our nation are not unique to the campus of Kent State University. The angry voice of dissent can be heard both on and off the campus and in the cities both large and small. But dissent in a democratic society does pose unique problems.

Universities have traditionally advocated the free and full expression of varying views and are committed to the concept of true academic freedom which in the unanimous view of our faculty senate includes academic responsibility. Because of this commitment to the full exercise of free thought and discussion, the university is particularly vulnerable to exploitation by the radical or an extreme.

The balance between the right of free speech and peaceful dissent is a delicate one. The right to dissent is not the right to destroy. The academic community is not to be considered a sanctuary for those who wish to disobey the laws. We hold no brief for law breakers or for disruptors. But neither is the academic community a place where ideas —no matter how offensive—are to be suppressed. The constitutional safeguards of the Bill of Rights and, in particular, the first amendment's rights of free speech, press and assembly are worthy of the utmost protection.

The comments in the Grand Jury report about campus speakers are judicially naive as well as fundamentally unworkable and ultimately undesirable. In a real sense the report leads into a censorship of points of view going quite beyond constitutional limits.

There has been and is a grotesque generalization of all of today's young people. We must be quite careful not to tar all students with the same brush.

We recognize the satanic alliance between the extremes of the left and extremes of the right in an assault upon the free and independent university. The effect has been growing polarization.

Society in general, with its courts and numerous law enforcement agencies, faces serious challenges from those who would protest alleged injustices. Despite the legal mechanism and personnel available, no happy solutions have been found. I would suggest that the solutions are even more difficult in the university setting. By the nature of their mission universities are without jails, without elaborate legal and judicial systems and are without large forces of security and police personnel.

This is not to say that universities are helpless or that their administrative and judicial procedures are not in need of review and repair. I simply point out that the problems are difficult and complex.

The administrative programs of Kent State University have undergone extensive review since last May. Since then the administrative structure has been altered, the security forces have been strengthened and better trained, the faculty have reviewed their role and responsibilities within the institution, and students have made their commitment to non-violence real and meaningful. The very numerous changes were generally well publicized and that all were not visibly apparent is by design.

Before closing, I want to make clear my belief that the panel of citizens who served in the difficult role of Grand Jurors made every effort to review testimony, to study evidence, and to report honestly their findings. At the same time, we must recognize that their general report reflects a frightening misunderstanding of the role and mission of higher education.

We are dedicated to the preservation of a free and open society. We must remain so dedicated if our democracy is to survive.

From *CBS Evening News with Walter Cronkite,* November 9, 1970.

CRONKITE: Ike Pappas, who covered the violence at Kent State last spring, returned to the campus this fall to examine the mood and the aftermath of the tragedy, and here is his report.

PAPPAS: Students took an economics test on the lawn outside of Franklin Hall last week, not because this was a particularly balmy fall day, but because of what has become a common occurrence on the Kent State campus—a bomb scare.

While it is apparent that someone is attempting to stir up trouble, none has developed on the Kent State campus. Generally students have refrained from demonstrations and the like, hoping to avoid a repetition of the horror of last spring, fearing that the next time there is real trouble at Kent State, the university will close forever.

"Keep Kent Open" stickers have been appearing everywhere in recent weeks, even on the lapel of university President Robert I. White. The stickers, designed and paid for by students, symbolize what appears to be a spontaneous movement that has taken hold here among the mass of students, a movement to discourage demonstrations.

WHITE: I don't know—who dreamed this up.

STUDENT: We were just sitting around and like it was a weekend before, you know, everything was supposed to happen, and like, there was just—one of my roommates and I, we just felt like, you know, we were sick of going to school every day underneath the threat of being bombed, you know, having a riot or something happening down here. We just didn't think like we had to live that kind of life.

PAPPAS: The closest thing to a mass demonstration took place in mid-October when Civil Liberties Action Day was staged.

FIRST SPEAKER: What Nixon and Rhodes are attempting to do after murdering students on this campus is to whitewash what they have done, to try to turn the victims into the criminals.

PAPPAS: But only some 2,000 of the 21,000 students that attend Kent State showed up at the meeting, called to protest a special state grand jury report that placed all of the blame for the Kent State tragedy on the university administration and students and absolved National Guardsmen. Most students elected to stay in class instead, and the attempt to make Kent State the rallying point for another round of campus demonstrations did not succeed.

STUDENT: If this university closes, then I'm out, you know, I'm out in the cold. You know, I may not be able to get another university. I'm a junior now and I got one more year to finish. I'd like to finish first, because I think I can help better with an education than without an education.

STUDENT: I feel that my civil liberties and my rights are to attend my classes and get an education, and some day, when I really have it together, I can go out and maybe do something permanent.

PAPPAS: Campus activists feel that students are as involved as ever, yet their protest is taking other forms; hence, a lack of interest in demonstrations. Robert Stamps was one of those wounded last May by National Guardsmen.

STAMPS: There was a time when the people who were bent on violence could get enough support to do what they want. But people around here have seen what violence can do and they don't want any more of it, and that's why, even if people—if people are bent on destruction they're going to have to do it all by themselves, because they're not going to get any help, and—and even if some people find out around here that someone's trying to blow up a building, then they're going to be against it, and so, you know, you're not going to see a situation where they're going to be spectators to violence.

PAPPAS: There seems to be a coming together now of the university family. Recently, Dr. Kenneth W. Clement and other members of the Board of Trustees gave President White a vote of confidence.

CLEMENT: I believe that the mobilization of support among the Board of Trustees, the community at large and the university community is sufficient that we will see not only a Kent State that stays open, but a Kent State that continues to serve the purpose that a great university should.

PAPPAS: Many people here have adopted a so far, so good kind of attitude, yet there is concern for the future and the question remains: will the restraint of a mass of students be enough to deter or discourage those that would bring violence back to this campus, and will that restraint indeed be enough to keep Kent open?

Ike Pappas, CBS NEWS, at Kent, Ohio.

From the *Akron Beacon Journal*, November 10, 1970.

Kent State Jury Never Saw Justice Department Report

By Jeff Sallot

. . . The chief special prosecutor for the Grand Jury probe, Robert Balyeat, said Monday the 15 jurors never saw a Justice Department report which said there is reason to believe Guardsmen fabricated the self-defense story.

In addition, a Guard captain who stood among his men as they fired was never called to testify.

The officer, Capt. Raymond Srp of G Troop, 107th Armored Cavalry, said his life wasn't in danger at the time of the shooting.

Srp and several unarmed guardsmen, according to the Justice Department memorandum, told the FBI "the lives of the members of the Guard were not in danger and that it was not a shooting situation."

During a Knight Newspaper investigation of the incident last May, Srp told the Beacon Journal, "I didn't feel threatened and I was in the center of it."

Srp's lawyer, C. D. Lambros, confirmed today the officer wasn't called to testify before the state Grand Jury that convened here Sept. 14.

If Srp had testified, his statement to the FBI would have run counter to testimony presented by men under his command who reportedly told jurors they feared for their lives when they fired.

Srp has been named as a defendant in a lawsuit filed by the parents of one of the slain students and the officer now declines to talk with newsmen.

But Lambros said Srp's statement to the FBI included only Srp's own assessment of the May 4 situation.

The Justice Department memorandum, a summary based on the investigation by the FBI, said, "We have some reason to believe that the claim by National Guardsmen that their lives were endangered by the students was fabricated subsequent to the event.

"The apparent volunteering by some Guardsmen of the fact that their lives were not in danger gives rise to some suspicions. One usually does not mention what did not occur."

Special Prosecutor Balyeat discounted the Justice Department summary, saying the Grand Jury depended on "first-hand evidence" presented orally by witnesses.

"We would not normally present to the Grand Jury conclusions reached by another investigative body such as the Justice Department," Balyeat said.

Balyeat said the Grand Jury used the investigative reports by the FBI, the Ohio Highway Patrol and other agencies "as guides" in determining who would testify.

At a press conference immediately after the Grand Jury released its report, Balyeat, queried about the FBI report, said:

"We had all evidence that the Scranton Commission had."

The Grand Jury report makes no mention of the jurors seeing the Justice Department summary of the FBI investigation, but it does thank the FBI, the Ohio Highway Patrol, the Ohio Bureau of Criminal Investigation and other police agencies for making available their investigative reports.

"Their reports and all pertinent information and evidence have been examined in detail," the Grand Jury's report said.

Jury Foreman Robert Hastings, a Ravenna insuranceman, said Monday, "We had access to the FBI report."

Asked about the Justice Department memorandum, Hastings said, "That was part of it. It was the last report."

Did the jurors see the Justice Department summary?

Hastings said, "I am not free to say what we did or didn't see. That's part of our oath of secrecy. Contact Balyeat."

Monday, Balyeat declined to comment on what specific testimony was heard or the omission of Capt. Srp from the witness list.

Others who did testify, however, told the Beacon Journal that the Grand Jury ignored points which several witnesses felt were important to an investigation of the KSU disorders.

A student government leader, Bruce King of Euclid, said that in his questioning session the prosecutors didn't ask him about the May 4 shooting incident which he witnessed.

King said that although he was in a position to see what happened, the prosecutors instead pressed him for information about a leaflet issued May 3 and signed by "23 Concerned Faculty."

The leaflet, which was distributed by King and others, condemned the burning of the campus ROTC building, but also called for the removal of National Guardsmen from campus.

The Jury's report tagged the leaflet as "irresponsible" and said it contributed to campus tensions.

The report said that Prof. Harold Kitner, dean for faculty counsel, lent his office and facilities to the authors of the leaflet.

Kitner denies the charge, saying the report was inaccurate by stating the leaflet was authored in his office.

He said the jury distorted and misrepresented his testimony concerning the meeting and "choose to ignore facts."

"The Grand Jury report stated that my office and facilities were used to prepare the document. This is not even technically true. The group met in an empty classroom and I do not know where the questioned document was prepared," Kitner said.

Kitner said his only connection with the leaflet was that he agreed "to serve as a repository for the signatures with one stipulation, that the list would be available to anyone who wanted to look at it."

The Grand Jury, according to Kitner, ignored his efforts to organize faculty peace marshals and attempted to paint a picture of an irresponsible faculty contributing to the turmoil.

Another professor, Dr. Jerry M. Lewis, said Prosecutor Balyeat asked extremely specific questions, thus preventing full explanation of what the professor saw during the shootings.

Lewis, a sociologist and an expert in group behavior, said Balyeat wasn't interested in the professor's analysis of why students gathered on the commons on May 4.

Although Lewis was close to the action at the ROTC building fire, he was not questioned on that incident, he said.

Another witness, a photographer, said he was asked to identify photographs he took at Akron University which were mistakingly presented to him as he testified and identified other pictures taken at Kent State.

Another photographer, student Howard Ruffner, said he was questioned about the shooting incident, but was never asked to identify any of his photos, including one which appeared on the cover of Life Magazine.

A journalism professor, Richard Schreiber, said the prosecutors asked no questions about his statement to the FBI that he saw a Guardsman fire a pistol shot over the heads of students several minutes before the fateful volley.

"They (the Grand Jury) seemed to have a preconceived idea and were trying to prove it," Schreiber said.

His sentiments were echoed by King and Lewis.

In one instance a wrong student was subpoenaed to testify.

The co-ed was served with a subpoena intended for another person with the same name but another address. The mistake was not discovered until questioning began.

One of the special prosecutors, Perry Dickinson of Ravenna, flew via an Ohio Highway Patrol plane to Florida to interview a 14-year-old runaway girl who had witnessed the shooting.

From the *Akron Beacon Journal,* November 10, 1970.

Oppose Those Indictments, Spock Urges

By Lou Mleczko

KENT—Warning Kent State University students and faculty that they are on the firing line, Dr. Benjamin Spock Monday night called for active opposition to the indictments issued by the special State Grand Jury.

"You aren't just protecting yourself from findings that go against the FBI report, you're helping protect all universities from prosecutors and state legislatures that are thirsty—eager—to blame students for America's ills," Spock said.

"The Grand Jury indictments are part of the new wave of repression, and if they get away with this, they'll close in on other universities."

Spock, the baby doctor turned anti-war protester, spoke before about 900 persons at KSU Auditorium.

He praised university president Robert I. White's speech Monday in Washington D.C., in which White criticized the Grand Jury report.

"I'm glad he made a strong stand on academic freedom," Spock said. "Getting at least part of the university administration on your side is very important."

The 67-year-old Spock challenged the students to organize politically and not become discouraged too easily.

"The only hope for America are young people insisting on radical change," Spock emphasized.

He urged his audience to "stand up for your legal rights:

"People who have gone to jail and those who protested here (at KSU) last May are the ones on the side of justice," Spock said.

Spock said that lawsuits, political involvement and other legal avenues of resistance will stop "ruthless retaliation by government against protest."

Speaking with Spock were Stanley Tolliver, a Cleveland civil rights lawyer, and David Ifshin, president of the National Student Association.

Tolliver who was agreed to aid in the defense of those indicted, received a standing ovation when he said, "We must save America—not for itself—but in spite of itself."

Tolliver said anyone that truly loves America should be a radical, adding:

"Webster's Dictionary says radical means change, and the status quo has got to go."

Tolliver called the Grand Jury report a "prostitution of the law."

Ifshin, former student body president at Syracuse University, said the nation was in a period of repression and intimidation.

From the *Akron Beacon Journal*, November 18, 1970.

KSU Jury Report Absurd—Brinkley

BALTIMORE (AP)—Newscaster David Brinkley has termed the Ohio Grand Jury report on the Kent State University killings "utterly absurd."

"The National Guard managed to kill four students," the NBC newsman said, "and the Grand Jury blamed everyone but the National Guard."

Brinkley made his comments Tuesday night at the Johns Hopkins University's Milton S. Eisenhower 1970 Symposium on Perspectives on Violence.

He said the official FBI report on the Kent State incident was ignored completely by the Grand Jury, even the part which said "there was no need for shooting."

In his speech Brinkley said a "classic revolution in the United States" by the radical left is "romantic nonsense." He said there is a real possibility of a violent confrontation but the radical left would be the victims. . . .

From the *Akron Beacon Journal,* December 10, 1970.

ONG: *"We Acted in Self-Defense"*

By Lacy McCrary
Beacon Journal Columbus Bureau

COLUMBUS—The Ohio National Guard has written the Kent State University shootings into its history as an act of self defense which took place during "a riotous condition."

National Guard Commander Sylvester Del Corso has filed an annual report with Gov. Rhodes in which the KSU tragedy of last May was summarized in less than 200 words.

The 114-page document features a picture on its cover of a National Guardsman wearing a helmet and gas mask and carrying a bayonet-tipped rifle.

The report is dated Nov. 1, but the governor's office did not release it until Wednesday—and quietly, at that. None of Rhodes' top assistants knew of the report and no news release was issued.

The report contains brief descriptions of the civil disturbances which brought out the guard during fiscal year 1970 ending last June 30.

The KSU section of the report is contained in one paragraph. Del Corso said it was intended to be a "summary" rather than a detailed description.

The report said the KSU disturbance "ended when National Guard troops acting in self defense fired their weapons killing four students and wounding several others."

It said the controversial events at KSU May 4 occurred because of a breakdown in law and order.

"Law and order continued to deteriorate during the following two days and on May 4 a riotous condition existed on campus," the report said.

The report said the KSU incident began when large groups of students "allegedly protesting the Southeast Asian war" created numerous disturbances.

The document contains several pictures of guard troops on duty at Ohio State University last May during disturbances there. But it contains no pictures of KSU.

Del Corso said he didn't think the KSU summary was controversial: "We didn't put it in there to stir it up again. Enough has been written about Kent already. We don't want to stir it up again."

EDITORIAL COMMENTARY

KSU Graffiti, Fall, 1970

—America—change it or lose it.
—The Guard was justified in firing.
—We'll be justified if we fire back.
—We don't need *more* killing.
—America already bombs babies in Viet Nam villages.
—What do you think the VC do when they go into a village?
—Love America or leave it but leave it the way you found it.

From the *Akron Beacon Journal,* August 9, 1970.

Now Record KSU Killings Album Topic

By Theodore Price

Art and politics have never really been separate from one another, even in the days when empire-minded popes were still commissioning Michelangelos to paint their chapels.

Or when Steinbecks were writing novels about the treatment of migratory workers.

Or now, when Flying Dutchman records releases a disc called "Murder at Kent State University" (FDS-127, stereo, $4.95). . . .

On the album, six of New York Post columnist Pete Hamill's columns comment on the tragedies at KSU and elsewhere in some jolting but colorful, provocative but sensational terms.

Read by Bill "Rosco" Mercer, an experienced disc jockey with a rolling voice midway between a ghostly frowl and a Greek theater orator, the sum total of Hamill's columns is this:

There is a direct relationship like cause-effect, between the words of President Nixon, Vice President Agnew, California governor Reagan and Spring 1970 violence in and out of the U.S. . . .

Hamill recommends impeaching both the President and Vice President. "There is no way this country can live when it has two neuters commanding power, devoid of true compassion or true ideas, dedicated to the irradication of opposition domestic and foreign." . . .

Hamill cites Gov. Reagan's call for a "bloodbath to solve campus disorder." "Well, now he has it," narrator Rosko snarls against droning bass dirges played by Ron Carter, with intermittent alto sax and flute interjections by James Spaulding.

Hamill's melodramatic clincher hides nothing: "At Kent State two boys and two girls were shot to death by men unleashed by a president's slovenly rhetoric."

If thoughts still are the prelude to words and actions—and it's clear many have become careless in thinking about possible consequences of their acts—then Hamill seems to be urging his audience to judge Nixon and Agnew by the standards of restraint, fairness and decency.

I wince not at Hamill's point of view, but at much of its sensationalism. He equates the hard hats' parade in New York with "a peculiar kind of distorted sexuality." . . .

In "The Army of the Young," he asks rhetorical questions that defy answer: "Could Nixon, in his hunched, tight style, wearing a dull banker's suit all his working hours . . . understand making love at the foot of the Washington Monument at midnight?"

He stoops to personality assassination: President Nixon is described as "a neurotic, without deep convictions . . . lusting after power." Hamill concludes Nixon is unfit for office because he visited a "shrink" (psychiatrist) while he worked for a New York City law firm.

Such slurs only drive middle-of-the-roaders to the extremes. And the extremes to which Presidential, vice-presidential and even some gubernatorial language descended just prior to the KSU tragedy are the very bullseye of Hamill's argument.

From the *Akron Beacon Journal,* October 2, 1970.

Doesn't Agnew Know He's Misrepresenting Report?

Spiro Agnew's Sioux Falls charges that the Scranton Commission was "irresponsible" and lacked "moral courage" were couched in arguments containing large flaws.

The vice president is an intelligent man, well trained in logical argument by his legal background, and well aware of both the exact meaning and the logical implications properly to be drawn from what he says.

It can only be assumed, therefore, that he is aware of the faults in his arguments, but considers it politically expedient to ignore them.

"To lay responsibility for ending student disruption at the doorstep of this President, in office 20 months, is 'scapegoating' of the most irresponsible sort," said Agnew.

First, the commission did not lay exclusive responsibility for this upon the President. It called for determined healing action from all concerned—students, faculties, school administrators, law enforcement agencies, public officials at all levels, the public at large—AND the President.

Agnew knows this.

Second: The commission was called into existence by the President himself, and prime among its duties was to come back to the President with recommendations as to what in its judgment he himself could do to improve things—if anything.

Its judgment, as expressed in the report, was that the President is in a position of influence uniquely qualifying him to point out for all of us ways toward solving the problem.

Agnew also knows this.

Is this, therefore, "irresponsibility"?

From the *Daily Kent Stater,* October 6, 1970.

Reality

The Scranton Commission has issued its "Special Report on the Kent State Tragedy." The document, a 150-page affair, contains an amazing amount of material gathered during the week that the commission spent on the Kent State campus.

The report states that the "indiscriminate firing of rifles into a crowd of students and the deaths that followed were unnecessary, unwarranted, and inexcusable."

We cannot more heartily agree.

The report goes on to say that "the conduct of many student and non-student protesters at Kent State in the first four days of May, 1970, was plainly intolerable. Violence by students on or off campus can never be justified by any grievance, philosophy, or political idea."

Once again, we can only agree.

From observations of the great efforts to organize groups for specific purposes on this campus since the fall quarter began, we feel it's evident that the student body of this university has learned that violence will only bring more violence and that the stone has never been, and will never be, the match for a .30 calibre rifle.

We feel that this campus has learned from its experiences of May 1–4. We feel that the matter, however loudly the "law enforcement" lobbies of the land may scream, should be quietly and solemnly buried like the bodies of our students who were slain here.

But we find that this is impossible.

According to the Scranton Report, "When (John) McElroy, Gov. James Rhodes' Chief assistant questioned (Portage county Prosecutor Ron) Kane's authority to close the school, Kane said he would worry about the legalities later."

It now appears that the legal powers in this state are in great contempt of the moral issues involved in the case.

The state, with its threats of over 200 indictments from the secret grand jury investigation going on in Ravenna now, has done more to keep the campus, the state, and the nation tense than anything else ever did.

A possibly unconstitutional muzzle has been placed over the mouths of private citizens who have been subpoenaed by the Grand Jury, prohibiting them from talking with the press for the "duration" of the time that Judge Edwin Jones deems it necessary.

We feel that these tactics and events are as uncalled for as the Scranton Commission and the Stater feel violence was in May.

We call for an end to violence on this university's campus and toward its students, just as much as we demand that the students of this university refrain from violence, themselves.

We feel our demands are rational. We wonder if others can make that claim.

From the *Kent-Ravenna Record-Courier*, October 6, 1970.

Blame on Both Sides

. . . There are two ways of looking at the conclusion reached by the [Scranton] Commission.

First, one could call it gutless and irresponsible because it evades the ultimate question of who really is to blame for the deaths. It is a typical bureaucratic fence-riding, designed to appease everybody.

The second view is that human occurrences, especially those as complex as the Kent State incident, cannot be simplified and guilt is not so easily distributed as the nation's Spiro Agnews would have us believe. Thus the only way of arriving at truth is to sort out the complexities and assign blame on both sides of the issue as it seems warranted.

Frankly we think the Commission's work deserves the latter opinion. While it provides no clear-cut good guys and bad guys, we think the Commission, in its assessment of the situation, came as close to the truth as it could possibly come.

Even if you don't agree with the findings of the Commission, we think you owe it to its members to respect it for telling it as they saw it, and not yielding to shouts from both sides that a bogy man be tarred and feathered for the Kent deaths.

And that, in our opinion, takes plenty of courage.

From the *Akron Beacon Journal*, October 6, 1970.

The "Analyzed" College Town

By Jeff Sallot

KENT—Perhaps no other town in Ohio, save for Wapakoneta, home of moonman Neil A. Armstrong, has been studied, probed and analyzed as much as this community.

It has been five months now since Kent, Ohio, became a name known around the world.

For one horrible moment on May 4, as four Kent State University students fell to the ground mortally wounded, the attention of mankind was focused on this Portage County community.

But even little Wapakoneta, nestled near the Indiana border, was under the microscope only once—July 21, 1969 when Armstrong took his "one small step. . . ."

Kent is under scrutiny again.

The newsmen want to know what the townspeople think of a Presidential Commission's opinion that both rock-throwing students and National Guardsmen with loaded guns bear some responsibility for what happened in this town last May.

"We're just sick to death of it," [says] a Coffeen dr. housewife.

"That whole incident has been exploited too much. The kids are dead now and there isn't anything anybody can do to bring them back," she says.

A W. Main st. gas station attendant echoes this sentiment. "'Darn right we want to forget it and just be left alone," he says.

"Right after the shooting incident all the newsmen swarmed over this place asking everybody in town what they thought of this and that and shoving microphones in people's faces and such," a kibitzer at a coffee shop explains.

"There's hardly a family I know who hasn't had some reporter ask somebody in the family a question or two," the man says.

As he finishes his coffee and sees the reporter's notebook, his last comment is "Don't use my name."

Although some Kent residents are reluctant to discuss their opinions with newsmen, that doesn't mean they don't hold strong opinions.

In spite of recommendations by the Scranton Commission, [the housewife] still feels Guardsmen should be armed with loaded guns.

"If they come at you to do you harm, you should shoot," she says.

And [the attendant] says he's "happy they (the Scranton Commission) placed some of the responsibility on the kids."

But the frustration of an over-analyzed college town shows through in the voice of a S. Depeyster st. housewife when she says: "I simply hate to talk about it."

From the *Kent-Ravenna Record-Courier,* October 17, 1970.

Most Residents Agree with Grand Jury Report

A random sampling of Portage area residents showed most agreed with the grand jury findings that the Ohio National Guard should not be prosecuted for the early May campus disorders in Kent. . . .

Area residents who were living in the community during the May 1–4 riots, labeled so by the grand jury, regretted the deaths of four students but emphasized the Guard's presence was the result of student rioting.

"The young people were doing the very things they said they were protesting," said [a Kent woman].

"They're supposed to be against all violence," she said, "but they caused the riots. The shootings wouldn't have occurred if there hadn't been trouble previously." . . .

[Another Kent woman] said the Guard was right in stopping the fight that the students started. She had a niece living in one of the dorms at the time and "she was scared to walk out of the dorm."

When [she] went to KSU to get her niece, the student ran to her crying. "That's something I'll never forget. She was scared. She didn't go out of her dorm for two days. She lived on cookies."

The niece did return to KSU this fall and "she goes about her business," her aunt said. "She said they'd have to show the others that 'we are stronger.' " . . .

[Another Kent woman] "I cannot understand how there can be such contradiction between the reports of the Scranton reports, the Knight newspapers and the grand jury report. I'm confused." . . .

When asked about the report's questioning the Guards' having no alternative weaponry than loaded rifles, [a contractor] said, "I don't think there's anybody who won't go along and say it was too bad young people were killed there.

"But I'm in favor of majority rule," he said, "and I think that report reflects that. Those college kids will too when they get a little older." . . .

[A high school English teacher] said he thought that the students and the KSU administration were somewhat to blame, "but I don't think it's right to put all the blame on them," he said. "Everybody was to blame in this."

From the *Akron Beacon Journal,* October 17, 1970.

Students: "They Kill Four Of Us So They Indict 25 More"

By Kathy Lilly

KENT—Students generally reacted with anger Friday to the report of a special Portage County grand jury which indicted students but no National Guardsmen in connection with disorders last May.

"It's only natural," said . . . a self-described independent radical. "They kill four of us so they indict 25 more."

. . . [A] graduate student in history called the report a political document and said he expects the trials equally to be political.

. . . [A] junior from Oberlin said the National Guard was not justi-fied in returning bullets for rocks.

"I was there May 4, and I would say the idea that the shootings were justified is totally wrong," he said. "It was murder." . . .

. . . [A] sophomore . . . said, "I feel there were people wrong on both sides last May, both the National Guard and the students. The fact that no National Guard were indicted indicates the prejudice of the grand jury."

. . . [A]n 18-year-old freshman . . . defended the National Guard: "If someone were trying to kill me, I'd be on the defensive. I think faculty had a lot of doing in the disturbances. I think a few (profes-sors) are rebels and they teach students to go out and rebel." . . .

From the *Dayton (Ohio) Daily News,* October 18, 1970.

Biased Kent Jury Report Deepens Campus Unrest

The state grand jury's report on the deaths and disturbances at Kent State university is a sordid misrepresentation of those tragic events and a biased assignment of responsibility for them.

The findings run counter to the careful study conducted by the President's Commission on Campus Disturbances and to the reported investigation by the FBI.

That 25 demonstrators were indicted is probably just, though each case will have to be judged individually, of course. Criminal offenses obviously were committed. The ROTC building didn't burn itself down, and rocks didn't take off on their own. The jury is right to insist that such acts require court action.

But the jury's report is grossly unfair when it whitewashes the fumbling, deadly performance of the National Guard and is frivolously fashionable when it pins major blame for tragedy [on] the university's "permissiveness."

Kent State officials were trying desperately to cope with the ex-traordinarily difficult events of early May. To blame them for failing to keep students in line is to blame them for failing to do the impos-sible. Only a police state can expect to compel the good behavior of its citizens. A city, for instance, can't force its residents to be always law abiding; it can only punish those who break the law.

Perhaps the Guard's fatal volley was technically in self-defense, as the jury ruled. The law in such matters is weighted heavily on the side of lawmen and their stand-ins. But if the Guard was legally in the clear, its performance still was indefensible and invited, in fact demanded, stern censure from the jury.

The guardsmen were in no mortal danger. They did not fire on command. They had an open fall-back route. No evidence has been found of the often-cited rooftop sniper, and even if there were evidence, that wouldn't excuse random shots into a crowd on the ground. The Guard's command was at serious fault for: 1. advancing troops in numbers too small for the situation, 2. deploying inadequately trained troops with loaded weapons and 3. losing control of the troops.

A society that wants to attract the substantial good behavior of its citizens has to be demanding on its own representatives and has to be fair minded. The grand jury had an opportunity, while properly enforcing the law, to express compassion for the students killed and wounded at Kent State, only a few of whom were anywhere near the disturbance, and to demonstrate some understanding of the causes of the riot.

The jury could have contributed to the solution of the problems at Kent State and other universities. Its one-sidedness and insensitivity instead will contribute to the problems.

From the *Kent-Ravenna Record-Courier,* October 19, 1970.

Grand Jury Report Not Unlike Public Opinion

Perhaps the most significant aspect of the long-awaited Grand Jury report on the Kent State campus disturbances is how closely the findings of that body parallel prevalent public opinion on the major facets of the May incidents.

Consider the following:

(1) Public opinion generally was that a riotous situation existed in the city of Kent and on the Kent campus in the period between May 1 and May 4. The Grand Jury reached the same conclusion.

(2) The public generally felt that the National Guardsmen were in a predicament that they couldn't avoid using their weapons, even though it deeply lamented the deaths that were the result.

(3) The public felt that those responsible for the burning of the ROTC building on May 2 and those who incited riots on campus were criminals. While we don't know exactly which individuals were counted in the 25 indicted and what they were charged with, it is safe to assume the Grand Jury came to the same conclusion.

(4) Perhaps most importantly, the public in general is fed up with what it terms permissiveness and lack of discipline on our campuses and in society in general. The Grand Jury made the same criticism of the administration at Kent State University, and warned that this permissiveness had created an atmosphere inviting trouble which still exists.

We don't mean to imply for a moment that the Grand Jury made an attempt to gear its findings to public opinion; on the other hand, we think that these men and women of middle class America came to their conclusions honestly after listening to and reading all of the evidence that was brought before them.

While we generally approve the Grand Jury report we think that it was unduly severe in blistering the university for "fostering an attitude of laxity, over-indulgence and permissiveness with its students and faculty to the extent that it can no longer regulate the activities of either."

The jury's statement that the conditions which prevailed on May 4 are the same today also startled us. The university has made important internal changes since May, including a beefing up in numbers and training of security forces and the rewriting of the Student Conduct Code to put it in line with Ohio's anti-disruptive law 1219.

Let us point out that Kent State has been the focal point of what has been a national disturbance.

The entire country has been in the throes of a permissiveness that has undermined many of our institutions.

In the face of this situation, we feel that the administration has done a tremendous job of grappling with the problem and holding the university together during its great period of crisis.

Whatever may have been the fault of those who guide and those who teach, they have responded with dedicated purpose to cope with the problems of the moment.

If the students will only study, the teachers teach and the administrators administer, we're certain that Kent will emerge from its great trial an even stronger institution of learning and democracy than it has been in the past.

No administration can be completely off the track if it can build and administer an institution of slightly less than 30,000 students on 10 campuses in nine counties in northeastern Ohio, as Kent has done.

Kent has played a major role in bringing education to the doorstep of all of those who want it in this corner of the state.

We believe that everybody—the students, the faculty, the administrators and the people as a whole—ought to help Kent in every way he can to live through this moment of adversity so that it can concentrate on its job of helping to make Kent, Ohio, and the nation a better place in which to live.

From *I. F. Stone's Bi-Weekly,* October 19, 1970. The complete text of the article appears in *The Killings at Kent State* by I. F. Stone, a New York Review Book, New York, 1971.

What's A Little Murder (Of Blacks and Students)?

The danger in the Jackson State and Kent State reports by the President's Commission on Campus Unrest lies in their very quality.

If they had whitewashed the killings, the findings would be angrily dismissed by blacks and students as more-of-the-same, but the hope would remain that a better investigation by better men might have produced better results. The destructive potential of the reports comes from the fact that they have honestly and thoroughly shown that the killings were unjustified and unnecessary. The established order mustered its best and they fulfilled their moral and political obligation. *And yet there is not the slightest chance that anything will be done about it.* The chairman of the Commission, Scranton, will turn up at the White House one of these days to be photographed with the President, an innocuous statement will issue from the White House, and that will be the end of the findings. The message to blacks and students will be that even when the established order does its highest best, there is no discernible effect. Disillusion will be deepened. The number of those who drop out, who abandon hope in normal politics and reason, will increase. The reports, by their very honesty and courage, will have demonstrated the impotence even of the conventional best elements in our society. What was intended to further reconciliation will end in provocation.

Where Scranton Failed

The Commission can be criticized on two points. Its main business was to investigate the killings at Jackson State and Kent State but it chose to issue its findings on these in two separate reports released several days after its main report. These two were released separately and without specially televised briefings. Governor Scranton and his colleagues could have put on the nation's television screens their conclusion that the killings on both campuses were unjustified and unnecessary. They chose instead to televise the safe and evenhanded generalities of their main recommendations, and left town before the other reports were issued. Apparently all the advance criticism orchestrated by the White House and Agnew had made them afraid of becoming too controversial. The other criticism is that these two reports do not put the spotlight on those responsible for the killings. The Commission had a valid excuse for this. As it said in the Kent State report, it did not wish "to interfere with the criminal process." Unfortunately the "criminal process" at Jackson State and Kent State is apt to end like the "criminal process" which grew out of the Orangeburg massacre in February, 1968. There three students were killed and 27 wounded by State Highway patrolmen at the all-black State College in Orangeburg, South Carolina. The nine highway patrolmen who did the shooting were acquitted last year (and promoted!). But Cleveland Sellers, the young SNCC worker whom the authorities arrested as the "outside agitator" responsible has just been convicted and sentenced to a year in jail though the original charges against him failed to stand up.

The killers—police, Guardsmen or state highway patrol—will go free and the only people punished will be selected scapegoats from among their victims. . . .

From the *Daily Kent Stater*, October 19, 1970.

Compare

Like a giant paint brush, the Ravenna Grand Jury has pictured the Guard in brilliant white and has dipped the administration in murky black.

The Scranton report, however, said the Guard was as guilty as the students.

The Grand Jury colored every day of May 1 through 4 as a riot which clearly "necessitated the request for assistance of the National Guard."

The Scranton report found very little justification for the Guard's presence.

The Grand Jury stated, "the National Guard . . . fired their (sic) weapons in the honest and sincere belief . . . that they (Guardsmen) would have suffered serious bodily injury had they not done so."

The Scranton Report condemned the Guard for its action, saying it was completely unjustified and that the Guardsmen's lives were not in danger.

The Jury said "the verbal abuse directed at the Guardsmen by the students . . . represented a level of obscenity and vulgarity which we had never before witnessed!"

The Scranton Report commented on the language, but didn't deem it necessary to practically hang the justification of the shootings upon the verbal barrage.

Both the Grand Jury and Scranton Report recommended the use of non-lethal weapons.

The "concerned faculty" letter signed by 23 professors, was condemned by the Grand Jury as "an irresponsible act clearly not in the best interests of Kent State University.

The Scranton Report notes the letter, but congratulates faculty members for their peace marshal work Saturday night, May 2.

Faculty members, some of whom had signed the letter, were congratulated by the Jury for their "efforts, May 4, (to) restore order and prevent further rioting after the shooting."

The Scranton report criticized the administration for three things: their handling of the Concerned Citizens' Committee, (CCC), in spring 1969; the confusion over who ordered the guard in May, 1970; and the ineffectiveness of the student conduct code.

The Grand Jury hung everything on the administration's neck. "The administrative staff has constantly yielded . . . to the extent it no longer runs this university," it said.

Now, who do you think came closer to the truth: a commission of professional men who spent three months on an exhaustive study of the time before, during and after the shootings, with such professional investigators as the FBI and Secret Service; or a jury of county people who spent 25 days studying the situation in an area of constant tension and unrest?

We support the administration policy to allow free thought on campus, condemned by the Grand Jury; we support the right of speakers of all political persuasions to speak on our campus, undercut by the Jury; and we support the right of a youth counter-culture involving music, language and ideas, completely repudiated by the Jury.

We don't want Kent State University to become Kent Police State University.

Not now! Not ever!

From the *Akron Beacon Journal,* October 21, 1970.

"Do Our Duty, Then This . . ."

. . . "I was graduated from Kent State but I don't recognize the place anymore." [said the father of an indicted student] "I had wanted my son to go there and get a business education. But he's going to stay home now." . . .

"I don't know what happened," he said.

"Holy God, I vote in every election. I keep out of trouble. I try to be a good citizen. My wife is active in civic affairs. She joins in the United Fund drives and Red Cross campaigns. We do our civic duty."

"And then this happens." . . .

From the *Akron Beacon Journal,* October 22, 1970.

Grand Jury Powers: Two Views

Curious, how far judges in the same state at the same time can differ on so general a question of law as the proper powers of a grand jury.

In the case of the Statehouse loan scandal, Franklin County's Common Pleas judges have ruled that the grand jury has no legal power to issue a general report on the matter it was assembled to investigate.

The jury, they say, has the legal power to return to the court its indictments and its no-bills, plus the power to issue reports on its findings as to current conditions in the county jail. Nothing more.

So, out of Columbus there will be no grand jury report on the Statehouse loan scandal—and the jurors remain barred, as usual, from disclosing what they heard.

In the case of the special state grand jury called in Portage County to investigate and take appropriate legal action on last Spring's disturbance at Kent State University, on the other hand, the judge followed the more general Ohio practice of allowing the jury free rein.

The result, as all in the area are aware, was both a group of indictments AND an extensive general report commenting on the jury's findings and its judgment as to where responsibility fell.

It is hard for the public to judge who is on sounder ground—the "strict constructionists" in Columbus with their (for Ohio) new view of jury powers, or the "traditionalist" in Ravenna.

But, with both cases coming virtually on election eve, there is a regrettable element here. The contrast in views will furnish ammunition to those critical of the machinery of justice. Watch for their comment:

"It just depends on what the case is and who is likely to be affected. For university people it's one kind of justice—for state officials, another."

From the *Kent-Ravenna Record-Courier,* October 26, 1970.

Ford Off Track

The remarks attributed to Seabury Ford, a special prosecutor in the State Grand Jury's investigation of the disorders at Kent State University last May, are hard to believe.

. . . He has been an attorney 45 years, a good one, and the rash statement attributed to him is irresponsible and is not in keeping with his long experience.

The intemperate remarks require that he be censured by Common Pleas Court Judge Edwin Jones, who has imposed a cloak of silence on witnesses and others involved in the special grand jury probe.

Furthermore, Attorney General Paul Brown who named Ford and two other attorneys as special prosecutors in the investigation, should give serious consideration to relieving Ford of his duties.

So should the Ohio Board of Regents, which named Ford a hearing officer for campus arrests made under public law 1219.

It's possible that Ford, known locally as a blustery, joke-loving man, made the statement to startle a couple of out-of-town newsmen looking for new leads in the Kent State investigation.

Or his personal feelings or emotions overcame his generally good reason.

Regardless, a man in his position should know better and should be administered more than a mild wrist slap by Judge Jones and Attorney General Brown.

Even if, as Ford claims, he was "over quoted," it seems to us necessary that he be separated from both his special prosecutor and campus hearing officer positions to remove any taint of prejudice in these serious matters.

Kent, which has been playing "catch up ball" trying to get its house in order since the May 4 tragedy, needs the help of thinking, understanding citizens, not new situations that will tear the community and students farther apart.

From the *Akron Beacon Journal,* October 26, 1970.

How Can a Bloodthirsty Prosecutor Be a Referee?

No wonder some students at Kent State University are bitter.

No wonder some members of the younger generation doubt that justice is even-handed.

Consider how disturbed they have a right to be about Mr. Seabury Ford. . . .

. . . Mr. Ford, sworn to uphold the Constitution and the laws under it, seems to believe it was right and proper to inflict capital punishment as a penalty for the crime of rioting.

Moreover, he seems willing to countenance punishment without trial—shooting the guilty and the innocent alike!

This is the man who is supposed to deal out even-handed justice on the Kent campus when new accusations are brought before him!

Aside from being shocked by what Ford says, Kent students have a right to wonder why *he* may talk freely while the university president and other jury witnesses remain under court order to keep silent.

Ford repeats the jury's overstated criticism of the university administration, adding the word "softies."

Mr. Ford is not the grand jury. President Robert I. White and others certainly have the right to respond to him. And surely, Judge Edwin Jones can no longer shield the jury itself from full and free comment and criticism by all interested persons, including witnesses.

Under the new law on campus disorders, the students and faculty members indicted by the grand jury are subject to an immediate hearing by the Regents' referee, who has authority to suspend them until their cases are heard by the trial court.

It would be highly inappropriate if Prosecutor Ford should put on his hat as Referee Ford and hear these cases—or any campus cases whatsoever.

If he doesn't have the grace to resign immediately as referee, the Regents ought to correct the error made in September when they appointed him. That means dismiss him.

Too much support has been given the cynical view of some students that the law and its administration are rigged against them.

The least the Regents can do now is to name an eminently fair-minded person as referee.

Excerpt from the *New Republic,* November 7, 1970.

Kent State Gag

By David Sanford

. . . Kent State University had been a school without national reputation; now it has a reputation it didn't want and doesn't know how to live with. After the school was closed last May, administrators speculated about how the riots, the burning of the ROTC building and finally the killings would affect fall enrollment. There were rumors that radicals from other universities would try to transfer to Kent to make trouble, or that many of Kent's own students would move to other schools and that enrollment would drop by five to ten percent. But in that month and a half in May and June, when Kent was closed, no one was in the registrar's office to talk to fearful parents or students considering transferring. The shut-down probably averted a drop in enrollment. When the school began its academic year in September, 21,370 students registered, a gain of 272 over last year. There were 100 fewer new transfer students than in 1969.

But at registration there was talk of bombs. On October 8–10, Homecoming, something was going to happen; on the 14th, the day a bomb exploded at Harvard, there'd be a bombing at Kent. All the rumors proved false. Kent opened and remained open. Communications at Kent have never been better. The university set up two telephone extensions last spring, before the demonstrations, to quell rumors and to dispense general information. Persons who dial extension 4000 hear a recorded message of the day's news. The five lines on the Code-a-Phones are almost always busy. Operators on extension 3000, the "rap line," are available to answer questions.

The night before the special grand jury indicted the Kent 25, operators handled 1200 calls asking for news of the impending report. October 24, "Dads' Day" at Kent, the Code-a-Phones were broadcasting a one-minute-twenty-second message about an actual bombing that morning which caused negligible damage to the building housing the Human Relations Center and the Black United Students. The visiting parents that day made the trip to the metal sculpture on blanket hill, which has a bullet hole in it. They strolled by the parking gate next to which Jeffrey Miller fell dead May 4, and the site of the burned ROTC building where new grass was planted but failed to take root. Except for such graphic reminders, the campus looks normal: a jumble of architectural styles, construction in progress, a new multi-story library, squirrels in three colors, couples making out on the grass. A sign in a dorm window reads, "Hitler is alive and living in Portage County"; another at the exit to Prentice Hall, a women's dorm, warns that: "Because of the security risk please don't use these doors after 7:30." (Someone transformed 0 in 7:30 into a peace symbol.)

A number of students wear round stickers which read "Keep Kent Open," seeming to confirm that the university's News Service Director Jim Bruss, is accurate in saying that the most prevalent feeling on campus "is keep the goddamn place open. We don't want people at either end of the spectrum to do anything to close the university." A few students wear "Kent Police State University" T-shirts, put on sale at Potpourri, a head shop some blocks from the campus. It sold out its supply of three dozen in about an hour. The money ($3.25 apiece) goes to the Kent Legal Defense Fund, Inc., hastily set up after the indictments. Tom Dubis, one of the fund's organizers, says they have raised about $2500, most of it in small contributions from students.

Local newspapers have reported surveys that suggest that in the city of Kent most people agree with the grand jury report, that the university's "permissive" treatment of students and faculty and the school's failure to exert proper discipline caused the rioting and violence of last May; the Guard was innocent.

If the press *is* representative of the community (some students call the *Record-Courier,* the Wretched Courier) there is little community appreciation of how apolitical and nonviolent the majority of Kent students are, even now. (The size of morning classes was undiminished October 23, the day the indicted student body president had designated as a national moratorium day of support for the Kent 25. Most students chose not to attend workshops on nonviolence.) The annual "Think Week" at the semester's start had as its themes, working within the political system, and nonviolent protest. But what the people of Kent know about KSU comes largely from the newspapers, and they play up the turmoil.

Kent's "situation" is a topic of conversation everywhere on campus, but few students are abandoning their way of life to become full-time activists. There is no SDS at Kent. The most visible "militant" organiza-tion is the Youth International Party which has done a lot to provide comic relief. YIP endorsed in jest the Republican gubernatorial candi-date Roger Cloud, and added to their own unwelcome support the affections of commie homosexuals. Last Saturday the Yippies staged a carnival on the famous Kent commons to raise bail money. They sold commie pinko bubblegum for a penny, fished for fake dope, threw painted rocks at paper pigs, and built a 10-foot penis out of papier-mâché. The Yippies have made serious demands on the university as well, opposing ROTC, government research, and they've put strains on the University's tightened rules for campus demonstrations. But in the main, they're the sort of revolutionaries that would frighten only a special grand jury in Portage County.

From the *New Republic*, November 2, 1970.

The Indicted Professor

By David Sanford

Dr. Thomas Lough is a 42-year-old associate professor of sociology at Kent, charged with inciting to riot on May 4. He assumes that at some point he will get to see a bill of particulars. What *did* he do on May 4? He can't talk about that, because in doing so he might put himself in contempt of court or violate the order of silence. So far 19 persons have been arrested. Lough turned himself in on Monday, October 19. How did he know he had been indicted, when the indictments were all secret at that point? Lawyers have a way of knowing these things. "I pleaded innocent and I am," Lough says. His bond was set at $5000.

John Kifner wrote in *The New York Times* that Lough is an avowed socialist. But Lough, who spent five years with the State Department in the Arms Control and Disarmament Agency, says that's not true. He describes himself as a "problem oriented" social psychologist. He teaches a social problems course at Kent in which he emphasizes ecology, poverty, the study of violence, gun control, "things like that." Lough got in trouble a couple of years ago when a student complained that he had passed out diagrams showing how to build Molotov cocktails, which he'd gotten from *The New York Review of Books*, as material for a lecture on "collective behavior." He was exonerated by a departmental investigation but nevertheless became known as the professor who teaches students how to make Molotov cocktails. Lough had told his students that he felt uncomfortable about the publication of the diagram, "because you're afraid it will get into the wrong hands."

Is there a historical precedent for what is happening to Lough, for the order of silence, the secret indictments, the ban on demonstrations, the new state law that provides for suspending arrested students and faculty pending trial? He doesn't think there is. These are new times and new things are being tried, by the courts, by prosecutors, and indeed by defendants. How has the university reacted to his indictment and arrest? There have been no repercussions. Lough, and the rest of the Kent 25 by virtue of their indictments have become campus heroes.

From *I. F. Stone's Bi-Weekly,* November 16, 1970.

When $in, $mut and $tudents Failed

The swiftest if most cynical way to sum up the election is that Nixon and Agnew misjudged the American people. Far too many of them may sometimes look and sound like morons. But they're not imbeciles. At a time when the country faces its gravest problems since the Civil War, Nixon and Agnew thought they could win by campaigning against sin, smut and students. They pitched their sales talk at the bright but mindless level of the TV commercials. They assumed—and no assumption could be more elitist, a favorite Agnew charge—that the un-poor, the un-black and the un-young were also the un-thinking. They had at least five times as much money to spend as the Democrats, and they still couldn't stampede the voters. The country proved better balanced, more humane, and far less susceptible to panic than Nixon and Agnew assumed. By their tactics, though inadvertently, they for the first time did something to create confidence in America. . . .

In the two States where campus violence was freshest in the minds of the electorate, the results show that whipping up hatred for students is not the vote getter Nixon and Agnew thought it was. Wisconsin and Ohio were among the States in which the Democrats made their dramatic sweep of the Governorships. Patrick J. Lucey, a McCarthy lieutenant in 1968, organizer of the New Democratic Coalition in 1969, was elected Governor of Wisconsin despite the effort to brand him, in alliterative Agnewism, as a coddler of campus terrorists. In Ohio John J. Gilligan was elected Governor despite a campaign in which the Republicans tried to exploit anti-student feeling in the wake of the Kent State shootings and accuse him of "permissiveness." Nixon's favorite, Governor Rhodes, by an inflammatory speech at Kent State had hoped and failed to win the Republican Senate nomination from the more moderate Taft who has now won the Senate seat. Best of all is what happened to the Attorney Generalship of Ohio, an elective office. Paul W. Brown, the Rhodes lieutenant who set up the whitewash special Grand Jury in the Kent State killings, will be replaced by a Democrat, Paul W. Brown. This may make a crucial difference in the struggle for justice at Kent State. . . .

From the *Daily Kent Stater,* November 10, 1970.

Bandwagon

The Stater congratulates Dr. Robert White for his firm attack on the Grand Jury report yesterday. We feel he was justified and spoke truthfully.

We also want to congratulate Professor Harold Kitner, the faculty ombudsman, who spoke out against the Grand Jury last Friday.

It's so comfortable to jump onto a moving bandwagon.

The Grand Jury report has been declared fair game and everyone is leveling their verbal barrages. . . .

Meanwhile, Glenn Frank is out on bond. He still can be sentenced to jail and fined for his comments of two weeks ago.

Nothing will happen to Dr. White, Ombudsman Kitner or any other outspoken orator.

Only Glenn Frank showed the courage and convictions to speak out when there was some legal clamp existing.

We find it ridiculous that the university administration was willing to let a Glenn Frank speak and face the consequences while the official leaders played a silent, waiting game.

Sure, after the target is wide open, no one can miss.

Dr. White overlooked the first opportunity he had in a long time to reassert his leadership.

All he would have had to do was open his mouth and protest the Grand Jury report; not harshly, not violently, just vocally.

As it stands now, only Glenn Frank will suffer any legal abuse for his comments.

So Dr. White, Dr. Kitner et al. can say and do as they please.

However, only Glenn Frank will have earned the students' and nation's respect.

From the *Akron Beacon Journal,* November 11, 1970.

Situation "Hopeful" at KSU—Michener

A "benevolent truce" now exists between Kent townspeople and Kent State University, author James A. Michener believes.

Michener, who has spent four months in Kent gathering information for a book on last May's disturbances, said Sunday the situation is "far more hopeful now than when I started."

Kent residents said "some dreadful things they really didn't mean" after the four days of disturbances that ended in four students being killed in a confrontation with the Ohio National Guard, the author said on the television program "Scene on Sunday" on WKYC [in a discussion with host Tom Haley and a group of KSU students].

Placing the number of those in favor of continued unrest on the campus at about 400—or 2 pct. of the student population of 20,000—Michener said he thinks many persons in the university and city don't want to see Kent State closed and are trying "to keep the system working."

The "radical element" has less influence now than last Spring, he said.

Michener said he thought the special state Grand Jury had made "an excellent report so far as the indictments are concerned." It could have indicted as many as 300, he added, but limited itself to those it thought were guilty.

But, the author contended, the jury "fell flat on its face" when it went on to criticize the university administration for allegedly allowing the situation to get out of hand.

He said it was "intolerable" to place all the blame for the disturbances on students. And he doubted if National Guardsmen could be charged legally with killing the four students and wounding nine others. But "the moral question is open," he said.

He said he doubted the complete FBI report of what happened at Kent State would ever be published.

From the *Daily Kent Stater*, November 12, 1970.

Kitner Defends Legal System

By Harold Kitner

Faculty Ombudsman

Having just read the editorial in the Tuesday issue of the Kent Stater, I find myself puzzled and frankly depressed.

The Editorial Board criticizes me (and President White) for not having spoken out sooner in regard to the slanted Special Grand Jury report. . . .

. . . [W]hat is most depressing is the expressed disdain for the operation of our judicial system. Civil disobedience is a time-honored procedure for human beings.

The power of the state (and the power of the press) can be grossly misused.

History in our own times is full of the examples of such misusage: therefore, Glenn Frank deserves all the praise that he has received.

He believed, and in my opinion, properly so, that Seabury Ford made statements that were shockingly callous and cynical.

The statements, as quoted in the Akron Beacon Journal were particularly reprehensible because they were made by an officer of the court.

Therefore, Glenn Frank made the personal decision to speak up. By doing this, no doubt, Frank personalized the issues raised by the Special Grand Jury report.

A hero and a villain were provided for the public. Through such personalization, the abstract issues were given a special human dimension.

No doubt this entire event contributed significantly to the moderate expression of the public during the last election.

However, the Editorial Board of the the Stater revealed a gap in its own education. There was another way—a way in which the long run must be honored if the laws of our society, basically decent laws, are to operate in a manner ultimately beneficial to all of us.

I was amazed that the Editorial Board could not see that it was also an act of faith and perhaps courage to wait, at some personal expense, so that the judicial system would have the opportunity to correct itself.

One of the happy highlights of the entire sordid mess that we have been through, was the fact that the Federal Court reversed the ban on free speech and thereby reaffirmed and strengthened this fundamental right in our society.

I would not be serving as an ombudsman if I were not entirely opposed to injustices, particularly those perpetuated by inflexible systems.

But we must not permit our outrage against abuses to cause us to move to the extreme where we express disdain or work actively to destroy a judicial system that so many people through the history of man sacrificed so much to create for us.

This system is far from perfect. Individuals and minority groups have had their rights violated.

All of us who desire humane treatment under law, therefore, are put at the point of a crossroad. We can decide to attempt to destroy that system or work hard to perfect it.

We have our personal decisions to make. I have made mine.

From the *Dallas Times Herald*, November 12, 1970.

The Real Enemy

Up from the bullet-scarred campus of Kent State University rises the full-throated cry of "Repression!" Or words to that effect. The cry proceeds from the throat of the university's president, Robert I. White, who won judicial permission a few days ago to comment on the Ohio grand jury report that substantially blamed his "permissive" administration for the violence of last spring.

"If pursued in all its nuances," quoth White, "(the report) would eventually destroy not only Kent but all major universities . . ."

In the mouth of a president whose university has suffered memorably from New Left ravages, such comments seem remarkable—until one reflects that White is only indulging in the inveterate sentimentality of academic liberals. The kind of sentimentality that refuses to see the SDS, the Weathermen, and their comrades-in-arms for what they are: a vicious, disciplined band of zealots, dedicated to pulling down American society.

White still can't believe it. And so he trains his salvo rightward—at the grand jurors who made so bold as to suggest that dissent should not "become the order of the day to the exclusion of all normal behavior and expression."

To White, evidently, the grand jury makes Joe McCarthy look like John Lindsay. "The academic community is not to be considered a sanctuary for those who wish to disobey the laws," he proclaims, "but neither is the academic community a place where ideas—no matter how offensive—are to be suppressed."

What White fails utterly to comprehend is that the greatest danger to "ideas" comes not from the right but from the far left—from that unwashed, steely eyed tribe who helped stir up the violence at Kent State; who may have destroyed Berkeley and Columbia; and whose totalitarian world-view can best be compared with Adolf Hitler's.

They are the enemy—not the middle-aged Ohioans who provoked White's wrath and indignation. Can't White understand that? Or is it simply that, good ivory tower liberal that he is, he really doesn't want to?

From the *Lynchberg* (Va.) *News*, November 13, 1970.

Defending Academic Freedom

The President of Kent State University this week accused the state grand jury of attacking academic freedom by exonerating the National Guard and indicting outside agitators and Kent State students for creating the disorders which resulted in the deaths of four students last May. . . .

The grand jury's report was a defense of academic freedom and an attack upon those who destroyed it during the disorders. For academic freedom can be preserved only by maintaining order—without which there can be no freedom of any kind. The jury did not "misunderstand" the role of the university. Instead, its report showed a profound understanding of that role and a determination to maintain it.

The grand jury properly placed much of the blame for the disorders upon the permissiveness and encouragement of White's administration. Liberal educationists have been encouraging the universities to take a more "activist" role in solving the problems of society. In so doing, they have changed the role of the university as a marketplace for the free discussion of ideas. They have turned universities into battlegrounds where ideas are contested physically instead of intellectually. When the activists win, the educationists proclaim a victory for free speech and academic freedom. When the activists lose, they charge censorship and the suppression of constitutional rights.

The grand jury sought to bring to justice those responsible for the disorders at Kent State. President White attempted to shift the blame to the National Guard—which would not have been called had he done his job.

From the *Orlando* (Fla.) *Evening Star,* November 20, 1970.

Brinkley's Latest Blast Injustice To Ohio Jury

That "Brandeis of the airwaves"—television announcer David Brinkley—slipped into his judicial robes the other night in Baltimore to rule on the Kent State case.

At his pompous best, Brinkley criticized the Ohio grand jury report on the Kent State University riots last spring.

Speaking at Johns Hopkins University's Milton S. Eisenhower 1970 Symposium on Perspectives on Violence, Brinkley described the grand jury's report as "utterly absurd."

Said Brinkley:

"The National Guard managed to kill four students and the grand jury blamed everyone but the National Guard."

There it is, Brinkley-style—neatly packaged, wrapped and tied together with a pretty red bow.

This same type of pitiful ignorance was a prime factor which led to the Kent State violence in the first place.

The Ohio National Guard did not "manage to kill" four young people.

First, the National Guard was called to the Kent campus because local police officials could not handle a dangerous situation. An unruly mob had taken control of the area.

The National Guard did not create the climate. If anything, from the standpoint of experience and history, the force sent to Kent was too little and too late.

Had heavy enough forces been sent initially, there would have been no killings at all.

Brinkley said the official FBI report on Kent was ignored completely by the grand jury, even the part which said "there was no need for the shooting."

But in making such a remark, Brinkley himself ignored a statement by J. Edgar Hoover in which he denied the FBI report said any such thing. . . .

As for Mr. Brinkley and his unfair condemnation of the Ohio grand jury which spent weeks listening to testimony, we leave him with three words:

Good night, David!

From the *Akron Beacon Journal,* November 22, 1970.

The Police Wife: She Worries

By Pat Ravenscraft

. . . Even though [a Kent woman] has been married to a Kent State policeman only a few months, she knows how demanding the law man's schedule can be. . . .

[She] said that her husband's usual duties are routine—parking tickets, etc.—and didn't worry her.

"But when the ROTC building was burned, someone broke his gas mask with a brick," she recalled. "I was scared. He is so easily identified with that uniform." . . .

From the *Akron Beacon Journal,* November 22, 1970.
Copyright *Los Angeles Times.*

The Boldest Ones of All

By Cecil Smith
Beacon Journal—Los Angeles Times

. . . David W. Rintels, who is 32, wrote and David Levinson, 31, produced "A Continual Roar of Musketry," the 2-part thinly disguised drama of the Kent State tragedy that occupies Holbrook as The Senator tonight and next Sunday night on NBC's The Bold Ones. The play's title is not accidentally from Paul Revere's description of the happenings at Concord in 1775. . . .

. . . To be relevant in a milksop medium takes guts . . . the guts to look at Kent State.

This one was the toughest of them all. Rintels wrote it at white heat, completing the 2-hour screen play in two weeks. Robert Day agreed to direct it if Rintels was on the set to make any changes.

But high in the black tower at Universal, lawyers were saying no way can you do this. Commissions were still studying Kent State and this play was drawing conclusions, placing blame.

Many blames. Rintels' technique is that of "Roshomon," where each of those immediately involved—the university chancellor, the mayor of the college town, the governor of the state, the commander of the guard, the soldiers and officers—tells what happened, each version differing according to the teller, the individual witness. . . .

From the *Akron Beacon Journal,* November 24, 1970.

The Distorting Mirror

That thinly disguised TV parody of Kent State's agony of May is a demonstration of the extent to which deep and terrible human problems can be turned into nauseating and truth-distorting tripe by translation into Madison Avenue-ese.

There is no good reason, in Madison Avenue's terms, not to hustle a buck by turning a still-open, still-angry wound into fourth-rate melodrama with cardboard characters from the world of slogans—like "Love that soap." No reason but conscience, a decent respect for truth and some kind of public morality involving a commitment to help us understand our own ills.

Here the truth is twisted and thrown out of focus just enough to make a stereotyped caricature out of every participant in the tragedy—the students and their leader, the Guardsmen, the college head, the governor, the mayor. And Hal Holbrook, who was a wow in the night club circuit with his impersonations of Mark Twain, comes out super-Scranton—the only sane human being in a nest of lunatics so far out that a bright 6-year-old would see through the errors in their grasp of reality.

The overall impression is like the images on those crooked mirrors in the fun house. But it's intended to be taken seriously—loaded with "significance."

Isn't there enough popular misunderstanding on this already without adding to it with boob-tube mythology?

From the *Akron Beacon Journal,* December 10, 1970.

Relevance Can Be a Nuisance

By Dick Shippy

The quest for story relevance within entertainment programs has caused some headaches for networks and television packagers other than disappointing audience ratings.

For example, that recent, two-part segment of NBC's "The Bold Ones" wherein Hal Holbrook's "Senator" chaired a committee of inquiry into a National Guard-student confrontation which resulted in two shooting deaths (obviously a fictionalized Kent State tragedy), brought a demand from the California National Guard about whether real Guardsmen were used in the dramatization.

Also, the Adjutant General's office wanted to know how the studio had obtained National Guard equipment.

Universal TV, in confirming the incident, said actors had played the part of Guardsmen and that equipment used in the dramatization had been rented.

A spokesman for the California Guard said that organization did not consider the program to be pro-Guard and insisted the depicted campus shootings could not have occurred with the state militia, which has riot instructions carefully delineating courses of action.

The studio emphasized no state had been identified in the drama. . . .

"The Beverly Hillbillies" don't make waves like this. . . .

"WITH ENEMIES LIKE YOU, WHO NEEDS FRIENDS?"

Opposite, above: Reprinted by permission of Charles W. Ayers and the **Daily Kent Stater.**

Opposite, below: Reprinted by permission of Don Wright and the **Miami News.**

Above: Reprinted by permission of Gene Basset and the Scripps-Howard *Newspaper Alliance.*

LETTERS

After his Washington speech, President White became more than ever the personal embodiment of the affair and its meaning. We again present a selection from the many letters received by White. We have noted that letters containing editorials and articles tended to be from writers who did not support White, while letters enclosing poems by the writers tended to support him. As before, letters from the public press follow.

From a Lima, Ohio, woman to Pres. White, November 2, 1970.

. . . I cannot comprehend that any decent, law-abiding person can really believe these killings were justified.

I would also like to quote a paragraph from a wonderful article in Redbook magazine, September issue, by a distinguished writer, Jessamyn West, called "Toward Peace."

> My generation must accept most of the burden of guilt for the killing of these students. [She is also referring to Mississippi and Georgia.] We cannot evade it with the citing of provocation: rocks, taunts, obscenity, unlawful assemblage. These are not punishable by death; and in any case the constabulary, be it local or national, is not a part of the judicial system. It was never intended that it mete out justice.

From an Elkhart, Ind., man to Pres. White, November 9, 1970.

. . . [My children] will never see the inside of your cesspool of liberalism. I would rather see them dead than brainwashed into nihilism through a diploma mill such as Kent State or Berkley.

After your statment recently, I place you with Jerry Rubin, Peter and Jane Fonda, Dr. Spock and others who are usurping our freedom and exploiting our system.

Go to Cuba. Here we have red blood.

From a Portland, Ore., couple to Pres. White, November 10, 1970.

We wish at this time to express our profound appreciation for your recent comments condemning the special grand jury's report. Though we are far from Ohio and not directly connected to Kent State in any way, we have felt ever since last May's tragedy that events there have portentous significance for colleges and universities all over the United States. Rarely has academic freedom been so threatened in this country, or the right to dissent politically so in jeopardy. It is as if the spectre of Joseph McCarthy has begun to haunt not only the halls of the White House and Congress, but the groves of Academe as well.

We cannot pretend, unfortunately, to have much hope for a reversal of the present frightening trend toward suppression of free inquiry in our colleges, especially those that are state-supported, but if there is even a shadow of a chance for such reversal, it exists because of men like you, who are willing to speak out even at the cost of certain persecution from the ignorant and the vicious elements in our society, willing to persist despite the scathing derision of those who would use tragedy as political capital.

For what it's worth, incidentally, we are both over thirty, decidedly middle-class, and have never stoned a policeman, planted a bomb, or burned a building; if obscenities have occasionally been wrung from us by the acts or speeches of politicians, they have been uttered in private. I cannot but think that many like us are also sympathetic to your position, though your mail will probably reflect the opposite—those filled with hate seem always more highly motivated to express themselves, sadly.

In any case, you have our full support in your fight to protect higher education from unwarranted repression. The books must not be burned; dissent must not be stifled; minds must not be closed. To borrow a phrase from the current college dialect, right on, President White.

From a University of Michigan (Ann Arbor) professor to Pres. White, November 11, 1970.

. . . I have been concerned for some time with another aspect of this question of "academic freedom" which I believe is at the basis of your concern and which I believe you have actually been quoted on radio news broadcasts. The aspect of "academic freedom" which disturbs me on many campuses in the United States with which I am familiar (and this does not include Kent State incidentally) is the very evident philosophic bias of the faculties in the direction of liberal left wing or radical liberal positions. On many campuses this situation is much more serious than a simple bias but rather an almost unanimous formulation of faculty having these viewpoints. I would of course not for a moment deny the right of an individual to hold these viewpoints so long as they are not in themselves treasonous or lead to acts of treason against our government. Nevertheless, it ought to disturb educators concerned with true academic freedom that there is not a more balanced presentation of political philosophies where such a presentation is appropriate by members of their faculties. Surely you must be aware that there is a large body of academically respectable and workable political philosophies from the other side of the political spectrum. I cannot but help to form the definite impression that for the past several decades probably, faculty screening committees composed of liberals have essentially ruled out the hiring of new faculty who do not hold similar political philosophies. I could be wrong but this seems to me to be quite a strong possibility. As a result, liberal beliefs generated more liberal beliefs and this position became implanted in the classroom and curricula which in turn generated more liberal Ph.D. graduates who then were hired by other faculties. Unfortunately the powerfully important concepts of true liberalism have become lost and gradually the political philosophies of many (and I believe most) liberal arts faculties moved leftward until today we have almost a monolithic structure of left wing philosophies among these faculties. . . .

It might also be wondered if the trouble which we have seen on our campuses and which almost invariably has come from the left wing side of the political spectrum is not in some way closely related with the left wing bias to which I have alluded. In many cases I think both you and I know there have been radical faculty members actively encouraging student disruptions and misbehavior far and beyond the point of even reasonably acceptable dissent. I am unsure as to the degree that this is really responsible for unrest but certainly it has been a very unsettling condition on the campuses. . . .

I am not writing to you with any intent of increasing your present burdens which I know must be great nor am I being critical or fruitlessly cynical. I am simply reciting what has been the consequence of my observations having close associations with campus life and students as a student or a faculty member on American campuses for the past quarter of a century.

From an Ohio man to Pres. White, November 11, 1970.

. . . You and your peers live in a world of fantasy and irresponsibility. You're not members of the working community; and, therefore, must be unable to cope with reality which is evidenced in your recent statements to the press. . . .

Where were you when the trouble on your campus was brewing? Probably home sipping martinis and reading poetry and slapping yourself on the back for the great job you WEREN'T doing for Kent State University.

I'm familiar with your kind of administrator. You probably allow your wife to wash the car and mow the lawn while you cook supper and clean the house. A real MAN! . . .

From an Ohio man to a school board (copy to Pres. White),
November 12, 1970.

The recent rebellions on the Kent State and other college campuses have had an adverse effect on the public and have, in my opinion, been one of the factors strongly influencing the defeat of school levies and bond issues in Ohio.

We were encouraged by the findings of the special grand jury which pointed the finger at the guilty parties and, in particular, demonstrated the failure of the administrative staff at Kent State University. We are now, however, beholden to the spectacle of that administration condemning the grand jury and anyone else who finds any fault whatever in the exceptionally poor performance of the faculty and the staff at Kent State University.

This is to suggest that we take formal action to congratulate the special grand jury on their efforts on behalf of all education in Ohio and to condemn president White for his irrational responses and to urge that the Board of Regents and the Board of Trustees at Kent State University take the necessary steps to ensure that people such as these can no longer besmirch the cause of education in Ohio.

From a San Francisco man to Pres. White, November 12, 1970.

I see your pinko friend Ramsey Clark is heading your way to try and get your little commie friends off the hook.

The grand jury hit the nail on the head, and put the blame where it belonged. Even a Phd should be able to figure out that the ones who started the riot are the ones responsible. Or is that too simple for our egg-headed prof?

The only place the grand jury failed is to indict the commie professors such as yourself who indoctrinate these bums, and instead of teaching these criminals how to make a living, try to make over our society according to Chairman Mao & Co.

Well, prof, you have a lot to learn, or should I say, unlearn? People are fed up with shelling out their hard-earned dollars, building buildings for you bums to loaf around in, smoke your damnable pot, tear up the flag, and thumb your nose at all of the good things in our wonderful country.

Make no mistake about it. The people are fed up. The general feeling is, too bad we only got four. Next time, maybe we will get you all. Your "college" is a cancer on society and should be burned to the ground; your "students" put at hard labor to learn the value of work, and the professors shot.

Get back to your books,

From a Jacksonville, Fla., man to Pres. White, November 13, 1970.

. . . We may not agree fully with the Kent State Grand Jury, however, it was a local representative body that investigated the disruptions that occurred on your campus and in Kent City. The report gives a fairly accurate insight as to the thinking of the vast majority of people from this county. In our type of democracy I would think that majority viewpoint should prevail over the minority point of view. Too many times the people from the outside—the pious do-gooders and Ivory Tower Philosophers spread more harm than good because they don't have to live with their advice and recommendations, right or wrong.

. . . In closing, I would like to suggest that the educators and law makers take a closer look to try and understand what the majority of the voters have been trying to say these past few years. Teachers and professors should spend more time teaching the basic rules of society along with their studies giving full measure of a good days work and less time on irrelevant matters.

From a San Francisco, Calif., woman to Pres. White, November 15, 1970.

. . . I do hope and wish for your own sake that you will find endless moral support from Presidents of other Universities to sustain your courageous battle in a country whose government must worry anyone who has grown up under dictatorship. Personalities of that type of civil courage were unfortunately silent during the rise of Hitler, which permitted basically the chaos of today's world.

From a Vienna (W. Va.) man to Pres. White, November 16, 1970.

I have noticed of late that our American Communist-controlled news media has been playing up your weak attempts to excuse your gutless, permissive actions both before and after the incidents of last May.

I have read that in your mouthings to the liberal and Commie press that you are denigrating the American grand jury system because the grand jury had the good sense and the guts to place some of the blame right where it belongs,—in your lap, brother! You warn of disaster if we do not "provide an open forum" for anyone who wishes to speak against America and her systems, even when such speakers go beyond the pale of sedition and treason! The disaster which faces us will be caused by so-called educators like yourself who believe that the students should run the educational system, the convicts should run the penal system, and the relief recipients should run the welfare system!

These "students" of yours were sent to college by their hard-working parents to gain an education,—not to riot and demonstrate in favor of our Communist enemies! Had they been in their dormitories studying, as they should have been, there would have been no "incident." I can tell you this: if I had been a Guardsman at Kent last May, and had been set upon by a wave of foul-mouthed weirdos, there would have been more than four dead bodies left lying on the campus!

You, sir, are a disgrace to America, and a disgrace to our educational system!

From a Kent mother to Dr. White, November 20, 1970.

. . . I do not blame the youth for becoming frustrated, but still believe that building, no matter how slowly, is the only way.

Actually I wanted to let you know one parent's view of your institution and educational freedom. I have children in special education. I have been allowed to attend discussions at the university with many of the prominent professional people and have found the openness, enthusiasm, and thirst for knowledge contagious. Anyone seeking an answer to problems is spurred on to seek an answer somewhere, somehow. Many of the teachers I have met in the field of special education (the ones I feel know their business) have this same attitude. That is, nothing is impossible and we'll keep trying until we come up with an answer. Their teaching is not limited to the books they have studied and their education not stopped with the awarding of a diploma.

If parents would build a firm foundation for a child in regards to moral right and wrong and inspire them to question any situation to find better methods, they would give them the best tools for life. For they would never stop learning and I feel this is what your university has attempted to do. Please keep your openmindedness and searching a major part of the curriculum. Anytime one presides over as many individuals as you do, [he] is bound to find extremes of all sorts. If the students are to develop into free thinking, mature, responsible adults, they must form and justify their own opinions of these extremes. But it appears that some of the older generation has reacted just as John Gardner warned in a speech of his, and that is, over-reacted, which is just as bad as a few students' acts of violence. And I believe this attitude will develop a society of injustice quicker than the attitude of a few extreme students.

I feel there must be many at the university working diligently to overcome the problems at Kent State and I hope they continue to do so. So please do not become disgusted with us silent majority. [My husband and I would like all our children] to learn in the "permissive" thinking atmosphere that a progressive university must have.

From "A Group of [183] Students in Several [Southern] Colleges"
to Pres. White, November 20, 1970.

. . . Did it ever occur to you that we are fed up with HAVING OUR RIGHTS AS STUDENTS WHO WANT TO LEARN AND BECOME GOOD AND ABLE CITIZENS taken from us by the minority of kooks and anarchists and enemy agents? And when CBS gives you time to jump on the Grand Jury whose members were willing, for once, to punish those who caused all this trouble in the first place, then it proves that the big TV media itself lacks responsibility and it is time we demanded some honor and honesty in this media. Why don't you actually read the Commission's report and then the Grand Jury's and you might see how right the Grand Jury was! . . .

From a Cleveland Heights, Ohio, man; the *Cleveland Press,*
August 1, 1970

Now that the FBI, America's finest guardian of the people, has blamed the Ohio National Guard for the murders at Kent State University, will the people who commended the Guard's actions still feel that the Guard was right? If these people still wish that more people had been killed, they indeed want a national police force of repression.

Do these people who favor repression feel that the FBI is an anarchistic organization because they have taken the blame of the Kent murders from the students? I tend to believe the FBI because they are protectors of all American's human rights.

From the KSU chapter of Young Americans for Freedom; the *Daily
Kent Stater,* October 6, 1970.

. . . When the university becomes partisan, even unintentionally, it takes upon itself the rights of deciding what evidence the individual can consider and, thereby, violates its own proper function. . . .

Thus, we are extremely disturbed at the gross bias shown in the selection of speakers for Think Week. . . . [T]he speakers do not even constitute a good representation of the sorts of opinions not favorable to the administration. Why not, for example, have invited a libertarian, an objectivist, or a rule-of-law constitutionalist? . . . The Democrat-leftward spectrum represented by Think Week speakers does not, by any stretch of the imagination, constitute a balanced approach. It appears that Think Week was intended not only to encourage students to think on the issue but also to decide for them what conclusions they are to draw.

That student government should be responsible for so limiting a range of views presented indicate that such a government has taken upon itself to decide for us which views are legitimate for a student to hold. That the faculty and administration should silently accept such a procedure is inexcusable.

In deference to the idea of the university as the sanctuary of the unbiased search for truth, society has given to the university special protection, support and respect.

If the university becomes a political tool, it is then only another partisan group not entitled to any special consideration. Looking at the Think Week program as an example of how partisan the university has become, we should not be surprised that already society is beginning to question whether the university is still entitled to its special benefits.

A DKS editorial suggests that, because the vast majority of students did not turn out to support the partisan program which the campus establishment arranged for them, these students do not care about the future of the university.

We believe that if the Kent State community really wishes to preserve the university, it will not support activities like Think Week designed to use the university as a political tool. Rather, it will insist that everybody practice politics by himself or through special interest groups. When, as was the case with the Think Week program, the university promotes ideas which are popular with those who control it, regardless of whether or not these ideas are called "dissenting," it is setting itself against truly free dissent and, consequently, against its own principles.

From "Over Fifty"; the *Kent-Ravenna Record-Courier,*
October 30, 1970.

We were shocked and dismayed at the decisions handed down by the "Kangaroo Jury" concerning the KSU tragedy. All the people responsible for the violence on property and human lives should have been indicted, but it looks like some were arrested for merely voicing an opinion.

How can there be justice shown when the man responsible for convening this jury said there would be no National Guard indictments even before the hearings? That is like having the Ku Klux Klan on a jury to try a black man in the south.

The FBI and the Scranton Reports said the deaths were uncalled for and unjustified and blamed both sides. We will go along with their decision, handed down by impartial dedicated men.

I agree with many who believe this insidious mockery of justice was planned for political reasons.

I can understand the apathy and indifference shown to the deaths of the four students by many of our "flag wavers" because they don't get uptight about the 44,000 killed in Vietnam, just so long as they can stay safe here and draw their big pay and overtime.

I really admire men like Prof. Glenn Frank who spoke out against this mockery of justice handed down by Judge Jones and the "Kangaroo Jury." Also the remarks by Seabury Ford. I have never heard such inhuman remarks by a public official. Anyone who would say such a thing will someday have to answer to his God. I hope the professors who were ordered to keep quiet will back Professor Frank and speak out.

I ask every fair-minded citizen to do as the Scranton Report said—

to reject all violence whether practiced by students, law enforcement men or by our jury system, and to bridge the gap between the young and old to try to erase this black spot on our community by the selfish inhuman acts of our fellowmen.

I urge all of you this November to vote for the candidates who will try to end this terrible war that has our young people so disenchanted.

I'm not signing my name because frankly I fear the repercussions from the "non-violent" segment of our society.

From a Bowling Green (Ohio) State Univ. Student; the *Cleveland Press,* November 11, 1970.

I think that the service given by today's news media is an absolute sin. The biased reporting on campus disorders serves as a means of advertising for the minute minority of campus radicals.

For example, a yippie rally at Kent State University produces a gathering of about 300 long-haired, unshaven hippies. On television, the technique of photography gives the impression that the whole campus is up in arms.

The percentage of students actually participating out of 22,000 is never given.

The camera never focuses on the great majority, the silent majority going to classes getting an education.

. . . I hope the news media will realize the responsibility that is on their shoulders—not to sell newspapers but to guide a young nation to an end not of revolution but of peace, intelligence and truth.

From an Akron man; the *Akron Beacon Journal,* November 1, 1970.

In the almost six months since the Kent State shootings, I have given up trying to find an objective point of view. A great number of the students I have talked to seem intent on making their dead comrades martyrs. A like number of adults seem to be looking for some sort of scapegoat on which to vent their fear, anger, and frustration over an unruly generation.

I have yet to meet the individual who can deliver a just and unbiased view on the events of last May. Nor can I honestly trust my own heart for judgment . . . I am little better than anyone else I have met.

This realization awakens my fear over the recent grand jury investigation. I fear greatly that we are trying to find fault for something in which we are not qualified to judge. I am even more afraid that we are missing the whole point of a very painful lesson.

Perhaps we should ask ourselves exactly what indictments and convictions are going to accomplish. By putting the blame on one group or the other are we going to call back the bullets of frightened young

Guardsmen? Are we going to ease the pain of the parents who have lost a child or make a young man crippled for life walk again?

In the end I can't help wonder if we shouldn't just let the matter drop. Justice herself has balked at lesser things, and perhaps we will do far more good to come to an understanding of the forces which were the making of this tragedy.

We can, of course, go on bickering, but then we will not be one inch closer to solving the problems that beset this nation. We can open our eyes or we can close them. But if we close them, perhaps more of our youth will pay the price in blood.

From a Barberton, Ohio, man; the *Akron Beacon Journal,* November 8, 1970.

"The KSU Debate Goes On and On" was your headline on the Sunday Forum [letters to the editor] (Nov. 1). Hiding behind this headline, the Beacon Journal piously seeks to blame the public for keeping the Kent State issue alive, when in fact, the Beacon Journal is guilty. Your biased investigations, your biased news items and your biased editorials have polarized this community; not this issue.

The Grand Jury report stemmed from hearings conducted in a calm atmosphere by a jury fairly selected from citizens at Portage County. I would dare say that a jury chosen from any place in this world would have rendered the same verdict. Prosecutor Ford did not render the verdict. Are you saying that a jury composed of average citizens is not fit to make a judgment on facts fairly presented?

I would hate to appear before a jury composed of pious, self-righteous newspaper publishers, editors and writers.

From a KSU student; the *Daily Kent Stater,* November 4, 1970.

I'm sick of hearing how repressed we students are. We are told that the only ones who are aware of our repression are those who are actively protesting; the others are merely ignorant of their state. Perhaps many of the "silent majority" don't believe in the concepts proposed for salvation by our self-appointed saviors. . . .

Do those students who are demanding realize that they are practicing what they say they hate—repression of individual freedom? I'm sure that not everyone agrees with all the demands made by protest; therefore individual freedom is repressed for someone if the demands are met. . . .

Sure, there are many mistakes that have been made in society and are still perpetrated today, but changes can be made without complete anarchy. Many of the great changes in societies throughout history have been the result of violent revolutions, but the only ones which produced better societies were those which had a fairly workable plan to put in place of the old one. . . .

Above all, dear dissident students, you need to begin to realize that there are many, many other people in the world and all at different intellectual levels. These people do deserve the same rights and respect as you do.

If changes are to be made for the good and last, they must be relevant for most of the people and understood by most of the people, not by just a few who feel they know all and others should also feel the same way to be "beautiful people."

From a KSU student; the *Daily Kent Stater,* November 4, 1970.

Witness the birth of the "Clown-priest-revolutionary" here in our midst: the emergence of the Yippie! . . .

One question is what have the "pigs" done to us. Another is what have we allowed to happen to ourselves. Why such a gloomy revolution? . . .

What the revolution needs is more Yippies (particularly as I understand them at Kent State). Oh, everybody doesn't have to run out and join up. Just put a little Yippie in your heart. . . .

The danger of the too serious revolutionary is that he may show up at the end of the revolution without any joy left.

Naive optimism is not the answer. Smiling passivity is not the answer. "Cheerful Pessimism," that's what is needed. A joy born out of a vital plunge into existence. Still, a realism that informs us that our brother is hurting.

This time is ripe for the "festive radical." The time is right for the circus to proceed where the revolution has failed. The time is ripe for a "creative and thoughtful buffoonery." Justice in socio-economic structures must be accompanied by a radical transformation of human consciousness.

Real revolution may mean learning how to dance again. Spiro, watch out! Joy is headed your way!

From a KSU professor; the *Akron Beacon Journal,* November 22, 1970.

. . . Whatever the outcome of the legal problems associated with the May disturbances, at least journalistic justice has been done. It is a rare thing when, in the face of what must be and have been enormous pressures—political, financical, and so on—a newspaper and its editor demonstrate so graphically a commitment to informing its readers. It is not an over-statement to say that without your dedication Kent might not have survived.

I hope you are aware that to many students—and faculty—the essential rightness of the American system is being demonstrated daily by the editorials and articles in your paper. . . .

From a Hudson, Ohio, man; the *Akron Beacon Journal,*
December 5, 1970.

. . . Publius Syrus (circa 42 B.C.) created this very cogent and timely maxim: "No one should be judge in his own cause."

Dr. White, president of KSU, should heed this wisdom. Instead, Dr. White judges his administration "totally blameless." This judgment, along with Dr. Frank's contempt of court episode backed by the Faculty Senate, is further proof that disrespect for law and order is still being taught at Kent.

Members of the administration continue, from what they regard as "privileged sanctuary" to hurl brickbats of anarchy over walls built for them by the Ohio taxpayers. Their target seems to be the procedure that makes our justice the fairest in the world, discrediting the jury system.

Isn't it past time that those accused of the legal responsibility by the Portage County Grand Jury be replaced?

From a Long Beach, Calif., man to *Newsweek,* November 16, 1970.

I cannot help but recall a similar moment in 1956 when the Communists who gunned down stone-throwing Hungarians were "acquitted" by the rest of the world on the ground that they were suppressing a criminal revolution by the people.

From a Kent man; the *Kent-Ravenna Record-Courier,* December
5, 1970.

What sort of response should one expect from the city, state, police, and Record-Courier when large numbers of persons, mostly young, do extensive damage to downtown property? It seems that it all depends on the nature of the cause of the disturbance.

In the much-celebrated case of the city of Kent on the night of May 1, 1970, when a variety of factors, chief of which was Nixon's Cambodian invasion, combined to send young people into the streets to do damage to plate-glass windows, the response was shock, outrage, a curfew, the formation of vigilante groups, headlines and angry editorials, and the summoning of additional police force from neighboring municipalities, the state highway patrol, and the National Guard. Add to this, the consequent killing and wounding of students by the Guard, all of which was "justified" by many citizens because of "what those hippies did to our town."

Compare the response to this event with the response to the disturbance which occurred in Columbus following Ohio State's football victory over Michigan. First, compare the events: The "victory celebration" lasted 12 hours (approximately three times longer than the Kent affair); police estimates place the Columbus "celebrants" at 40,-000 (approximately 40 times larger than the Kent "rioters"); 60 Columbus commercial establishments reported losses according to the Associated Press, totaling "tens of thousands of dollars" or at least $30,-000, but including the damage to automobiles, utility poles, the Ohio State Stadium's $2,000 goal posts, and the cost of cleaning up the "thousands of beer cans, wine bottles and other debris" (UPI) (as compared with the $10,000 damage done to Kent—the estimate, admitted to be liberal, by the Kent Area Chamber of Commerce); dozens of persons in Columbus suffered injuries, some in fist fights, and one was shot in the back by a policeman (there were no reported injuries in the Kent "riot").

Did the city of Columbus slap a curfew on its citizens? Did the Governor go on TV and accuse the football fans of being "brown-shirted anarchists"? Did irate citizens organize vigilante groups to protect their property? The answer in each case is negative.

How did the police respond? According to the Record-Courier: "Although dozens of campus-area store windows were smashed, cars damaged and even steel utility poles uprooted by the fans, police for the most part stayed away from the area. Plain clothes officers mingled with the crowd and dozens of riot-trained patrolmen were on standby at a nearby command post in case the celebration got completely out of hand. They were never called into action." Police blamed most of the disorders on drinking (not on Communists, SDS, or drugs), and one officer was quoted as saying: "I'm sure glad this only happens once in a while!"

Finally, how did the Record-Courier respond? A headline and an outraged editorial? Hardly. It carried a brief story on p. 21, entitled "It must have been a great party"! The only editorial comment is a brief paragraph submerged in a congratulatory editorial, entitled "OSU victory 'just great'." The editorial righteously laments the "incident" as "the only negative factor about the game."

What incredible hypocrisy! Little wonder that growing numbers of persons, especially the young, are unimpressed by the cries of alarmed concern coming from the "Establishment" regarding law and order, the sanctity of property, permissiveness, and radical behavior on the part of students. If the "Establishment" wants to be taken seriously it had better examine carefully its own prejudices, inconsistencies and system of values, and ask itself how it is that it is willing to tolerate and minimize one "riot" but not another.